The Arab–Israeli Conflict
Third Edition

In this concise yet comprehensive survey, Kirsten E. Schulze analyzes the causes, course and consequences of the Arab–Israeli conflict, exploring the particular dynamics of this conflict and the numerous attempts at its resolution. Covering pivotal events ranging from the creation of the State of Israel to the first and second Lebanon Wars and the Arab Spring, the book traces the development of the conflict from its intellectual roots in the nineteenth century to the present day.

This third edition has been revised throughout to bring the text up to date with recent events, including:

- a completely new chapter on the Gaza Wars from 2006 to 2014
- new material on the Arab Spring and its implications for Israel
- an updated discussion of the ongoing negotiations for peace.

Containing a diverse collection of primary source documents, a chronology of key dates, a glossary, a guide to further reading and a who's who summarizing the careers and contributions of the main figures, this book is essential to understanding the background to and worldwide significance of the continuing violence between Israel and Palestine and is valuable reading for all students of the Arab–Israeli conflict.

Kirsten E. Schulze is Associate Professor in International History at the London School of Economics. Her recent publications include *The International History of the Twentieth Century and Beyond* (2014, 3rd edition, co-authored with Antony Best, Jussi Hanhimäki and Joseph A. Maiolo) and *The Jews of Lebanon: Between Coexistence and Conflict* (2008, 2nd edition), as well as articles on Israeli–Lebanese relations in the 1950s, Israel's 1982 invasion of Lebanon and the al-Aqsa *intifada*.

Introduction to the Series

History is narrative constructed by historians from traces left by the past. Historical enquiry is often driven by contemporary issues and, in consequence, historical narratives are constantly reconsidered, reconstructed and reshaped. The fact that different historians have different perspectives on issues means that there is also often controversy and no universally agreed-upon version of past events. *Seminar Studies in History* was designed to bridge the gap between current research and debate and the broad, popular, general surveys that often date rapidly.

The volumes in the series are written by historians who are not only familiar with the latest research and current debates concerning their topic, but who have themselves contributed to our understanding of the subject. The books are intended to provide the reader with a clear introduction to a major topic in history. They provide both a narrative of events and a critical analysis of contemporary interpretations. They include the kinds of tools generally omitted from specialist monographs: a chronology of events, a glossary of terms and brief biographies of 'who's who'. They also include bibliographical essays in order to guide students to the literature on various aspects of the subject. Students and teachers alike will find that the selection of documents will stimulate discussion and offer insight into the raw materials used by historians in their attempt to understand the past.

Clive Emsley and Gordon Martel
Series Editors

The Arab–Israeli Conflict

Third Edition

Kirsten E. Schulze

Routledge
Taylor & Francis Group

LONDON AND NEW YORK

Third edition published 2017
by Routledge
2 Park Square, Milton Park, Abingdon, Oxon OX14 4RN

and by Routledge
711 Third Avenue, New York, NY 10017

Routledge is an imprint of the Taylor & Francis Group, an informa business

© 1999, 2008, 2017 Kirsten E. Schulze

First edition published 1999 by Pearson Education Limited

Second edition published 2008

British Library Cataloguing in Publication Data
A catalogue record for this book is available from the British Library

Library of Congress Cataloging-in-Publication Data
A catalog record for this book has been requested

ISBN: 978-1-138-93334-7 (hbk)
ISBN: 978-1-138-93335-4 (pbk)
ISBN: 978-1-315-44080-4 (ebk)

Typeset in Sabon
by ApexCovantage, LLC

Printed and bound in Great Britain by
TJ International Ltd, Padstow, Cornwall

MIX
Paper from
responsible sources
FSC
www.fsc.org   FSC® C013056

Contents

Acknowledgements

No book is ever the product of one person alone. So I would like to thank the following friends and colleagues for their comments, suggestions and support: Fred Halliday, Avraham Sela, Abigail, Rona, Catherine, Melissa, Elizabeth, Kate, Gary, Yussi and Tim. For useful comment on the second and third edition I would like to express my gratitude to Jeroen Gunning and Adam Stahl, respectively. And last but certainly not least I would like to thank my students for making the Arab–Israeli conflict a subject worth teaching and writing about.

Figures

Maps

Chronology

1951	20 July, King Abdallah is assassinated
1952	23 July, Free Officers coup
	11 August, King Talal is succeeded by King Hussein
1953	14 October, Qibya raid
1955	28 February, Gaza raid
1956	26 July, Nasser nationalizes the Suez Canal
	29 October, Israel invades Sinai
	5 November, Britain and France invade Suez Canal zone
	6–7 November, Britain, France and Israel agree to ceasefire
1957	5 January, Eisenhower Doctrine
1958	February, UAR created
	14 July, Iraqi monarchy is overthrown
1964	January, PLO is created
	May, First PNC in Jerusalem
1966	November, Syrian–Egyptian defence pact
	13 November, As-Samu raid
1967	April, Israeli–Syrian air clash
	13 May, Soviet Union tells Egypt of pending Israeli attack on Syria
	17 May, Nasser mobilizes troops
	18 May, UNEF asked to withdraw
	23 May, Blockade of Straits of Tiran
	30 May, Egyptian–Jordanian defence pact
	5–10 June, Six Day War
	September, Khartoum summit
	22 November, UN Resolution 242
1968	21 March, Battle of Karameh
	October, Hafez al-Asad assumes leadership of Syria
	December, Beirut raid
1969	February, Yasser Arafat is elected PLO chairman
	War of Attrition begins
	8 March, Nasser proclaims War of Attrition
	9 December, Rogers Plan
1970	25 June, War of Attrition ends
	September, Black September
	28 September, Nasser dies; Anwar Sadat assumes the presidency
1971	27 May, Soviet–Egyptian Treaty of Friendship
	28 November, Wasfi al-Tell is assassinated
1972	March, King Hussein's Confederation Plan
	July, Sadat expels Soviet advisors
1973	6–22 October, October War
	22 October, UN Resolution 338
	11 November, Israeli–Egyptian ceasefire
	21 December, Geneva Peace Conference

1974	1 January, Israeli–Egyptian disengagement agreement
	31 May, Israeli–Syrian disengagement agreement
	October, PLO becomes sole legitimate representative of the Palestinian people
	13 November, PLO granted UN observer status
1975	April, Lebanese civil war begins
	1 September, Sinai II Agreement
1977	9 November, Sadat is prepared to go to Jerusalem
	19–20 November, Sadat addresses Knesset
	25–26 December, Begin meets Sadat in Ismailia
1978	14 March, Operation Litani
	5–17 September, Camp David Summit
1979	26 March, Israeli–Egyptian Peace Treaty is signed
	31 March, Arab League expels Egypt
1981	7 June, Israel bombs Iraqi nuclear reactor
	6 October, Sadat is assassinated
	14 December, Israel annexes Golan Heights
1982	6 June, Israel invades Lebanon
	August, Multinational peacekeeping force enters Beirut
	14 September, Bashir Gemayel is assassinated
	17–18 September, Sabra and Shatilla massacres
	9 October, PLO–Jordanian negotiations start
1983	10 April, PLO–Jordanian negotiations break down
	17 May, Israeli–Lebanese Agreement
	16 September, Israel begins withdrawal from Lebanon
1984	21 February, US forces leave Lebanon
	5 March, Lebanon abrogates agreement with Israel
1985	11 February, Jordanian–PLO negotiations
	July, Israel completes withdrawal to security zone
1986	March, King Hussein breaks relations with Arafat
1987	April, Arafat abrogates agreement with Jordan
	9 December, *intifada* erupts; Hamas is created
1988	16 April, Khalil al-Wazir is assassinated in Tunis
	31 July, Jordan severs ties to the West Bank
	15 November, Palestinian state is declared
	14 December, PLO renounces terrorism
	US–PLO dialogue begins
1989	6 April, Israel announces election plan for the Occupied Territories
	22 May, Egypt is re-admitted to the Arab League
	September, Mubarak announces 10-point plan
1990	20 June, US suspends dialogue with PLO
	2 August, Iraq invades Kuwait
	12 October, Arafat supports Saddam Hussein
1991	16 January, Operation Desert Storm is launched

Scud missiles are launched against Israel and Saudi Arabia

27 February, Bush announces liberation of Kuwait

March, Baker's shuttle diplomacy begins

30 October, Madrid Peace Conference is convened

1992   July, Yitzhak Rabin forms new Israeli government

1993   Spring, Secret PLO–Israel negotiations in Oslo

July, Operation Accountability

13 September, Israel–PLO Declaration of Principles

1 October, Washington conference on the Middle East

1994   25 February, Jewish settler kills Palestinian worshippers in Hebron

Israel–PLO talks suspended

31 March, Israel–PLO talks resume

29 April, Israel–PLO agreement on framework for economic ties

4 May, Gaza–Jericho Agreement

18 May, Israel completes withdrawal of troops from Gaza

25 July, Summit meeting in Washington between Rabin and King Hussein Washington Declaration

29 September, Oslo Declaration

1 October, Secondary and tertiary boycotts of Israel are lifted

9 October, Hamas gunmen kill 2 and wound 13 in Jerusalem

19 October, Hamas suicide bomber kills 22 and wounds 26 on Tel Aviv bus

26 October, Jordanian–Israeli Peace Treaty

18 November, Palestinian police fire on demonstrators in Gaza, killing 12

10 December, Rabin and Arafat receive Nobel Peace Prize

1995   22 January, Islamic Jihad kill 19 and wound 62 in an attack on Beit Lid junction

4 November, Assassination of Israeli Prime Minister Yitzhak Rabin

5 December, Yigal Amir is charged with premeditated murder of Rabin

10 December, Israeli troops redeploy from Palestinian city of Tulkarem

21 December, Talks between PNA and Hamas end unsuccessfully

27 December, Israeli troops withdraw from Ramallah

1996   5 January, Israeli security services kill Hamas activist Yahya Ayash by booby-trapping his mobile phone

20 January, Palestinian elections; Arafat is elected president of the PNA

25 February, Hamas suicide bombs on Jerusalem bus and in the city of Ashkelon, killing 25, injuring 77

4 March, Suicide bomb explodes outside Tel Aviv shopping centre, killing 12, wounding 126

7 March, Newly elected PNC is inaugurated in Gaza City

27 March, Yigal Amir is convicted of murdering Rabin

11–26 April, Operation Grapes of Wrath

5 May, Israeli–Palestinian final status negotiations scheduled for completion by May 1999

29 May, Israeli elections; Benjamin Netanyahu becomes prime minister by 50.4% to 49.6%

June 16, Netanyahu issues policy guidelines stating opposition to a Palestinian state, the strengthening of settlements, the retention of Jerusalem and the Golan Heights

23–28 September, Temple Mount riots

2 October, Two-day White House Mideast summit ends without results

1997   15 January, Netanyahu and Arafat agree to the withdrawal of 80% of Israeli troops from Hebron and other areas of the West Bank by mid-1998

17 January, Hebron reverts to Palestinian control

4 February, Two Israeli helicopters transporting troops to South Lebanon collide, killing 73

13 February, Clinton urges resumption of Israeli–Syrian talks

17 February, Netanyahu vows to strengthen his hold over Jerusalem

26 February, Knesset approves of construction of Har Homa settlement

5 March, Arafat tells Jewish leaders in New York that Palestinian Covenant has been changed so that it no longer calls for the destruction of Israel

13 March, Jordanian border guard fires on Israeli schoolgirls, killing 7 and wounding 6 more

31 March, Arab League freezes relations with Israel and reinstates economic boycott

30 July, Two suicide bombs explode in Jerusalem market Mahane Yehuda, killing 13 and wounding 150

4 September, Three suicide bombers explode bombs in Jerusalem's Ben Yehuda Street, killing 4 and wounding 180

5 September, Netanyahu announces that he no longer considers Oslo Accords binding

26 September, Mossad agents try unsuccessfully to assassinate Hamas political leader Khaled Meshal in Jordan

1 October, Israel releases Hamas founder Sheikh Ahmad Yassin (imprisoned since 1989)

13 November, Arafat states that he will declare statehood in 1999 regardless of the status of negotiations with Israel

1998   24 October, An Israeli–Palestinian summit is held at Wye; it produced the Wye Accord, which stipulated that Palestinians remove the clause calling for the destruction of Israel from their charter and that Israel cede another 13% of the West Bank

1999   7 February, King Hussein of Jordan dies

May, First direct Israeli prime ministerial elections in which Ehud Barak is elected

November, Resumption of formal Israel–Palestinian negotiations

December, Israeli–Syrian negotiations formally re-open

2000   January, Israeli–Syrian negotiations take place at Shepherdstown but no agreement is reached

26 March, Clinton and Asad meet in Geneva in a final attempt to bridge the gap between Israel and Syria

24 May, The IDF withdraws unilaterally from southern Lebanon

10 June, Hafez al-Asad dies

11 July, Camp David Summit starts

28 September, Sharon visits the Temple Mount to shore up the claim over a united Jerusalem; the Al-Aqsa *intifada* erupts out of protests against Sharon's visit

2001   21 January, Israeli–Palestinian talks open in Taba, Egypt; despite coming closer than ever no agreement is reached

February, Special Israeli election which Barak loses and Ariel Sharon is elected prime minister

2002   28 March, Arab League Summit in Beirut adopts Arab Peace Plan; suicide bomber kills 30 people in the Park Hotel in Netanya

July, The Quartet drafts the Roadmap

Autumn, Work begins on the West Bank barrier

2003   April, Mahmoud Abbas is elected Palestinian prime minister; the Roadmap is officially initiated

1 December, Yossi Beilin and Yasser Abed Rabbo put forward the Geneva Accord as an alternative to Sharon's disengagement plan; the Geneva Accord constitutes a draft permanent status agreement

2004   November, Yasir Arafat dies

2005   9 January, Mahmoud Abbas is elected Palestinian president

14 February, Lebanese Prime Minister Rafiq al-Hariri is assassinated

12 September, 21 settlements in Gaza and 4 in the West Bank are forcibly evacuated in the implementation of Sharon's disengagement plan

2006   4 January, Sharon suffers a haemorrhagic stroke and falls into a coma; Ehud Olmert takes over as acting prime minister

25 January, Hamas wins the legislative elections, taking 74 out of 132 seats

30 January, The Quartet makes international aid contingent upon Hamas accepting the Roadmap

19 February, Israel imposes economic sanctions on Gaza

29 March, Investiture of Hamas government

7 April 2006, EU suspends direct financial aid to the Palestinian government

14 April, Olmert is elected prime minister

8 June, Israel resumes its policy of targeted killings with the assassination of Hamas Interior and National Security Minister Jamal Abu Samhadan

9 June, Israel conducts air strikes against Gaza beach; Hamas consequently breaks its 16-month ceasefire

24 June, IDF abducts 2 brothers Osama and Mustafa Muamar, deeming them responsible for rocket attacks against Israel

25 June, Palestinian commando unit abducts Israeli soldier Gilad Shalit

28 June, Israel launches Operation Summer Rains; one of the aims is to free the kidnapped soldier

12 July, Hizbollah launches an ambush on an Israeli patrol, capturing two soldiers and killing three others

30 July, Qana in southern Lebanon is bombed by Israel, killing 28 civilians

1 November, Operation Summer Rains is replaced by Operation Autumn Clouds

26 November, Operation Autumn Clouds ends

2007   February, Fatah and Hamas sign Mecca Agreement

10–15 June, Battle of Gaza in which Hamas ousts Fatah from the Gaza Strip

19 September, Israel declares the Gaza Strip a hostile entity

28 October, Israel imposes economic sanctions on Gaza

26–28 November, Annapolis summit between Israeli prime minister Ehud Olmert and Palestinian president Mahmud Abbas; these are the first talks after 7 years, the aim being to implement the Roadmap and conclude a final status agreement in 2008

2008   27 February, Rockets are fired at the Israeli city of Ashkelon, killing one Israeli

28 February, Israel launches Operation Hot Winter

3 March, Operation Hot Winter ends

19 June, Israel and Hamas agree to a 6-month ceasefire through Egyptian mediation; Israel agrees to gradual lifting of the blockades imposed upon Gaza

4 November, Israeli infantry unit enters Gaza and shoots dead 6 Hamas gunmen; Hamas responds with rocket attacks into southern Israel

19 December, Hamas announces end of ceasefire as Israel has not lifted blockade

27 December, Israel launches Operation Cast Lead with the stated objective to put an end to the firing of rockets into Israel

2009 3 January, IDF ground offensive starts

6 January, Israel bombs 3 UN-managed schools; at least 43 Palestinians killed

9 January, UNSC calls for ceasefire

17 January, Israel announces unilateral ceasefire, giving the IDF a week to withdraw from Gaza

2 April, A Palestinian attacks a group of Israeli children with an axe, killing 1 and injuring 3

24 December, Rabbi Meir Hai is killed in a drive-by shooting later claimed by the Al-Aqsa Martyrs Brigades

2010 10 February, A PA police officer stabs an Israeli soldier to death

May, Turkish activists with the Free Gaza Flotilla try to break Israel's naval blockade of the Gaza Strip; when the IDF intercepts them and boards the ship, 3 Israeli soldiers are taken hostage; 9 Turks are killed by the IDF in the ensuing struggle

2 September, US-facilitated talks between Israel and the PA in Washington

14 September, second round of Israel–PA talks in Sharm al-Shaykh

2011 11 March, Two Palestinians enter the town of Itamar and kill 5 members of the Fogel family while asleep in their beds, including three young children

15 March, Israel seizes the ship *Victoria* carrying missiles from Iran

23 March, The bombing of a bus stop in Jerusalem kills 1 Israeli and injures another 39

7 April, Hamas militants bomb an Israeli school bus, killing one teenager

18 August, Palestinian and Egyptian militants carry out a cross-border attack on southern Israel, killing 6 Israeli civilians, 2 Israeli soldiers and 5 Egyptian soldiers

September, The PA puts forward a resolution for the recognition of Palestinian statehood in the UN

November, the vote on Palestinian statehood is postponed as it had no support from the US, France and the UK; However Palestine is given UNESCO membership

2012 9–15 March, Some 300 rockets, Grad missiles and mortar shells are fired into southern Israel, wounding 23 Israelis; Israel retaliates with air strikes, killing 22 Palestinians

21 September, Militants carry out an Egyptian–Israeli cross-border attack, firing upon Israeli soldiers and civilian workers, killing one

14 November, Israel launches Operation Pillar of Defence

21 November, Hamas and Israel conclude ceasefire through Egyptian mediation

29 November, The UN upgrades Palestine to non-member observer status

2013   23 January, A Palestinian woman is shot dead by an Israeli soldier; another is wounded

30 April, An Israeli is killed by a Palestinian

26 August, Three Palestinians die in clashes in the West Bank

21 September, An Israeli soldier is abducted and killed in Beit Amin

22 September, An Israeli soldier is killed by a Palestinian sniper in Hebron

2014   23 April, Hamas and the PA form a national unity government; Netanyahu withdraws from US peace efforts in return

12 June, Israeli teenagers Naphtali Fraenkel, Gilad Shaer and Eyal Yifrah are kidnapped by a rogue Hamas cell led by Marwan Qawasmeh and Amer Abu Aysha

17 June, Israel launches Operation Brothers' Keeper to find the 3 teenagers

30 June, The bodies of the 3 teenagers are found buried near Hebron

2 July, Palestinian youth Mohamed Abu Khair is abducted by 3 Israeli settlers and burnt to death

8 July, Hamas fires M-75 rockets at Tel Aviv and Jerusalem; Israel launches Operation Protective Edge

17 July, Start of Israeli ground operation

26 August, Hamas and Israel agree to a ceasefire through Egyptian mediation

2015   September, A new wave of Palestinian violence erupts in Jerusalem, which the media labels 'intifada of the knives'. Between 13 September and 9 December, according to the Israeli Foreign Ministry, Israelis were killed in 90 stabbings, 33 shootings and 14 car rammings

Who's who

Abbas, Mahmoud (b. 1935): Palestinian politician. *Nom de guerre* Abu Mazen. Key figure in the PLO; founding member alongside Yasser Arafat; architect of 1993 Oslo Accords; PLO Executive Committee member since 2004; first Palestinian Prime Minister March to October 2003; elected Palestinian President in January 2005.

Abdallah (1882–1951): Second son of the Sharif of Mecca; Amir of Transjordan 1921–46; King of Transjordan 1946–48; King of Jordan 1948–51. Regarded as a collaborator with the British and the Jews, he was assassinated on 20 July 1951 by a Palestinian while entering the al-Aqsa Mosque in Jerusalem.

Abu Jihad: Palestinian guerrilla. Second in command to Arafat; assassinated in Tunis.

Ali, Ahmad Ismail: Egyptian Defence Minister during the 1973 October War.

Arafat, Yasser (1929–2004): Palestinian guerrilla leader and politician since 1958; founding member of Fatah; became Chairman of the PLO Executive Committee in 1969; was appointed Commander-in-Chief of Palestinian Arab guerrilla forces in 1970; signed the Oslo Accords with Israel in 1993; elected Palestinian President in 1996.

Al-Asad, Bashar (b. 1965): Syrian politician; son of former President Hafez al-Asad; Syrian President since his father's death in 2000.

Al-Asad, Hafez (1930–2000): Syrian officer and politician of Alawi origin; appointed Commander of the Syrian Air Force in 1963; led coup d'état in 1966; Syrian Prime Minister 1970–71; Syrian President 1971–2000.

Ashrawi, Hanan Michail (b. 1946): Palestinian politician; member of the Palestinian delegation to the Madrid peace conference; elected to the Palestinian Authority in 1996.

Barak, Ehud (b. 1942): Israeli politician and retired general; Prime Minister 1999–2001; most decorated Israeli soldier.

Begin, Menachem (1913–92): Zionist underground leader and Israeli politician. Head of the militant underground organization Irgun 1943–48; founder of the Herut Party in 1948; minister without portfolio in the 1967 National Unity Government; resigned post in 1970; elected first

Likud Prime Minister in 1977; withdrew from politics after the Sabra and Shatilla massacres in Lebanon in 1982; resigned from office in 1983.

Beilin, Yossi (b. 1948): Israeli politician; member of Knesset for the Labour Party; Deputy Finance Minister 1988–90; Deputy Foreign Minister 1992–95; Minister of Justice 1999–2001; architect of Oslo Accords; participated in 2001 Taba Talks; author of the Geneva Accord.

Ben Gurion, David (1886–1973): Israeli politician. First Secretary-General of the Histadrut in 1920; elected chairman of the Zionist Executive and Jewish Agency in 1935; became first Israeli Prime Minister and Defence Minister in 1948; left the government in 1953; returned first as Defence Minister and then Prime Minister in 1955; resigned in 1963.

Bernadotte, Count Folke (1895–1948): A Swedish nobleman and president of the Swedish Red Cross; appointed UN mediator for Palestine in May 1948; recommended merger of Arab Palestine with Jordan; suggested that Haifa be made international port and Lydda international airport; he was assassinated on 17 September 1948 by Jewish extremists.

Breznev, Leonid (1906–82): Soviet officer and politician. Elected deputy to Supreme Soviet of USSR in 1950; elected to Central Committee of the Communist Party in 1952; President of the Supreme Soviet 1960–63; elected First Secretary of the Central Committee of the Communist Party of the Soviet Union in 1964; title changed to General Secretary in 1966.

Carter, Jimmy (b. 1924): US politician. Entered state politics in 1962 after seven years' service as a naval officer; US president 1977–81.

Clinton, Bill (b. 1946): US politician; Served 12 years as governor of Arkansas; 42nd president of the United States 1993–01.

Dayan, Moshe (1915–81): Israeli military and political leader; lost his eye in 1941 in an Allied operation against Vichy France in Lebanon; led the IDF to victory in the Sinai campaign; left army in 1957 to enter politics; Minister of Agriculture 1959–64; Minister of Defence in June 1967.

Dulles, John Foster (1888–1959): US Secretary of State under Eisenhower; Cold War hardliner; wanted to create a Middle East defence organization; played a decisive role in US Middle East policy during the Suez Crisis.

Eisenhower, Dwight (1890–1969): US general and politician. Commanding general of US forces in Europe during the Second World War; assumed supreme command over NATO forces in 1951; US president 1953–61.

Eshkol, Levi (1895–1969): Labour Zionist leader and Israeli politician. Minister of agriculture 1951–52; Minister of Finance 1952–63; Prime Minister 1963–69; Defence Minister 1963–67.

Farouk, King of Egypt (1920–65): Son of King Fu'ad; educated in England and Egypt; inherited the throne in 1936; deposed in July 1952 by the Free Officers; went into exile to Italy.

Ford, Gerald (b. 1913): US politician. Elected to Congress in 1948; became vice-president under Nixon; became US president in 1974 upon Nixon's resignation; US president 1974–77.

Gemayel, Bashir (1947–82): Lebanese politician and militia leader. Appointed political director of Kataib Party (Ashrafieh district) in 1972; became Commander-in-Chief of the Kataib Military Council in 1976; appointed head of unified command of Lebanese Forces in 1976; became Commander-in Chief of Lebanese Forces in 1980; elected Lebanese President in 1982; was killed before he could assume office in September 1982.

Haig, Alexander (1924–2010): US officer and politician. Supreme Allied Commander in Europe 1974–79; Secretary of State under Reagan 1981–82.

Haniyyeh, Ismail (b. 1963): Hamas politician; dean of Islamic University in Gaza 1993; Palestinian Prime Minister in 2006.

Herzl, Theodor (1860–1904): Father of political Zionism; founder of World Zionist Organisation; author of *Der Judenstaat* (The Jewish State); organized the first Zionist Congress in Basle in 1897.

Hussein, King of Jordan (1935–99): Born in Amman; educated in Egypt and England; crowned in 1953; signed defence treaty with Egypt in May 1967; expelled PLO from Jordan in 1970; signed peace with Israel in 1994.

Al-Husseini, Hajj Amin (1894–1974): Palestinian political and religious leader; headed anti-Jewish demonstrations in 1920; became Mufti of Jerusalem in 1921; elected president of the Supreme Muslim Council in 1922; elected president of Arab Higher Committee in 1936; led Arab revolt 1936–37; escaped to Syria and then to Germany where he worked for the Nazis as a propagandist; tried to form an 'All Palestine Government' in Gaza in 1948; moved to Lebanon.

Khalaf, Salah (1933–91): Palestinian guerrilla. Fatah leader upon the establishment of the resistance movement in 1957.

Kissinger, Henry (b. 1923): US politician. Served in the Army 1943–46; member of faculty of Harvard University 1954–69; received Nobel Peace Prize in 1973; US Secretary of State 1973–77; Assistant to President for National Security Affairs until 1975.

McMahon, Henry (1862–1949): British High Commissioner in Egypt 1914–16; accepted principles of Arab independence in correspondence with Sharif Hussein of Mecca.

Meir, Golda (1898–1978): Zionist leader and Israeli politician. Active in the Histadrut; member of the Political Department of the Jewish Agency in 1936; met secretly with King Abdallah of Jordan in an effort to reach an agreement in 1947; member of Knesset since 1949; Minister of Labour 1949–56; Foreign Minister 1956–66; appointed Secretary-General of Mapai in 1965; Prime Minister 1969–73.

al-Moualem, Walid (b.1941): Syrian diplomat; Foreign Minister in 2006; former Syrian Ambassador to the United States.

Mubarak, Hosni (b. 1949):   Egyptian officer and politician. Vice-president under Sadat; became president upon Sadat's assassination in 1981.

Muhieddin, Zakariya (1918–2012):   Egyptian officer and politician. Joined Free Officer coup in 1952; Minister of Interior 1953–56; Prime Minister 1965–66; Vice-President 1966–67; removed from government 1968.

Nasser, Gamal Abdel (1918–70):   Egyptian officer and politician. Participant in 1952 Free Officers coup; Deputy Secretary of the Revolutionary Council in 1953; Prime Minister in 1954; elected president in 1956; promoted doctrine of Arab Socialism.

Netanyahu, Benjamin (b. 1949):   Israeli politician. Israeli Ambassador to UN 1984–88; elected Likud Member of Knesset in 1988; elected Israeli Prime Minister in 1996.

Olmert, Ehud (b. 1945):   Israeli politician; elected member of Knesset in 1973; mayor of Jerusalem 1992–03; became Acting Prime Minister in January 2006; elected Prime Minister in April 2006.

Peres, Shimon (b. 1923):   Israeli statesman. Deputy Director of the Ministry of Defence in 1952; Director General of the Ministry of Defence 1953–65; Defence Minister 1974–77; acting Prime Minister after Yitzhak Rabin's assassination November 1995–May 1996.

Pyrlin, Evgeny: Head of the Egypt Department, Soviet Foreign Ministry, during the 1967 June War.

Rabin, Yitzhak (1922–95):   Israeli general and politician. Chief of Staff in 1964; Israeli Prime Minister 1974–77; Defence Minister in 1984; Prime Minister 1992–95; signed Oslo Accords with PLO.

Sadat, Anwar (1918–81):   Egyptian officer and politician. One of the leaders of the Free Officers; participated in 1952 coup; Chairman of the National Assembly, 1959–69; appointed Vice-President in 1969; succeeded Nasser as president after Nasser's death in 1970; signed peace with Israel in 1979; assassinated by Islamists in 1981.

Samuel, Sir Herbert (1870–1963):   British liberal statesman. Helped prepare the ground for the Balfour Declaration; first High Commissioner of Palestine 1920–25; drafted 1922 White Paper; after Second World War opposed partition of Palestine.

Sharett, Moshe (1894–1965):   Labour Zionist leader and Israeli politician. Appointed head of the Political Department of the Jewish Agency in 1933; chief Zionist spokesman to the British and the Arabs; Israeli Foreign Minister 1948–56; Chairman of the Zionist and Jewish Agency Executive 1960–65.

Sharon, Ariel (1928–2014):   Israeli general and politician. Elected Likud Member of Knesset in 1974; Special Advisor to Rabin 1975–76; Minister of Agriculture 1977–81; Minister of Defence 1981–82; Minister without portfolio 1982–84; Prime Minister 2001–06; suffered a haemorrhagic stroke on 4 January 2006.

Al-Shukayri, Ahmad (1907–1980):   Palestinian politician; headed Palestinian propaganda office in the United States in 1946; member of Syrian delegation to the UN 1949–50; Under-Secretary for Political Affairs of the Arab League 1951–57; Saudi Arabian Minister of State for UN Affairs and Ambassador to UN 1957–62; Palestinian Representative to Arab League in 1963; Chairman of PLO 1964–69.

Vance, Cyrus (1917–2002):   US politician; Secretary of State under Carter 1977–80; resigned over Carter's decision to attempt a rescue of the hostages in Iran.

Wazir, Khalil (1935–1988):   Palestinian guerrilla; Fatah leader upon the establishment of the resistance movement in 1957.

Weizmann, Chaim (1874–1952):   Chemistry professor and Zionist leader; president of the Zionist Organization 1920–48; supported partition on the grounds of parity in Palestine; first President of Israel 1948–52.

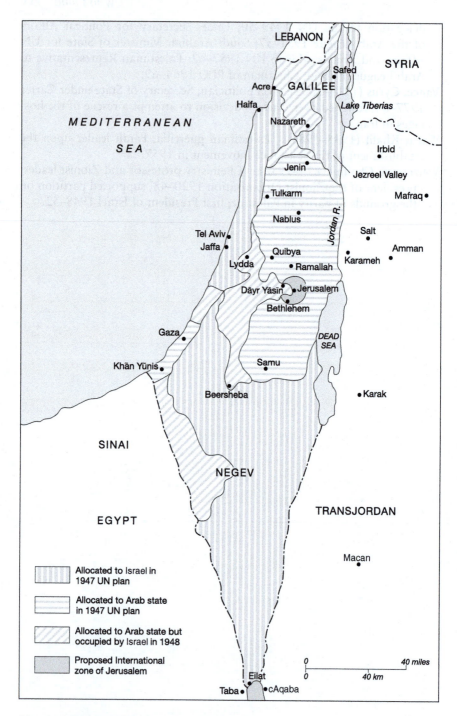

Map 1 Palestine and Transjordan, 1947–48

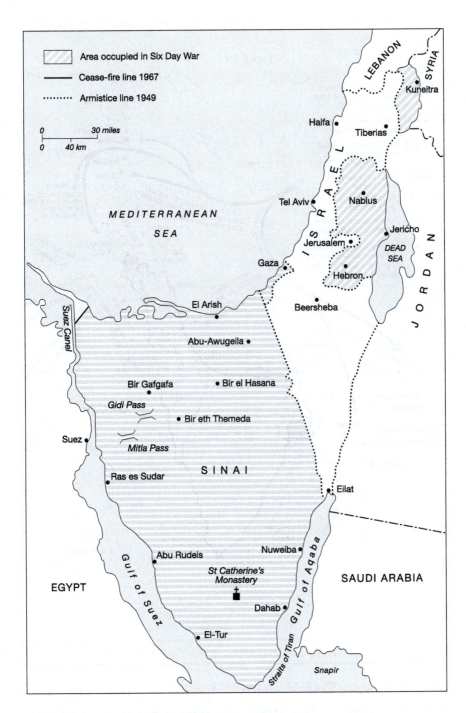

Map 2 The revised borders after the Six Day War

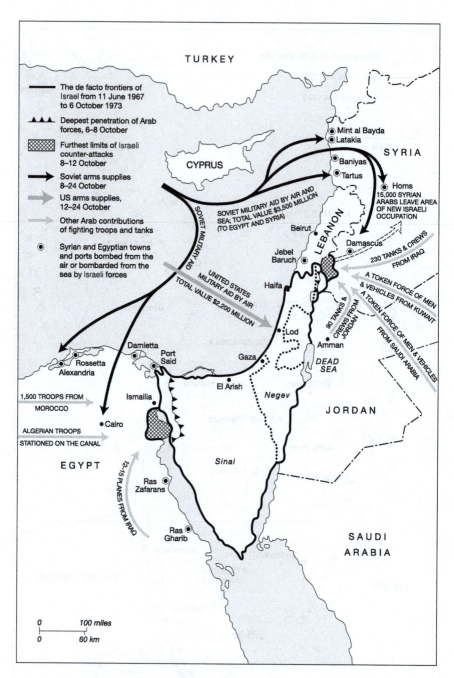

Map 3 The October War, 6–24 October 1973

Source: Adapted from Gilbert, Martin, *Atlas of the Arab-Israeli Conflict* (© 2002, Routledge), reprinted by permission of Taylor & Francis Books UK.

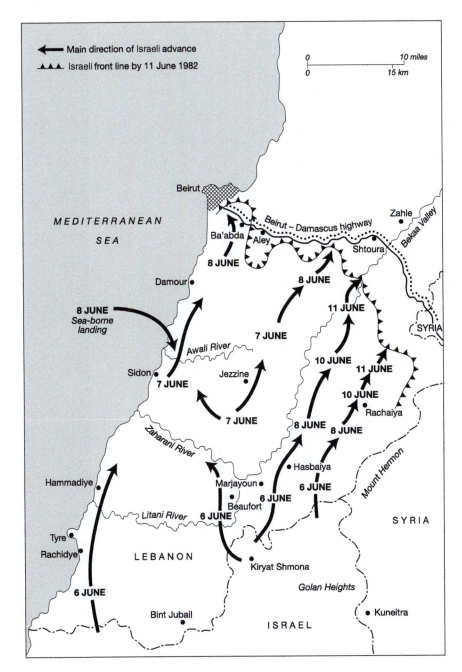

Map 4 The war in Lebanon, 6 June–21 August 1982

Source: Adapted from Gilbert, Martin, *Atlas of the Arab-Israeli Conflict* (© 2002, Routledge), reprinted by permission of Taylor & Francis Books UK.

Part I
Background

1 The origins of the Arab–Israeli conflict

The origins of the Arab–Israeli conflict have been the subject of numerous debates. Biblical enmity between Abraham's two sons Isaac and Ishmael, the advent of Islam, the prophet Mohammed's quarrel with the Jews of Medina, the emergence of Zionism in the nineteenth century and British colonial policy in the early twentieth century have all been considered appropriate starting points. While a case for these points of departure can be made, it will be argued here that the Arab–Israeli conflict emerged with the advent of nationalism in the Middle East and that the conflict, in simplistic terms, is one of competing nationalisms.

Zionism and Arab nationalism

Zionism and Arab nationalism embarked upon a course of almost parallel development in the nineteenth century as predominantly secular political ideologies based on emancipation and ultimately self-determination. Both started in intellectual circles as a response to political challenges from Europe during that period (Tessler, 1994), and both evolved around the concepts of identity, nationhood, history, religion and culture.

When looking at Zionism it is imperative to distinguish between classical Zionism and modern political Zionism. Classical Zionism was rooted in the traditional ties Jews in the **Diaspora** proclaimed to the Land of Israel and the belief that Jewish independence would be restored with the coming of the Messiah. Modern political Zionism saw the Jewish people as constituting one nation and saw a Jewish state as the solution for the Jewish problem in Europe. It rejected assimilation, which it believed was neither desirable nor deemed to be possible. Anti-Semitism could only be overcome by physical separation from Europe and by self-determination. And for the vast majority of Zionists religious and cultural ties to the Land of Israel made Palestine the logical territory for this Jewish state.

As a political ideology modern political Zionism was a fusion of ideas and formative experiences from both Eastern and Western European Jewish thinkers. Thus it combined many of the ideas born out of the European enlightenment and the French Revolution, such as concepts of social contract, secularism, equality and citizenship, but was also a response to centuries of inequality and persecution on the other hand (Laqueur, 1974).

It was the series of pogroms which swept through southern Russia in 1881 that crushed any hopes the Eastern European Jewish intelligentsia had nurtured for reform and assimilation. These pogroms triggered Jewish emigration, mainly to the United States, but also gave birth to the Zionist movement with the first Zionist publication – *Auto-Emancipation* – written by Leo Pinsker, a Jewish doctor from Odessa, in 1882. *Auto-Emancipation* saw a territory for Jews as the answer to the burden of life as a Jewish minority among Gentiles and as the means to regain lost dignity and self-respect. Drawing upon Pinsker's ideas, the first Zionist organization *Hibbat Zion* (Lovers of Zion) was formed to channel small groups of idealist settlers to Palestine. They were part of what became known as the first *Aliyah*, which lasted from 1882 to 1903 and founded the first Jewish settlements of Rishon LeZion, Petah Tikva, Rehovot and Rosh Pina.

Pinsker was soon joined by **Theodor Herzl**, who came to similar conclusions but from a completely different starting point. Herzl was a Western European–assimilated Jew who lived in Vienna. In 1894 he was in France as a journalist and reported on the trial of the French Jewish officer Alfred Dreyfus, who had been falsely accused and convicted of treason. Herzl was shocked by the anti-Semitism in a country as cultured as France and the birthplace of the French Revolution. So in 1896 Herzl wrote a book titled *Der Judenstaat* (The Jewish State) [Doc. 1, p. 131]. In it Herzl called for the creation of a Jewish state, as assimilation had not produced the hoped-for end to anti-Semitism. Only a state of their own could provide a rational solution to the Jewish experience of rejection, humiliation and shame. Only a state of their own could provide a permanent solution to the problem of the Jews. Through a state of their own, the Jewish people could finally occupy an equal place among nations.

Herzl's activism and his ideas resulted in the convening of the First Zionist Congress in 1897 in Basle, Switzerland. It was here that the ideas of a Jewish state were linked to the ideas of returning to the Land of Israel. Interestingly, neither Pinsker nor Herzl had been particularly committed to Palestine as the territory for their Jewish state. Indeed, both were, in principle, prepared to accept land elsewhere such in Argentina or in British East Africa. However, Herzl found himself quickly outnumbered by those who favoured Palestine and thus the World Zionist Organization, which was established at this Congress, called for the 'creation of a home for the Jewish people in Palestine to be secured by public law'. This aim was to be achieved through the acquisition of land, the immigration of European Jews to Palestine and the settlement of Palestine. This Jewish settlement in Palestine became known as the *Yishuv*.

Zionism saw two further developments which are of long-term interest for the Arab–Israeli conflict. The first was the introduction of socialist principles and ideas of class struggle. These ideas were fused with Zionism by thinkers such as A.D. Gordon, giving rise to Labour Zionism. These ideas infused the second Aliyah between 1904 and 1913, which included mainly Russian and East European Jews fleeing the renewed persecution following the 1905 aborted Russian revolution. An estimated 2.5 million Jews left Russia at that time, of which 60,000 settled in Palestine (Tessler, 1994). This second Aliyah created the first Zionist institutions in Palestine, including the agricultural cooperative or **kibbutz** which clearly embodied socialist ideals. This second Aliyah is also conventionally credited with laying the institutional foundations of the *Yishuv*.

The second development in Zionist ideology was the introduction of right-wing nationalist principles in the 1920s and 1930s, again reflecting broader trends in European nationalism. These recast the rational Enlightenment-based Zionism of Herzl into a romantic-exclusivist, much more ethnic nationalism, which openly acknowledged both its colonial nature and the impossibility of co-existence with the Arabs living in Palestine. The key proponent of this strand of Zionism, which became known as Revisionist Zionism, was Vladimir Ze'ev Jabotinski, who in his treatise 'The Iron Wall' [Doc. 2, p. 132] emphasized the need for Jewish soldiers and self-defence.

Zionism as a modern nationalist movement came into direct competition with Arab nationalism and later with Palestinian nationalism, as both Jews and Arabs laid claim to the same territory. Arab nationalism is the belief that the Arab people constitute a single political community or nation, which should be either independent and united under a common government (Goldschmidt, 1996) or a set of independent allied Arab states. Modern Arab nationalism emerged within the context of the Arab renaissance or awakening, which began at the end of the eighteenth century. This renaissance was in part a response to the challenge of modernization but also an engagement with European nationalist ideas of freedom, independence, equality, and progress. Arab nationalism embodied both elements, embracing modernization but at the same time stressing that European colonialism was superfluous in its attainment (Tessler, 1994).

Like Zionism, Arab nationalism started to develop in intellectual circles. The first Arab nationalist party, in fact, was a small secret society founded around 1875 by graduates of the American University of Beirut. Other societies and literary clubs soon followed and disseminated Arab nationalist ideas of unity, language and culture.

At the core of Arab nationalism, like any other nationalism, was the concept of self-determination. This quest for independence emphasized three elements in Arab nationalism. First, there was a strong anti-Turkish sentiment as a reaction to centuries of Ottoman control, but also to the 1908 Young Turk revolution. Second, the entrance of European colonial powers and foreign control of Arab land led to an anti-colonial and anti-imperial element. Third, the interaction and competition with Zionism also provided it with an anti-Zionist ideology.

Despite these common aims the Arab nationalist movement was by no means unified. There were differing views on the degree of autonomy, the territorial unit and the type of political system. For instance, at the first Arab

Congress organized in 1913 in Paris, the stated aims were the establishment of administrative autonomy, Arab participation in the Ottoman central government, making Arabic an official language and generally striving towards unity – but all still within the framework of the Ottoman Empire. Other Arab nationalists, however, demanded full independence. There were also leadership struggles. As a result Arab nationalism saw both the emergence of pan-Arabism and separate localized nationalisms following the dismemberment of the Ottoman Empire by the victorious European powers after the First World War. And like Zionism it also saw a degree of fusion with other ideologies, giving birth to Arab socialist ideas such as those advanced by Michel Aflaq and Salah al-Din al-Bitar, or the 'romantic' Arab nationalist ideas of Sati al-Husri.

That leaves the question of Palestinian nationalism and at what point a distinctly Palestinian nationalism started to emerge and to what extent this was in reaction to the Jewish immigration to Palestine and Zionist institution building between 1882 and 1913 or the British mandate after the First World War. A look at Arabs in Palestine at the turn of the century reveals that indeed the majority of them did not define themselves in national terms, but rather by family, tribe, village or religion. However, it is equally evident that a process of nationalist self-definition had begun among intellectuals, and this can be traced back to the Ottoman reforms of 1872, which established the independent *sanjak* of Jerusalem and gave rise to the local urban notables. This predated the first Aliyah by a decade. Yet, at the same time, a more cohesive Palestinian discourse did not emerge until the 1936–39 Arab Revolt, which was a reaction to the Zionist state project and British colonialism.

The impact of the First World War

The outbreak of the First World War in 1914 ushered in important changes for the achievement of both Arab nationalist and Zionist aspirations, mainly as a result of Britain's policy of alliances. The Ottoman Empire had entered the war on the side of Germany. This meant that in the Middle East Britain was effectively fighting the Ottomans. In order to prevent the latter from taking the Suez Canal, Britain started to cultivate local Arab allies who would aid its war effort (Goldschmidt, 1996). In 1915 the British High Commissioner in Cairo, Sir **Henry McMahon**, negotiated the support of the **Hashemite** leader and the Amir of Mecca, **Sharif Hussein**, in return for the promise of future Arab independence. Embodied in a set of letters known as the Hussein–McMahon Correspondence [**Doc. 3, p. 133**] is the promise that the Arab territory of the Ottoman Empire be returned to Arab sovereignty, with the exception of the districts of Mersina and Alexandretta, as well as the districts west of Damascus, Homs, Hama and Aleppo, which were not purely Arab. The excluded territory, according to Arab interpretation, referred to present-day Lebanon and parts of Syria only. It did not include Palestine, despite Britain's later claim that it did.

The promise of Arab independence and statehood was not the only British pledge made in the context of First World War alliance policy. By the summer of 1917 the British government had also started to consider the Zionist movement as a potential ally (Fraser, 1995). The key player on the Zionist side was the Russian-born chemist **Chaim Weizmann** who was teaching at Manchester University. Before the war he had already had contact with a number of liberal and conservative politicians, including former Prime Minister Arthur Balfour. Weizmann furthered Zionist aspirations in two important ways: first, he was an excellent diplomat and eloquent spokesperson for the movement; second, he was involved in the synthesizing of acetone, hitherto imported from Germany, and essential for making explosives and consequently for Britain's war effort. Both enabled him to convince British decision makers that the Zionists were important for Britain's war effort. The Zionists could help sustain the Russian front, which was collapsing from internal Russian revolutionary turmoil, and they could help galvanize the desperately needed American war effort. The result of Weizmann's diplomacy and powers of persuasion was a declaration issued by Foreign Secretary Balfour on 2 November 1917, stating that 'His Majesty's Government viewed with favour the establishment in Palestine of a national home for the Jewish people' [Doc. 4, p. 133].

Some observations should be made at this point. The Balfour Declaration did not state that Palestine should be turned into a Jewish state. In fact, the word 'state' had initially appeared in the earlier drafts of the statement but was changed due to pressure from British Jews who feared that this would prejudice their rights and citizenship within the United Kingdom. Further, neither the Balfour Declaration nor the Hussein–McMahon Correspondence was specific about the actual borders of the territory promised to both Jews and Arabs. The result was that both Zionists and Arab nationalists believed Palestine had been promised to them; the seeds for conflict had been sown.

British policy and the Palestine mandate

British troops entered Palestine in 1918 and set up a provisional military government in Jerusalem. Britain had thus physically laid claim to a territory not only promised to the Arabs and Zionists, but also to one designated as an international zone in the secret 1916 British–French Sykes–Picot Agreement [Doc. 5, p. 134]. Anticipating the future dismemberment of the Ottoman Empire, Britain and France had carved the Middle East into spheres of influence to prevent a power vacuum and Russian entry into the region. British military presence from 1918 onwards assured Britain that it was granted the mandate over Palestine by the League of Nations in 1922, fulfilling its strategic aims of 'assuring access to the Suez Canal and the East, preventing French ambitions in Lebanon and Syria from drifting South, and creating a land bridge from the Mediterranean Sea to the oil fields of Iraq'

(Tessler, 1994: 7). The mandate provided Britain with the responsibility for placing the country under

> such political, administrative, and economic conditions as will secure the establishment of the Jewish national home . . . and the development of self-governing institutions, and also for safeguarding the civil and religious rights of all the inhabitants of Palestine, irrespective of race and religion.

British policy was caught between conflicting promises and different views within its own establishment right from the beginning. Popular perception of this period is that Britain was a more than inadequate mandate power which managed to stir up Arab resentment and at the same time was hostile to the Zionist state-building project. A policy acceptable to both Arabs and Zionists was never achieved, and British policy on the ground was further complicated by often contradictory positions in world politics. For instance, in the international arena Britain tended to support Zionism, while in Palestine, British officials favoured the Arabs, often influenced by concern for Muslim opinion in neighbouring countries and India (Goldschmidt, 1996). Arab and Jewish suspicions of each other and of British intentions flourished in such an environment. Many Arabs believed that Britain was planning to hold on to Palestine until a Jewish majority had been achieved. Many Jews believed that Britain was secretly aiding and arming the Arabs, as well as restricting Jewish immigration and land purchases in order to prevent the creation of a Jewish state. While British Palestine policy stumbled from one crisis to another, inter-communal violence rose, starting with the first Arab disturbances in 1920 and 1921.

The inter-war period

The period between the two world wars was characterized by institution building in Palestine. Britain's first civilian governor, **Sir Herbert Samuel,** encouraged both Jews and Arabs to form their own institutions. The Zionist Commission, which had been established after the Balfour Declaration, evolved into the Palestine Zionist Executive in 1920 and became the **Jewish Agency** in 1928–29. Foundations laid earlier by the Zionist Organization were expanded and built upon. The majority of institutions, which later served as the framework for the new Israeli state, were established during this time, including political parties, the general labour federation or **Histadrut,** the underground defence organization or **Haganah** and the Hebrew University of Jerusalem. These institutions constituted a proto-state which made the transition to full statehood in 1948 easier.

Arab or, indeed, Palestinian institution building did not take place at the same rate. Despite the fact that the British military and civil administration encouraged Palestinian Arabs to mobilize, resulting in the formation of the

Figure 1.1 The arrival of Sir Herbert Samuel as high commissioner of Palestine. © Universal History Archive/UIG via Getty Images

Arab Executive in 1920, the Arabs remained divided by religious, family and regional loyalties. Consequently the local Arab Executive was a feeble vehicle for their aspirations, beset by feuds between followers of the two leading notable Jerusalem families, the Husseinis and Nashashibis, who, amongst other issues, were split over the degree of Arab cooperation with the British authorities. In the 1930s the feud was clearly won by the Mufti of Jerusalem, **Hajj Amin al-Husseini**, who emerged as the unrivalled leader of the Palestinian cause. In addition to local rivalry, the emergence of Palestinian nationalism, which needed to counter the advances of the Zionist project on the ground, competed directly with the Arab nationalist agenda promoted by the Hashemites.

In the early days under Samuel it looked as if Jewish–Arab differences would be resolved in the near future. The number of Jewish immigrants had started to decrease, and some immigrants decided to leave Palestine for the greener shores of the United States (Goldschmidt, 1996: 248). A limited amount of Arab–Jewish co-operation and the absence of widespread violence supported this perception. In 1929, however, the situation changed drastically with the **Wailing Wall or Western Wall** incident. The disturbances which erupted in response to benches being set up in front of the Wailing Wall resulted in 133 Jewish deaths and 116 Arab deaths (Fraser, 1995: 11). It was followed by the massacre of most of the Jewish residents of Hebron. The British attempt to calm the situation further exacerbated inter-communal tension. Colonial Secretary Lord Passfield issued a White Paper blaming the Jewish Agency land purchases for the disturbances. Restrictions on Jewish immigrants were consequently tightened. The Jewish reaction was outrage. In an attempt to assuage the Jews, the British Prime Minister Ramsay MacDonald then issued a letter explaining away the White Paper, which, in turn, angered the Arabs.

During the 1930s British policy started to shift from the 'status of umpire to that of advocate and finally paternal defender of Arab rights' (Tessler, 1994: 81). At the same time the rise to power of Adolf Hitler in Germany and his anti-Semitic ideology made the Zionist need for a Jewish state more pressing. Restrictions on immigration into the United States left Palestine as the only alternative. The number of Jewish immigrants started to increase again. Between 1930 and 1936 alone the Jewish population rose from 164,000 to 370,000. Thus it is no surprise that the local Arab population became more and more convinced that their aspirations would ultimately be sacrificed for German ambitions. This feeling of anger and impotence among the Arabs led to a new phase in Arab nationalism, which can be seen as the first popular expression of a distinctly Palestinian nationalism.

Arab opposition to this increased immigration found expression in the Arab Revolt, which began on 15 April 1936 with the murder of a Jew near the town of Nablus. The **Arab Higher Committee** was formed under the leadership of Hajj Amin al-Husseini and found support in the wider Arab nationalist community. The initial strike turned into a large-scale rebellion, paralyzing Palestine for months. The revolt tied up British military resources at a time when belligerence was increasing in Europe. An end to the Arab Revolt had to be achieved in order to avoid being caught in a two-front war. The Palestine Royal Commission was set up under Lord Peel in order to determine the causes of the conflict and find a way of dealing with the grievances of both Arabs and Jews. The Arabs, however, boycotted the commission until just before its departure, effectively leaving the floor to the Zionists. In 1937 the commission published its recommendations [**Doc. 6, p. 134**], stating that co-existence was impossible and that partition was the only solution. Arab opposition to partition was inevitable, and as war in Europe was only a matter of time, the goodwill of the Arabs needed to be reestablished quickly. Colonial Secretary Malcolm MacDonald thus issued a White Paper in 1939 [**Doc. 7, p. 135**], which not only limited Jewish immigration to 15,000 per year until 1944, but also made it contingent upon Arab consent thereafter. For the Jews the 1939 White Paper represented the deepest act of betrayal at the time of their greatest peril (Fraser, 1995: 14). It ensured that the limited number of Jews who were able to escape the death camps of the Holocaust had nowhere to go.

The impact of the Second World War

The Second World War broke out when the German army invaded Poland on 1 September 1939. As most Arab countries were still under some form of mandate control at that time, the official Arab position was one of neutrality. Arab sentiments in Palestine, however, were more ambiguous. Hajj Amin al-Husseini had made contacts with Germany, seeing the Nazis as a tool to free Palestine from both the British and the Zionists. The Germans, conversely, saw Husseini as a vehicle for recruiting Bosnian Muslims into the SS. While Husseini's decision not to remain neutral was by choice, neutrality for the Jews was an option not afforded them. The unravelling events in Germany and Eastern Europe made it imperative for the Jews to join the Allied war effort. Palestinian Jews enlisted in the British Army in large numbers despite their resentment against British policy in Palestine. Zionist leader and future prime minister of Israel, **David Ben Gurion**, summed up the Jewish attitude in Palestine quite aptly when he said: 'We must assist the British in the war as if there were no White Paper and we must resist the White Paper as if there were no war' (Goldschmidt, 1996: 251).

Assistance in the war came through the contribution of a Jewish legion, which fought alongside the British Army in the Middle East and Europe (Garfinkle, 1997). Resisting the White Paper came in the form of illegal immigration. In 1940 alone an estimated 40,000 Jews entered Palestine illegally (Zweig, 1986: 47). British reaction was to suspend the quota allowed under the White Paper in October 1940 and to intercept ships and deport refugees. The stream of immigrants declined sharply in 1941 when Germany gained control of the Balkans, but increased again with the end of the war and the liberation of the concentration camps. Britain's attempts to stifle immigration resulted in the confiscation of ships, preventing ships from sailing by diplomatic means, intercepting ships and diverting them to Cyprus (Hadari, 1991) – a policy pursued until the expiry of the mandate.

The Second World War had a number of dramatic effects upon the conflict in Palestine. First, Britain's empire was clearly in decline. Maintaining colonies, protectorates and mandates was becoming increasingly difficult in the face of the worsening economic situation in the United Kingdom. Maintaining the Palestine mandate and containing the increasing conflict were becoming too costly, politically, economically and financially, at a time when the British government's priority was post-war reconstruction. Thus, from 1945 onwards, Britain started to look for an honourable way out.

Second, concomitant with the decline of British influence was the rise of US influence in the region. Lobbying by Jewish Americans and a broad American-Zionist network resulted in the Biltmore Program at a conference in May 1942, which called for a Jewish state in Palestine. This programme did not find immediate support within the US administration, as President Roosevelt was worried about Arab oil supplies during the war. Yet, in the 1944 presidential elections, keeping the ethnic vote in mind, both Democratic and Republican election platforms endorsed the Biltmore Program. The stage for post-war US policy had been set.

Third, the Holocaust and the mass murder of 5,600,000 to 6,900,000 Jews led the survivors of the camps and the Zionist Movement to push even harder for a state. It had become clear that only a state of their own could provide the Jews with security. The Holocaust also engendered international sympathy, which the Zionist cause needed for the final stage in its struggle for statehood.

Fourth, as a result of the war Europe was faced with a refugee problem of enormous proportions. This created pressure for increasing the number of Jewish immigrants to Palestine and for ending the restrictions on land purchases. These two issues were the key recommendations of the 1946 Anglo-American Committee of Inquiry.

And fifth, the situation in Palestine had deteriorated rapidly towards the end of the war and had developed into an almost full-scale Jewish uprising against the British, as well as inter-communal Arab–Jewish tensions bordering on civil war. By October 1947, Jewish attacks had killed 127 British soldiers and wounded 133 others (Garfinkle, 1997: 52). British policy had become untenable.

These five key factors created the environment which made British withdrawal almost inevitable and the establishment of a Jewish state in Palestine possible. It also convinced both Jews and Arabs that ultimately there would be war.

Partition

The British withdrawal from Palestine and the decision to hand Palestine over to the newly established United Nations was the result of Britain's inability to settle the conflict between Zionists and Arabs, as well as Britain's need to address more pressing matters at home. The United Nations set up a Special Committee for Palestine (**UNSCOP**) and sent it on a mission of inquiry during the summer of 1947. Like the 1937 Peel Commission and the 1946 Anglo-American Commission, UNSCOP set out to listen to both Arabs and Jews in Palestine, as well as to consider the submissions of other Arab leaders of the region. But believing that the commission was already biased towards the Zionists, the Arab Higher Committee boycotted it. This Arab perception was to some extent correct, as the visible horrors of the Holocaust and the alliance of Hajj Amin al-Husseini with Adolf Hitler had already reduced UNSCOP's choice (Pappé, 1994). These perceptions, however, were only reinforced by the Arab boycott.

Like the previous commissions, UNSCOP, too, came to the conclusion that both Jewish and Arab claims were of equal validity, that their aspirations were irreconcilable and that the only viable solution to the conflict was the separation of the two communities by partitioning the territory and creating both an Arab and a Jewish state.

The Partition Plan drawn up by UNSCOP divided Palestine in accordance with the existing settlement pattern and population centres. The proposed Arab state was to consist of the coastal strip of Gaza; Galilee in the north; and the area around Nablus, Hebron and Beersheba. The proposed Jewish state was to consist of the coastal area around Tel Aviv and Haifa, the Negev in the south, and the Jezreel and Hule valleys. The city of Jerusalem, according to the UN partition plan, was to come under international control [Map 1, p. xxvi]. One problem with the plan was the territorial fragmentation of both proposed states, as well as the notion that while partition was necessary, economic unity should be retained. Another problem was the Arab population 'trapped' in the proposed Jewish state.

Although Zionist politicians did not like the status of Jerusalem or the lack of territorial contiguity, they accepted the plan as a first step to statehood. The Arab leadership, on the other hand, could not find any redeeming aspects in a plan that allotted part of their territory to the Zionists. **Arab League** members met to adopt a common strategy and decided to go to war to prevent the creation of a Jewish state. Beyond the public facade of unity, however, Arab leaders were as divided as ever. King Abdallah of Transjordan concluded a secret deal with the Zionists to partition the Arab sections of Palestine (Shlaim, 1988). Egypt and Syria also had territorial as well as leadership ambitions. When the Partition Plan was passed in the General Assembly on 29 November 1947 by a vote of 33 in favour, 13 against (including the United Kingdom) and 10 abstentions, it was not surprising that the five Arab member states opposed it.

Part II
Wars and peace

2   The 1948 war

The first Arab–Israeli war began in December 1947 and lasted until January 1949. This war went down in Israeli history as the War of Independence during which the State of Israel was proclaimed, survived the subsequent attack by its Arab neighbours and even expanded its territory. In Arab history this was the 1948 Palestine war, a war that saw defeat of the Arab armies and subsequent delegitimation of the governments involved. In Palestinian history this war is referred to as *an-Nakba* or 'the catastrophe' as the Palestinians lost the territory of their state and were dispersed as a nation of refugees. Attempts to apportion responsibility for the refugee situation, the conduct of forces during the war and the inability to reach a peaceful settlement in its aftermath have resulted in controversy between traditionalist and revisionist historians in Israel, as well as disputes between Arab, Israeli and Palestinian scholars and politicians.

The first Arab–Israeli war

The 1948 war can be divided into two very distinct phases. The first phase began almost immediately following the UN General Assembly vote on the partition of Palestine on 29 November 1947. The emerging inter-communal conflict between Jews and Arabs in Palestine was partially driven by the way that the territory of Palestine had been divided between Arabs and Jews. The loosely connected bits of land that were to form the territory of the Arab and Jewish states, respectively, were neither properly contiguous nor did they have defensible boundaries. They also included pockets of 'enemy population'. The emerging conflict was driven by the mutual assumption that conflict was inevitable. Thus both Jews and Arabs started to arm themselves while the Arab Higher Committee called a strike for 2–4 December reminiscent of the strikes that had characterized the 1936–39 Arab Revolt. It was these strikes that provided the spark for the first inter-communal clashes, which soon turned into a full-blown Jewish–Arab civil war in Palestine. The months before the end of the mandate were characterized by bitter fighting and large numbers of civilian casualties – including the massacre at the Arab village of Deir Yassin by the **Irgun** and **Lehi,** which killed 250, and the Arab ambush on a Jewish medical convoy killing 75 (Morris, 1987).

During this first phase of the war, armed Palestinians augmented by Arab irregulars, which at their height numbered 6,000 to 7,000 and became known as the **Arab Liberation Army,** targeted outlying and less defensible Jewish settlements and towns. They also sought to cut the main roads connecting Jewish areas. They scored some early successes as the Zionist leadership struggled with arms procurement and the difficulties of coordinating an 'army' consisting of European refugees and local Jews. The situation was particularly critical in the Galilee where Jewish settlements were surrounded by Arab villages, as well as in Jerusalem, where the Jewish population was almost completely under siege and running out of food, water and ammunition. It was with this situation in mind that the controversial Plan D or **Dalet** [**Doc. 8, p. 136**] was drafted. 'To win the battle of the roads, the *Haganah* had to pacify the Arab villages and towns that dominated them: pacification perforce meant either the surrender of the villages or their depopulation and destruction' (Morris, 1987: 62). The main question Plan Dalet raises is to what extent the plan constituted a blueprint for the expulsion of the Palestinian Arabs and can thus be seen as the cause of the Palestinian refugee problem.

The second phase of the 1948 war started with the end of the British mandate; Israel's declaration of independence [**Doc. 9, p. 141**] on 14 May 1948; and the subsequent declaration of war by Egypt, Jordan, Lebanon, Syria and Iraq, turning the on-going Zionist–Palestinian civil war into an Arab–Israeli inter-state conflict.

The newly established State of Israel was on the defensive for the first month of this inter-state war as Arab soldiers attacked it from all sides. This, however, changed with the first ceasefire on 11 June 1948, which was ordered by the **United Nations Security Council** and supervised by UN mediator **Count Folke Bernadotte.** Bernadotte proposed a new political compromise, calling for a Palestine Union to consist of separate Jewish, Palestinian and **Transjordanian** units. Although this proposal was not acceptable to any party to the conflict and Bernadotte's efforts cost him his life when he was shot by members of the Jewish underground organization Lehi on 17 September 1948 (Peretz, 1996), the ceasefire was used by all parties to try to regroup despite the UN embargo.

Israel was able to import a significant amount of rifles, machine guns, armoured cars, field guns, tanks and ammunition. This allowed the Israel Defence Force (**IDF**) to seize Nazareth between the resumption of fighting on 8 July and the second truce on 19 July. Following the second truce Israel went on the offensive, and by December 1948 it had successfully broken the Egyptian blockade in the Negev, seized most of Galilee and crossed the border into southern Lebanon.

Why did Israel win the war despite being attacked by five Arab states? Contrary to conventional Israeli accounts, Israel's victory and the defeat of the Arab armies were largely the result of the military balance during

Figure 2.1 Israeli Prime Minister David Ben Gurion (1886–1973) reading Israel's declaration of independence in Tel Aviv, flanked by members of his provisional government. © AFP/Getty Images

the 1948 war. The soldiers of the Haganah and later the IDF were highly motivated as they saw this as an existential war, knowing that a defeat most likely meant the loss of state. They were also better trained, as many officers and enlisted personnel had gained combat experience in the British army during the Second World War. Although they had problems at the beginning procuring weapons, this was resolved with the arms shipments during the first ceasefire. Israel also attained numerical superiority as Jewish refugees continued to enter Israel in large numbers during the war. In mid-May 1948 Arab troops were estimated at 20,000 to 25,000 while the **IDF** had mobilized 65,000. By September that number had risen to 90,000, and by December it peaked at 96,441 (Shlaim, 1995: 294). In comparison, the Arab armies were badly trained, ill equipped and had logistical problems, except for Transjordan's **Arab Legion** (Peretz, 1996).

Their leaders were also divided. While the official aim of the Arab states was the liberation of Palestine, a closer look at the dynamics reveals that each state was pursuing its own political and territorial aims. **King Farouk** of Egypt joined the war effort in order to check the leadership ambitions of Transjordan's King Abdallah. Transjordan, Egypt and Syria also had their eyes on territorial expansion at the expense of establishing a Palestinian state. Moreover, King Abdallah had entered into a secret agreement with the Zionists that 'laid the foundations for mutual restraint' (Shlaim, 1988:1). The lack of unity at the leadership level was further compounded by false expectations of an easy victory and spoils of war, which, on the one hand, led to a lack of preparation (Bregman and El-Tahri, 1998: 38) and, on the other hand, to a decline in morale among the Arab soldiers when these expectations were not fulfilled. In fact, morale was so low that only a month later, in June, the Arab campaign to liberate Palestine had already lost its momentum.

The post-1948 war changes to the region were quite dramatic. Not only was Israel there to stay, but during the course of the war it had increased its territory to such an extent that a contiguous and therefore defensible border had been created [**Map 1, p. xxvi**]. Israel had increased its territory by 21 per cent compared with the partition resolution boundaries. Its demographic make-up comprised 716,700 Jews, of which 591,400 were of European (**Ashkenazi**) origin and 105,000 were of Oriental (**Sephardi**) origin, as well as 165,000 Arabs, of which 19 per cent were Christian and 10 per cent **Druze** and **Circassian** (Garfinkle, 1997: 74). The Arab states, too, had increased their territory, revealing that the Arab states had not been motivated by solidarity with the Palestinians, but were competing with each other for power and territory. Transjordan gained the West Bank and Egypt the Gaza Strip. The Palestinians in contrast had lost any possibility of a state of their own. The defeat of the Arab states had important domestic repercussions as well. It de-legitimized the existing leadership, leading to revolutions, military coups and instability. Last but not least, the Palestinian Arab population had been divided: 150,000 came under Israeli rule and were granted Israeli citizenship, 450,000 came under Transjordanian control becoming Jordanian citizens and 200,000 came under Egyptian control. The total number of Palestinian refugees at the end of 1948 was somewhere between 550,000 and 800,000.

The Palestinian exodus

When fighting broke out following the UN partition resolution, Palestinians started to leave their homes in areas directly affected by the inter-communal violence. Middle- and upper-class families were the first to leave for neighbouring countries. Their departure was considered temporary, as they hoped to return to their homes after the fighting had died down. The Palestinian exodus was accelerated after the Deir Yassin massacre and the Palestinian broadcast which followed it. The Palestine National Committee under the leadership of Dr Hussein Fakhri El Khalidi attempted to make Arab governments send troops by exaggerating the Deir Yassin atrocities in a subsequent radio broadcast. 'We want you to say that the Jews slaughtered people, committed atrocities, raped, and stole gold' (Bregman and el-Tahri, 1998: 33). The broadcast had a devastating impact on everyone in Palestine, and the exodus began. It was retrospectively described as the biggest blunder that could have happened. When the Arab states finally invaded Israel, 200,000 (Peretz, 1996: 44) Palestinians had already left. After the war, the UN estimated the total refugee population at 750,000 by the beginning of 1949, and 940,000 by June of that year, coming from 369 Palestinian towns and villages.

There are three main points of contention with regard to the refugee issue. The first is a dispute over how many Palestinians left. Estimates vary greatly from one source to another, whereby Israeli sources have tended to underestimate and Arab sources have tended to overestimate the numbers. Both sides, however, concur that only about 150,000 Palestinians remained inside Israel (Tessler, 1994). The second point of contention concerns the circumstances surrounding the Palestinian exodus. Israel has blamed the Arab states for the departure of the Palestinians, maintaining that the invading Arab armies had urged the Palestinians to temporarily vacate their villages in order to smooth the path for the advancing troops. The Arabs, in turn, charged Israel with expulsion of the Palestinians as part of a systematic campaign of ethnic cleansing. Both accounts are true to some degree. Although there may not have been a Zionist plan for systematic expulsion, there were cases of expulsion such as in Lydda and Ramle. Credence must also be given to the argument that military plans such as Plan Dalet did not occur in a vacuum, but that Zionist and later Israeli politicians and commanders clearly understood that the future of the Jewish State would be far better secured if fewer numbers of Arabs remained in its boundaries (Khalidi, 1988; Masalha, 1992). On the other hand there were also examples such as Haifa where the Jews pleaded with Arab residents not to flee, or where Arab residents after surrender were permitted to stay, such as in Nazareth. Similarly, on the Arab side, there is evidence of local Arab leaders encouraging flight, but no official call upon the Palestinians to evacuate the area for the advancing Arab armies. The Palestinian exodus was also partially the result of the quick collapse of Palestinian society resulting from the lack of political leadership as the highly factionalized notables fled, from the socio-economic dislocation caused by the transition from feudalism to modernity, and from the loss of military leaders and fighters during the 1936–39 Arab Revolt (Khalaf, 1991; Khalidi, 2001). Indeed, the Palestinian exodus developed a momentum of its own driven by war, fear, massacres, Arab encouragement and Zionist intimidation.

This leads directly to the third issue of solutions to the refugee problem. Attributing responsibility for the refugee problem was crucial as it ultimately determined whether these refugees would be permitted to return to their homes or had to resettle in the neighbouring Arab states. The Arabs demanded that the Palestinian refugees should return to their homes – after all, Israel had illegally expelled them. Israel, conversely, maintained that the Palestinians should be integrated into the Arab states – after all, they had left voluntarily. Moreover, Jews living in Arab countries had migrated to Israel after 1948, so there had been a population exchange (Tessler, 1994). Ultimately, because Israel felt it could not realistically re-admit hundreds of thousands of Palestinians without placing at risk political and economic stability as well as the Jewish character of the state, Israel did not permit the refugees to return. As a result, the refugee problem became one of the most important issues for future attempts at negotiating Arab–Israeli peace.

Palestinian refugees emigrated to the Persian Gulf, Europe and North America. Some were integrated into the business communities of neighbouring Arab capitals such as Beirut, Amman, Damascus and Cairo. However, most of them settled in camps close to the Israeli border or on the outskirts of major Arab cities. The inability and to some extent unwillingness of the Arab states to absorb these refugees placed the responsibility for these Palestinians in the hands of voluntary relief organizations. It also created an environment conducive to the development of a distinct Palestinian national identity based on the right to return and the demand for a Palestinian state. Palestinian organizations started to develop, including numerous political movements with paramilitary wings aimed at liberating Palestine through armed struggle.

The importance of the Palestinian defeat and expulsion for the Palestinian national psyche cannot be overestimated. Historical accounts, literature, art and politics from 1948 to the present day have evolved around dispossession, economic dislocation, political disenfranchisement and dispersion. Palestinian refugees, despite Arab and Israeli attempts to ignore them, played an increasingly destabilizing role within their Arab host countries, within Israeli-administered territory from 1967 onwards and in the Arab–Israeli conflict as a whole. The Palestinian refugee issue became a stumbling block in Israel's quest for legitimacy and secure borders, as well as an obstacle to regional peace.

Peace negotiations

The armistice negotiations resulted in an Israeli–Egyptian armistice on 24 February 1949, followed by an Israeli agreement with Lebanon on 23 March 1949, with Transjordan on 3 April 1949 and with Syria on 20 July 1949. Israeli politicians expected a full peace to follow soon thereafter. Official channels were established by the UN, such as the Mixed Armistice Commissions and the Lausanne Conference, semi-official contacts were made through mediators and secret negotiations between Israel and its Arab neighbours followed the armistices. Arab–Israeli peace, however, remained elusive.

One interpretation of this period of early negotiations is that Israel wanted peace but since the Arab states were unwilling to recognize the Jewish state, there really was no one to negotiate peace with. Another reading of the situation is that Israel was intransigent and unwilling to compromise. Both reflect aspects of Israeli–Arab relations during this time, but neither is an adequate explanation for the failure to find a settlement after the 1948 war. An alternative and more comprehensive explanation can be found in state–society relations. Both Israel and the Arab states had only just moved towards independence, and consequently nation and state building were higher up on the list of priorities than peace. Both had a strong society and a comparatively weak state and were still in the process of construction and legitimization.

The defeat in the 1948 war led to instability in the Arab states as a result of domestic challenges to the leadership which had lost the war, rivalry between the Arab states in pursuit of regional hegemony, the rise of Arab nationalism and an emerging tendency towards more revolutionary ideologies. The extent of instability becomes clear when looking at the years between the first Arab–Israeli war and the 1956 Suez war. Egypt's monarchy was overthrown in the 1952 Free Officers coup. King **Abdallah** of Jordan was assassinated in 1951 and succeeded by his eldest son, Talal, who reigned until May 1953 when he was deposed and succeeded by Hussein. In 1951 Lebanon's Prime Minister Riad as-Sulh was assassinated, and in 1952 President Bishara al-Khoury was deposed in a bloodless coup and replaced by Camille Chamoun. In Syria, General Husni Zaim staged a military coup in May 1949. He was overthrown a few months later by Sami al-Hinnawi, who in turn was deposed by another coup in December 1949 by Adib Shishakli. In 1954 Shishakli was overthrown and forced to flee. Hashem al-Atassi then held the presidency until 1955 when he was replaced by Shukri al-Kuwatli. In comparison, Israel was more stable. That did not, however, mean that there was no tension within the decision-making elite. In fact, a major rift was emerging between Prime Minister David Ben Gurion and Foreign Minister **Moshe Sharett** over the direction of Israel's foreign and defence policy. Ultimately, Ben Gurion's hardline security-driven policy – as opposed to Sharett's 'softer' diplomatic approach – won the upper hand in 1955.

In light of these instabilities, tensions and leadership challenges, it is not surprising that major Arab–Israeli diplomatic initiatives did not result in peace (Rabinovich, 1991). Immediately following the 1948 war, Israel initiated a diplomatic offensive to start secretly negotiating with Jordan. Jordan was seen as the Arab state most likely to sign peace with Israel based on the Zionist–Jordanian alliance during the war. Contacts between Israeli leaders and King Abdallah had always been amicable and, from an Israeli perspective, it was therefore not surprising that in February 1950 a non-belligerence agreement between the two was concluded. Jordan, however, never ratified this agreement. The main stumbling block in the search for peace was King Abdallah's insistence on territorial concessions. Israel had only just acquired the territory it needed to achieve territorial contiguity and defensible borders. The notion of land for peace was unacceptable from an Israeli perspective. Territorial concessions were also the main point of contention in Israel's secret negotiations with Syria and Egypt. Syria demanded half of the Sea of Galilee, and Egypt wanted parts of the Negev desert in return for full peace.

One final observation should be made at this point. Both official diplomatic initiatives and secret negotiations reveal that while attempts were being made to resolve the dispute between Israel and the Arab states, the Palestinian dimension had been completely marginalized. In fact, it could be said that Israel used contacts with its Arab neighbours to bypass the Palestinians, while Arab leaders, it turn, only played the Palestinian card to consolidate their own political position domestically and regionally. Indeed, Jordan's annexation of the West Bank in April 1950 made it very clear that there was little Arab support for a separate Palestinian state.

Conflicting expectations, aims and perceptions, as well as intransigence on both sides, led to discord in the early Arab–Israeli negotiations. The aims of the Arab states were the acquisition of territory and the repatriation of Palestinian refugees. Israel's aims were recognition and peace without giving up territory. At the same time the weakness of state and government and the strength of society discouraged risk taking by political representatives and shifted the political agenda towards state consolidation. Despite perceptions that peace would be achieved in due time after the armistice agreements, the right conditions for conflict resolution simply did not exist. The Arab states might have lost the war, but they were not defeated to such an extent that they were 'forced' to make peace at all costs. Israel, conversely, while desiring peace and recognition, was also not ready to make territorial concessions. International mediation, which could have brought the parties in the conflict closer to a settlement, was indecisive. The great powers were far from impartial brokers, being preoccupied with the emerging Cold War. There were no incentives or, indeed, benefits for Arab–Israeli recognition and acceptance of each other. The lack of 'stateness' did not provide leaders and diplomats with sufficient security and stability to pursue peace. In short, the so-called ripe moment had not come.

3   The 1956 Suez–Sinai campaign

The inconclusive outcome of the first Arab–Israeli war and the inability to conclude a peace agreement led both Israel and its Arab neighbours to believe that ultimately there was going to be a second round. Israeli diplomats had been unsuccessful in attaining the recognition and international legitimacy Israel desired, and Israel's army was unable to fully secure its borders. The Arab regimes, in turn, were suffering from domestic challenges as well as regional insecurity. Arab–Israeli tensions were further exacerbated by the unresolved issue of Palestinian refugees and influenced by the emerging Cold War in the Middle East. The latter had set in motion the on-going debate over whether the Cold War was imposed upon the region by the superpowers or whether it was imported by regional actors for their own ends.

The 1952 Egyptian coup

On 23 July 1952 Egypt's monarchy was overthrown by the Free Officers whose six-point charter called for 'ousting the king, ending colonialism, strengthening the army, social equality, economic development and free education for all' (Bregman, 1998: 44). Egyptian journalist and diplomat Mohamed Heikal describes the reasons for the coup as follows:

> Discontent in the armed forces had been smouldering for a long time. At the beginning of 1946 there had been massive demonstrations by students and workers in Cairo, Alexandria, and other towns, involving loss of life. Then had come the defeats and humiliations of the Palestine war. Two prime ministers had been assassinated, as had been Hassan al-Banna, the Supreme Guide of the Moslem Brotherhood, the latter by members of the special police. All this continuing unrest and frustration increased the contempt felt by the armed forces for their nominal head, King Farouk.
>
> (Heikal, 1986: 28)

Reasons for the revolution further included the old regime's association with the colonial powers as well as its inability during the 1948 war to supply adequately the Egyptian army with arms in order to defeat Israel. After the Free Officers coup, King Farouk went into exile while Egypt under the leadership of President and Prime Minister Mohammed Naguib and his deputy **Gamal Abdel Nasser** instituted far-reaching socio-economic reforms. Nasser replaced Naguib in October 1954, and through his policies of non-alignment, Arab unity and Arab socialism propelled Egypt into a position of leadership in the Middle East and the Third World.

Both Israel and the West initially regarded the new Egyptian government with favour. It was seen as more reasonable than the **Wafd** nationalists had been. Nasser appeared to be a moderate leader with vision, idealism and honour. The new regime was welcomed by the United States in particular, which had been looking for popular pro-Western leaders (Fraser, 1995). American aid, numerous invitations to send Egyptians on training missions and a strong US diplomatic presence marked this honeymoon period (Hei-kal, 1986). Israel, too, saw the change of government as a new opportunity for settlement.

> The Israelis were hopeful of a breakthrough. Much of their optimism centred on one man, Gamal Abdel Nasser . . . he had participated in the cease-fire talks with Israel in 1949 and had expressed a desire to resolve the conflict.
>
> (Oren, 1992: 14)

In fact, intense secret Israeli–Egyptian diplomatic efforts were initiated and pursued until 1956. The perceptions of Nasser changed, however, when he refused to join the Baghdad Pact and negotiated the Czech arms deal in 1955. Hopes for peace gave way to distrust, animosity and finally war.

Israeli–Egyptian tensions

The 1949 armistice agreement did not result in a stable border situation. Indeed, Israeli historian Benny Morris asserts that 'even before the ink on the armistice agreements was dry, there arose in the Arab capitals a clam-our for an avenging second round' (Morris, 1993: 9). This second round was aimed at redeeming the Palestinians and defeating Israel. 'Second round thinking', however, was also evident in Israel, where it was seen as a way to establish a more defensible border as well as achieve territorial expansion.

The permeability of Israel's border exacerbated tensions. Palestinians infiltrated Israel from their camps in the Gaza Strip, as well as from Jordan and Syria. The motivations for crossing into Israel ranged from attempts to reunify families, harvest fields and orchards left behind, regain property and trade, to sabotaging Israel's infrastructure and attacking civilian and military targets. As the Palestinians were becoming more organized in the mid-1950s, paramilitary, or *fedayeen*, raids on Israel became more frequent and successful. In 1950, 19 Israeli civilians were killed and 31 wounded;

in 1951, 48 were killed and 49 wounded; in 1952, 42 were killed and 56 wounded; in 1953, 44 were killed and 66 wounded; in 1954, 33 were killed and 77 wounded; in 1955, 24 were killed and 69 wounded; and in 1956, 54 were killed and 129 wounded (Morris, 1993: 98). In the face of these figures, Israeli decision makers opted for a policy of retaliation, shoot-to-kill orders, mining of border areas and expulsion operations. The first major retaliatory strike was the Qibya raid on 14 October 1953 which was ordered by Ben Gurion in retaliation for an attack on the settlement of Yehud, during which an Israeli mother and her two children were killed (Oren, 1992). The perpetrators' tracks led to the Jordanian border. The village of Qibya had regularly appeared in Israeli intelligence reports as a base for infiltrators, and thus became the target for Israeli retaliatory action aimed at 'blowing up houses and hitting the inhabitants' (Morris, 1993). Forty-five houses were destroyed and 69 people killed, half of them women and children (Fraser, 1995).

Egyptian–Israeli relations were also deteriorating over border clashes and infiltrations. Egyptian efforts to curb infiltration along the Gaza Strip were unsuccessful. By mid-1953 Israeli intelligence asserted that Egyptians were employing minelayers and saboteurs, using Bedouin as guides (Morris, 1993). Israel accused the Egyptian authorities of instigating the infiltrations. Closer analysis of Egyptian policy, however, suggests that Egyptian support for saboteurs only started after the 1955 Gaza raid.

Tensions were further exacerbated in July 1954, when a group of Israeli agents in collaboration with Egyptian Jews tried to sabotage British and American property in Egypt in order to create discord between the Egyptian government and the West and to persuade the British that their military presence was still needed (Tessler, 1994). British withdrawal from the Suez Canal Zone would effectively remove the buffer between Egypt and Israel and, worse still, Egypt would become eligible for US military aid (Bregman and el-Tahri, 1998: 51). The Israeli operation failed when the saboteurs were apprehended, resulting in Israeli–Egyptian tension, as well as jeopardizing the secret talks in Paris. The so-called Lavon affair, as it came to be known, provided Ben Gurion with the opportunity to manoeuvre himself back into the premiership. With him the activist approach to foreign and defence policy returned in full force.

In February 1955 an Egyptian intelligence-gathering squad entered Israel and killed an Israeli cyclist near Rehovot. In retaliation, Israel launched the Gaza raid on 28 February, killing 38 Egyptian soldiers. Retrospectively, it has often been asserted that this particular infiltration only provided Israel with the 'pretext for an operation designed to show Israel's military power both to the West and a nervous public opinion' (Fraser, 1995: 64). Nasser considered the Gaza raid to be the turning point in Israeli–Egyptian relations and maintained that Israeli action was the primary reason for Egypt turning to the Soviet bloc in search for arms. Indeed, Egyptian accounts of the raid describe it as 'an action of unprovoked aggression carried out with deliberate brutality'. The raid was intended as a message from Ben Gurion to Nasser, and Nasser understood the message (Heikal, 1973: 66).

Nasser's response was the Czech arms deal and the closure of the Straits of Tiran in 1955, which in the eyes of Israel changed the regional balance to a much less favourable one. The deal provided Egypt with 100 self-propelled guns, 200 armoured personnel carriers, 300 tanks, 200 MiG 15 jets and 50 Ilyushin-28 bombers (Fraser, 1995: 66). In an attempt to redress the situation, Israel courted French military aid, resulting in the supply of 12 Mystère IV fighters in April 1956, followed by another 72 Mystères, 120 AMX light tanks and 40 Super Sherman tanks.

The Czech arms deal also set in motion Israeli deliberations on a pre-emptive war. Ben Gurion's reaction to the deal was recorded in Moshe Sharett's diary as follows: 'If they really get MiGs – I will be for bombing them!' (Sharett, 1978), and **Moshe Dayan** in his diary of the Sinai campaign stated that 'if the Arab states, led by the ruler of Egypt, had not pursued a policy of increasing enmity towards her, Israel would not have resorted to arms' (Dayan, 1967: 11). Dayan's statement is interesting in that it obscures a crucial debate taking place in the Israeli decision-making elite, which has carried over into the historiography of the conflict. At the heart of both debates is the issue of Israeli interventionism. In short, to what extent was Israeli policy only reactive?

The Israeli foreign and defence policy debate

In the years immediately following the establishment of the state, Israel firmly established itself regionally and internationally. The state successfully absorbed Jewish refugees from Europe and embarked upon the more long-term integration of Jewish immigrants from Asia and North Africa. The priority of the fledgling state, however, remained its security, placing a large burden on society, politics and the economy. It also triggered an intense debate between the Israeli Prime Minister and Defence Minister David Ben Gurion and Foreign Minister Moshe Sharett.

Ben Gurion's approach to foreign policy was based on large-scale intervention and resorting to covert operations in order to inject disunity into the enemy camp. It was aimed at keeping the Arabs off balance and retarding their efforts to modernize their military (Shlaim, 1995). At the core of Ben Gurion's activism was the belief that the Arabs were incapable of accepting peaceful co-existence. Israel's security, therefore, took precedence. It was within this context that Ben Gurion advocated retaliation, the use of force and pre-emptive war. His main challenger within the Israeli decision-making elite was Sharett, who advocated a much more cautious approach. Long-range implications were the focus of this view. With peace as the ultimate goal for the region, Sharett argued that Arab disunity was against Israel's interests, as Arab consensus was needed in furthering the cause of peace (Schulze, 1998).

Simplistically, it was a debate between 'hawks' and 'doves', which was enforced by tensions in the personal relationship between Ben Gurion and Sharett, who had shared the governance of the Jewish state project since the 1930s.

> Sharett admired and respected Ben Gurion – but also felt overawed, overshadowed, and occasionally, jealous. Ben Gurion, for his part, while respecting Sharett's analytical and diplomatic skills, and his mastery of languages, was envious of Sharett's man-of-the-world sociability and *savoir-faire*. People liked and respected Sharett; they 'merely' admired Ben Gurion and stood in awe of him.
>
> (Morris, 1993: 230)

Ultimately, Ben Gurion's activist approach prevailed because of the strong involvement of the security sphere and defence establishment in decision making. Sharett's unsuccessful attempt at the premiership followed by the Sinai Campaign settled the debate in Ben Gurion's favour.

The importance of this debate emerges when returning to the Czech arms deal from a historiographical perspective. The conventional view sees the Sinai Campaign as the result of the influx of Soviet arms and the blockade of the Straits of Tiran. This view has been challenged by historians such as Motti Golani who claims that 'on the contrary, the arms deal temporarily blocked Israel's efforts to launch a war' (Golani, 1995: 804). This implies that war was on the cards much earlier, setting the parameters of the debate: When did Israel plan to go to war? And was the war the result of a broader interventionist policy?

British–French–Israeli collaboration

The 1956 Suez–Sinai war consisted of two separate military operations, one Anglo-French and one Israeli, with the overarching aim to depose Nasser. It was the result of a convergence of interests and similar perceptions of Nasser rather than a long-standing strategic relationship. Indeed, Israeli–British relations had been rocky as Israeli interests prior to 1956 had often been diametrically opposed to those of the United Kingdom (Levey, 1995). France and Israel, on the other hand, had already developed a cordial relationship with the premiership of Pierre Mendes-France, which was strengthened by Egyptian–French tensions over the Algerian war. Ben Gurion saw Nasser as a direct threat to Israel, while France considered Egypt to be the main support to Algerian nationalists fighting for their independence from France. As a result of their mutual antagonism, Israel was able to acquire French war planes as well as assistance in developing its first nuclear reactor (Peretz, 1996).

In spring 1956 French decision makers came to the conclusion that the only way to control the Algerian revolution was to overthrow Nasser. Plans for an assault on Egypt were deliberated at length. The nationalization of the Suez Canal on 26 July 1956 made French–Egyptian collision almost inevitable. Moreover, France was no longer isolated in its opposition to Nasser, but had been joined by Britain and Israel. French shuttle diplomacy between the British and Israelis in September and October resulted in the sought-after tripartite alliance.

Britain's perception of Nasser did not differ much from that of the French. British influence in the Middle East had been in decline since 1945, and the British share of oil production had decreased from 49 per cent to 14 per cent (Ovendale, 1992: 154). The Suez Canal consequently became the major focal point of, and Egypt the main obstacle to, British Middle East policy. In addition, Nasser's pursuit of neutralism had stood in the way of Anglo-American attempts to create a Middle East defence organization along the lines of **NATO**, and Nasser's determination to reform and modernize Egypt, not only economically but also militarily, provided the Soviet Union with an entry point. Moreover, Nasser was able to mobilize support against the remaining conservative Arab regimes in the Middle East, which were Britain's traditional allies, as well as against the British presence in Africa. The conclusion was simple: Nasser had to go.

British perceptions of the Egyptian problem were twofold. First, Egypt's refusal to join the Baghdad Pact followed by the Czech arms deal was seen as a sign that Egypt was coming increasingly under Soviet influence [**Doc. 10, p. 141**]. Second, the nationalization of the Suez Canal not only deprived Britain of its profits, but was also perceived as a political and even military challenge. Much of British shipping, especially oil tankers, had to pass through the canal. The British decision underlying military action can to some extent also be traced back to the failure of its appeasement policy in Europe.

The key to understanding Nasser's decisions, in comparison, can be found in his policy of neutralism and his assumption that military action following the nationalization of the Suez Canal would not necessarily follow. The period of maximum danger, according to Nasser, was the first few days. Then international opinion would eliminate this risk (Heikal, 1973). After all, when the Anglo–Iranian Oil Company was nationalized on 1 May 1951, Britain 'only' imposed sanctions, while the United States even supported it wholeheartedly. Moreover, Nasser needed to nationalize the canal in order to finance the Aswan Dam, a project of great prestige and personal legitimacy which the United States had stopped funding in July 1956 in an attempt to humiliate and control Nasser.

The nationalization of the Suez Canal on 26 July 1956 in order to obtain the financing for the Aswan Dam provided the *casus belli* for Anglo-French decision makers, in the way that the Czech arms deal and the complete sealing of the Straits of Tiran in September 1955 had provided the *casus belli* for Israel. Britain and France refused to recognize Egypt's sovereignty over the canal. As early as 29 July 1956 France started to consider military cooperation with Israel against Egypt. Although there were no obstacles in the relations between France and Israel, British–Israeli relations were strained as the result of the British–Jordanian defence arrangement. Jordanian–Israeli border tensions were high, and the instability in the Hashemite kingdom of Jordan prompted the British to suggest moving Iraqi troops into Jordan during the forthcoming parliamentary elections. Israel saw this as a direct threat, as Iraq was the only state not to have signed the 1949 armistice. In light of the tripartite plans against Nasser, Israeli decision makers found Britain's attitude incomprehensible. Only on 16 October at a meeting in Paris was the situation finally resolved. Britain agreed to Israel's participation in the Suez war and called off its Jordanian plans.

The plan [**Doc. 11, p. 142**], which has been described as 'ill-conceived both in organization and purpose' (Fraser, 1995), called for Israel to seize the Suez Canal. Britain and France would then ask Egypt and Israel to withdraw from the canal. Counting upon Egypt's refusal to do so, Anglo-French troops would be forced to intervene in order to protect the canal. Ben Gurion wanted to delay the campaign until after the US presidential election on 6 November in order to secure American backing. Yet Dayan set the invasion date for 29 October. In his diary Dayan describes the situation with the United States as 'complicated, and not at all agreeable'.

> Israel, wishing and needing to maintain close ties of friendship with the US, finds herself in the difficult position of having to keep from her – and even be evasive about – her real intentions. . . . The US is adamantly opposed to any military action on the part of Israel, yet she does not – perhaps she cannot – prevent anti-Israel action on the part of the Arabs. Moreover, the US consistently refuses to grant or sell us arms, thereby exposing us to aggression by the Arabs who have open access to arms from the Soviet bloc.
>
> (Dayan, 1967: 74)

On 30 October, Israeli troops reached the canal. Britain and France issued an ultimatum for both Israeli and Egyptian forces to withdraw from the area. Nasser, as predicted, rejected the ultimatum and thereby 'provoked' the British and French bombing of Egyptian airfields on 31 October. For the next two days 200 British and French fighter-bombers destroyed economic targets in Egypt as well as Egypt's air force. British and French paratroops subsequently invaded, only to be forced to halt their military operation as a result of US pressure.

Ironically, despite US opposition to the tripartite attack on Egypt, the American analysis of Nasser was not necessarily different from that of Britain, France and Israel. The lack of American support for an Anglo-French military operation was not based on the belief that Nasser should remain in power, but to a large degree on US President **Dwight D. Eisenhower's** election campaign. The use of force had to be delayed until its successful conclusion. Consequently it is not surprising that Eisenhower, hearing of the Israeli attack while on a campaign trip to Florida, felt deceived. He told US Secretary of State **John Foster Dulles** to 'tell them goddam it, we are going to apply sanctions, we are going to the United Nations, we are going to do everything that there is to stop this thing' (Eisenhower, 1965: 73). Eisenhower erroneously suspected that Ben Gurion had deliberately chosen the timing in order to assure Israel of US approval through pressure from the Jewish lobby. He felt even further betrayed when Britain and France joined in the Suez war.

Israel was condemned for aggression, economic sanctions were applied and the severing of US–Israeli relations was threatened should Israel decide to stay in Sinai. On 2 November 1956 the UN General Assembly approved a US-sponsored resolution for an immediate ceasefire and withdrawal of all forces from Egyptian territory. Israel, under severe US pressure, was forced to accept the ceasefire, leaving Britain and France in a difficult situation. Britain and France were still in the midst of their invasion and had not seized control of the canal. Financial pressure brought to bear on Britain finally forced Anthony Eden to give in to mounting Cabinet pressure and agree to a ceasefire as well, and Guy Mollet, the French prime minister, reluctantly went along.

The American intervention to halt the joint British–French–Israeli operation can be explained, first, by the belief that a full-scale war would result in Soviet intervention in the Middle East. US Secretary of State John Foster Dulles, for example, saw the Suez Canal as the crucial link for oil supplies to NATO, and an opportunity for the Soviet Union to restrict the canal would weaken Western European resistance to communism (Alteras, 1993). The second factor was the US policy of even-handedness in the Arab–Israeli conflict, which was motivated by oil interests as well as preventing an arms race. The third element was Eisenhower's 1956 election campaign on a peace platform. And fourth, the fact that the United States had condemned Soviet intervention in Hungary not only made it difficult to support intervention in Egypt, but the latter also diverted attention from Soviet action. The underlying US mistrust of Soviet motives became clear on 1 November, when Eisenhower and Dulles at a National Security Council meeting stated that 'if we were not now prepared to assert our leadership in this cause, leadership would certainly be seized by the Soviet Union' (Bar On, 1994: 273). Indeed, the convergence of the crisis in the Middle East and events in Hungary created an atmosphere in which the fear of a possible US–Soviet nuclear confrontation spread (Alteras, 1993).

The results of the war

The war ended in a resounding military defeat for Nasser. Yet from a regional post-war perspective, Nasser clearly emerged on the winning side. Dismissing Israel's Sinai campaign as non-existent, he was hailed as the only Arab leader able to challenge the West and to expel the British and French imperialist forces, as well as Israel, from Egyptian territory. From this position Nasser expanded his regional influence and established Egypt's leadership of the Arab world. He had been able to hold on to the Suez Canal. During the war he had also been able to nationalize the remaining British and French holdings, providing funds for the Aswan Dam and the modernization of Egypt. He had even acquired an international army, **UNEF**, to protect Egypt from Israeli retaliatory policy.

Israel, too, had gained from the war, despite its failure to depose Nasser. UNEF guaranteed freedom of shipping in the Gulf of Aqaba, providing Israel with a Red Sea port. UNEF also provided some limited control over the *fedayeen* infiltrations. Most importantly, however, Israel's military reputation had been further enhanced. The speed with which Israeli troops were able to advance on the Suez Canal elevated Israel's status to that of regional superpower. It could even be argued that the Sinai campaign was able to deter a further Arab–Israeli war and thus provide Israel with the space to complete its nation building and state building.

France and Britain are generally considered to be the losers of the war. Egypt remained in total control of the canal, and the perception that Nasser had successfully challenged the former colonial powers led to a further decline of British and French influence in the Middle East as well as in Africa and Southeast Asia. Neither Britain nor France was able to counter the damage to an already declining diplomatic position. The United States and the Soviet Union, in comparison, were able to step into this vacuum and emerged as the two 'new' foreign powers in the Middle East. As a result the Arab–Israeli conflict had become an arena for the Cold War. In addition, it raised a further point of scholarly contention: the question to what extent the Cold War had been imposed upon the region by the United States and the Soviet Union – and to what extent the Cold War was imported into the region and manipulated by regional leaders for their own ends (Gerges, 1994: 118).

4   The 1967 June War

The 1967 June War, referred to by Israelis as the Six Day War and by Palestinians as *al-Naksa* – the setback – was the third Arab–Israeli war in less than two decades. It was triggered by a growing intensity in attacks on Israel as well as increasing Israeli retaliation against its Arab neighbours in late 1966 and early 1967. It was a war that took many in the international community by surprise, a confrontation that neither Israel, Egypt, Syria and Jordan nor the United States and the Soviet Union claim to have wanted. Yet the decline into confrontation seemed almost inevitable from 1966 onwards. Israel's perception of vulnerability; hostile Israeli, Egyptian and Syrian rhetoric; continuing border tensions; and finally Egyptian troop movements to the Sinai, the withdrawal of UNEF, and the closing of the Straits of Tiran left little room for diplomatic manoeuvring. It has, however, left room for quite an amount of speculation in the search for an explanation.

In Israeli historiography the blame for the war clearly rests with Nasser who, by closing the Straits of Tiran, left Israel with no alternative but to fight. Another version advanced in the historiographical debate is that Nasser did not intend to go to war. His threats were not aimed at Israel, but at his fellow Arabs to whom he wished to prove that he was still the champion of pan-Arabism. Accordingly, it was misplaced Israeli reaction that led to war. A third explanation of events is embodied in the so-called 'accident' theory, which lays the blame for the conflict on regional dynamics as a whole rather than one particular player. The 1967 June War was the result of Egyptian–Israeli brinkmanship that went over the brink. Neither wanted war, but both had to keep up with the other's hostile rhetoric. The final historiographical contender to be mentioned here is the argument that the war was really the result of US–Soviet manipulation of regional powers, seeing the Cold War as the defining context.

The creation of the Palestine Liberation Organization

The 1956 Suez crisis had once again shown the focus of Arab leaders to be on their own foreign and domestic problems rather than on the conviction to liberate Palestine. The Arab world and the international community seemed to have forgotten about the plight of the Palestinian refugees. It was this realization that led to a Palestinian political and military revival. Building on earlier underground nationalist groups, **Fatah** was formed in 1957 in Kuwait, and renewed Palestinian resistance was organized under the leadership of **Yasser Arafat, Khalil Wazir** and **Salah Khalaf**.

In an attempt to control the Palestinian *fedayeen* and to prevent their actions from completely destabilizing the region, Nasser established the Palestine Liberation Organization (**PLO**) in January 1964 at an Arab summit meeting in Cairo. This new Palestinian organization also provided Nasser with leadership credentials in his regional rivalry with Syria and Iraq. Thus it is not surprising that the PLO soon became the object of an inter-Arab struggle for influence between Egypt, Syria and Iraq, as well as an Arab–Palestinian struggle for control.

From its establishment onwards the PLO served as an umbrella for all Palestinian resistance groups, providing political and military coordination when needed, but essentially leaving individual groups free to act. Its main political institution was the Palestine National Council (**PNC**), which met for the first time in East Jerusalem in May 1964 to draft its Covenant [**Doc. 12, p. 143**]. The covenant was a political manifesto and a constitution at the same time, laying claim to Palestine as a future state and designating armed struggle as the means to this end. During its first few years of existence the PNC comprised only 100 members, but as the PLO expanded and embarked upon a clear path of emancipation from the Arab states, PNC membership increased to 600. Real power, however, lay with the small Executive Committee, which consisted of the top PLO leadership.

The first head of the PLO was Palestinian lawyer, **Ahmad al-Shukayri**, who had served as Saudi Arabia's UN representative and was personally chosen by Nasser. Indeed, up until 1967 the PLO remained very much under Arab and particularly Egyptian control. Units of its official army, the Palestine Liberation Army (**PLA**) were trained and to some extent integrated into the various Arab armies. Yet Arab control was never all-pervasive, and soon after 1964 independent Palestinian *fedayeen* operations against Israel started to increase again, reinforcing Israel's feeling of vulnerability.

On the brink of war

The 1967 June War was the result of political developments, which began with the change of government in Syria on 23 February 1966. The rise to power of militant Ba'thists resulted in increasingly hostile rhetoric at a time when already bad Syrian–Israeli border relations were deteriorating. The road to conflict, however, was not really embarked upon until August 1966, when Israel and Syria clashed in a fierce battle in the area of the Sea of Galilee (Tessler, 1994). This was followed in November by Egypt signing a mutual defence pact with Syria. The pact boosted Syria's confidence, but, at the same time, increased Israel's threat perception. Syrian and Egyptian moves were compounded by continued *fedayeen* operations against Israel from Jordan. In light of this triple threat, Israeli decision makers adopted a more hardline security response. On 13 November, Israel launched its most extensive operation since the Sinai Campaign when the IDF raided the West Bank villages of as-Samu, Jimba and Khirbet Karkay. Three Jordanian civilians and 15 Arab Legion soldiers were killed, and another 54 civilians and military personnel were wounded. A clinic, a school and 140 houses were damaged. Thus it is not surprising that by the end of the year the region was once again on the brink of war.

The tensions continued through the first half of 1967. In April, Israel and Syria engaged in an air battle over Syria, in which Syria lost six MiGs. A future all-out military confrontation seemed almost unavoidable. The final factor to set the ball rolling was a Soviet intelligence report. On 13 May, Soviet President Nikolai Podgorny told Nasser's aide **Anwar Sadat**, who was on a visit to Moscow, that Israeli troops had mobilized and intended to invade Syria (Black and Morris, 1991). With this report Soviet intelligence confirmed earlier reports from Syria. As Nasser was bound by the mutual defence pact, he decided to act immediately, despite the fact that Israel, as confirmed by a UN inspection team, had not mobilized or deployed (Tessler, 1994). The false Soviet intelligence report has ever since been the subject of intense speculation. One possible motivation for planting this information is that the Soviet Union wanted to take pressure off Syria (Fraser, 1995), believing that both Israel and the Arabs would stop short of war (Black and Morris, 1991). Another explanation is that it was simply an inaccurate and poorly evaluated report. A third possibility is that the Soviet Union was deliberately misled by Israel, either to intimidate Syria or to draw Egypt into the fight. The fourth possibility is that the Soviet Union wanted a war (Brown, 1996). This explanation is supported by **Evgeny Pyrlin**, head of the Egypt Department of the Soviet Foreign Ministry at that time, who claims that Soviet decision makers believed

> that even if the war was not won by our side – the Egyptians – a war would be to our political advantage because the Egyptians would have demonstrated their ability to fight with our weapons and with our military and political support.
>
> (Bregman, 1998: 65)

A final explanation is based on a Cold War globalist perspective, according to which the Soviet Union deliberately issued false information in order to create another conflict for the United States so as to weaken the American position in Vietnam.

Regardless of Soviet motives, Nasser reacted swiftly. On 14 May, Egyptian troops moved into the Sinai. It has been claimed that this move was purely a measure of deterrence aimed at Israel as well as assuring Syria. 'Dangerous though it seemed, this troop deployment did not signal that war was imminent' (Fraser, 1995). Nasser's request for the partial withdrawal of UNEF confirms this to a degree. UN Secretary-General U Thant's insistence on either 'no withdrawal or complete withdrawal' instead left the Egyptian–Israeli border without a buffer. Nasser, who had been taunted by rival Arab leaders that he was hiding behind the UN, had no choice but to opt for complete withdrawal. Yet the specific Egyptian request for UNEF to withdraw from Sharm al-Sheikh, from where Egypt could close the Straits of Tiran to Israeli shipping, could also be interpreted as a deliberate act of war – and indeed was by Israel.

Following the withdrawal of UNEF from Sinai, U Thant urged Israel to accept UN troops on its side of the frontier in order to maintain a buffer (Tessler, 1994). As such a move did not prevent Egypt from closing the Straits of Tiran, the offer was rejected. On 22 May, Nasser proceeded to close the straits, later claiming that he had no choice if he wanted to return 'things to what they were in 1956' (Laqueur, 1972). Interestingly, he did not believe that his action would lead to war. Rather, he would gain a political victory and deflect Arab criticism (Smith, 1996). As Egyptian Minister of War Shams Badran recalls:

> The Arab countries kept on saying that we were allowing Israeli ships to go through Eilat, and that Eilat was the main port for Israeli exports. The attack against us – in Jordanian and Saudi propaganda – was fierce, and showed us that we had to do something to stop the Israeli ships going through the Straits.
>
> (Bregman, 1998: 68)

Israeli decision makers, having stated their position repeatedly since 1956, regarded this act as a clear *casus belli*. Indeed, from the Israeli perspective, Egypt's aggressive intent was confirmed when Jordan joined the general mobilization on 21 May, followed by the signing of a mutual defence agreement with Egypt on 30 May. By that point, Israel, too, had started to mobilize, with the overall result of 80,000 Egyptian troops and 900 tanks, 300 Syrian tanks, 300 Jordanian tanks, and some 250,000 Israeli troops, 1,093 tanks and 203 planes ready for action. War seemed inevitable.

All through May, Israeli public anxiety and military frustration increased while diplomats tried to diffuse the crisis. Israeli attempts to negotiate the opening of the straits with Egyptian Vice-President **Zakariya Muhieddin** in Washington on 3 June failed against the backdrop of increasingly hostile rhetoric from all belligerents. The Israeli public demanded action, and Israeli Prime Minister **Levi Eshkol** more and more felt the need to assert himself vis-à-vis Ben Gurion's constant criticism from the comfort of retirement. As a result, on 4 June, Israel's national unity government was established. Eshkol was forced to hand over the defence portfolio to Moshe Dayan, who then took the decision to go to war. It was clear that if Israel did not strike first, the Arabs would.

Figure 4.1 King Hussein of Jordan (left) and President Gamal Abdel Nasser after signing a Jordan–Egyptian defence agreement in Cairo, June 1967. © AFP/Getty Images

The pre-emptive strike

On 5 June 1967 Israel launched its pre-emptive strike. The Israeli air force destroyed 304 Egyptian, 53 Syrian and 28 Jordanian aircraft, mostly on the ground (Black and Morris, 1991: 222–3). The IDF crossed into the Sinai and into the West Bank. Syria, Jordan and Egypt counter-attacked the same day. The three Arab states became embroiled in a land battle with the Jewish state, which continued until 10 June. However, without air cover for troops and tanks, the Arab forces were easy prey. The war with Egypt ended when Israeli forces occupied Sharm al-Sheikh and reached the Suez Canal. Having lost 2,000 soldiers in the fighting with Israel and another 10,000 in the retreat, Egypt had no choice but to agree to a ceasefire on 8 June. Jordan's position was no better. **King Hussein** recalled his troops coming back in small groups, deprived of air cover and defeated. 'I saw all the years I had spent since 1953 trying to build up the country and army, all the pride, all the hopes, destroyed' (Bregman, 1998: 91). The battle on the West Bank ended when Israel captured East Jerusalem on 7 June and troops moved to the Jordan River before King Hussein agreed to the ceasefire later in the day. Syrian–Israeli fighting did not even start until 9 June. Indeed, Israel only attacked Syria once Jordan and Egypt had been defeated. 'Shortly after midnight on the ninth, Syria, which had contributed so much to the crisis and nothing to the conflict' also agreed to a ceasefire (Smith, 1996).

The war left Israel in control of Jordan's West Bank, Egypt's Sinai Peninsula and the Gaza Strip and Syria's Golan Heights [**Map 2, p. xxvii**]. Israel's air superiority was the most important factor in Israel's victory, followed closely by the lack of Arab coordination which enabled Israel to deal separately with Egypt, Jordan and Syria rather than having to fight a genuine three-frontal war.

By 10 June, Syria, Jordan and Egypt had agreed to ceasefires. Egypt had lost 12,000 soldiers, Israel 766. As in 1948, this war proved decisive in its consequences, both increasing Israel's territory and tilting the strategic balance unequivocally in Israel's favour.

The aftermath of the war

Israel emerged from the war victorious and had increased its territory three-fold. The acquisition of this additional territory provided Israel with strategic depth and consequently more security. Nasser had been resoundingly defeated and was no longer considered to be the main threat. In the wake of his demise, the more radical Ba'athi regime in Syria started to emerge as Israel's main regional rival, ultimately resulting in a Syrian–Israeli arms race which, in turn, provided the opportunity for greater superpower involvement. The prestige of the Soviet Union, as Egypt's and Syria's ally, had also been damaged, while the United States started to see Israel as a valuable asset in the region through which to counter Soviet influence (Yapp, 1991).

US support for Israel was based primarily on Israel's military strength and reliability, as well as Israel's opposition to the radical Arab states, which were perceived as Soviet clients. Added to this was an element of affinity derived from shared moral and political standards (Lipson, 1996).

As a result of the war, Israel emerged as the dominant power in the region. The Arab regimes, despite proclaiming a victory, had been humiliated, which triggered another period of domestic challenges and instability. Egypt was forced to abandon its involvement in the Yemen war, and Nasser saw his claim to leadership of the Arab world greatly reduced. In 1968 Syria had another military coup, while Egyptian–Israeli hostilities continued as the War of Attrition 1969–70. With the 1967 June War, regional dynamics had also changed. Pan-Arabism started to decline and had to compete not only with the emergence of political Islam but also with strengthened local nationalisms, including Palestinian nationalism. Thus, by discrediting Nasser and 'ejecting Arab rule from those parts of mandatory Palestine which had been saved in 1948', the Israeli victory contributed to the re-focusing on particularistic Palestinian nationalism as well as placing the Palestinians back on the international agenda (Heller, 1983).

The 1967 June War also provided the international community once again with the opportunity to attempt the conclusion of a regional settlement. Disagreement between the United States and the Soviet Union, however, revealed an almost unbridgeable gap. In light of this superpower stalemate, the diplomatic focus shifted to the United Nations. The result of numerous sessions was UN Security Council Resolution 242. It emphasized 'the inadmissibility of the acquisition of territory by war' and acknowledged 'the sovereignty, territorial integrity and political independence of every state in the area and their right to live in peace within secure and recognised boundaries free from acts of force' [Doc. 13, p. 145]. The resolution also called for a just and lasting peace based on the Israeli withdrawal from territories occupied during the war, and reaffirmed the necessity of a 'just settlement of the refugee problem'.

Resolution 242 embodied all those key elements which had to be addressed for conflict resolution: recognition, inadmissibility of acquiring territory by war, freedom from acts of force, peace and the Palestinian refugee problem. These, however, were not seized upon until the Madrid peace process some 25 years later. In the meantime, the Arabs insisted that 242 called for Israeli withdrawal from *all* territories, while Israel insisted it had to hold onto *some* of the territories in order to live within secure boundaries.

In the immediate aftermath of the war, both Israel and the Arab states were divided with regard to how to proceed. The initial view of the Israeli government was that the conquered territory could be returned for peace, with the exception of those areas which Israel saw as strategically vital, as well as East Jerusalem. Opposition to territorial compromise was only expressed by **Herut** and the **National Religious Party**. Yet, as time proceeded without any indication of meaningful negotiations, 'the Israelis seemed increasingly reluctant to accept a formula which would require their complete withdrawal from territories occupied in war, even if their objectives of secure frontiers, non-belligerency and freedom of navigation were conceded' (Lall, 1968).

On the Arab side, the more hardline states advocated a continuation of the conflict in order to liberate all of Palestine. Others, however, such as Nasser and King Hussein, preferred a diplomatic solution. The Arab summit in Khartoum in September 1967 decided the debate in favour of the hardliners: no peace with, no recognition of and no negotiation with Israel [Doc. 14, p. 146]. Despite the Khartoum resolution, the cause of the failure to resolve the conflict after the 1967 June War was not Arab intransigence. Rather, it can be found in the continuing mutual distrust and in the enormous asymmetry of Israelis and Arabs, which precluded conditions conducive to negotiations from the beginning. Added to that was Israel's continued circumvention of the Palestinian refugees and their political representatives. Israel's strong position after the war did not encourage concessions, while the Arabs' weak position made it impossible to become an equal negotiating partner.

5 The 1973 October War

The unresolved Palestinian question, continuing border tension, the change in leadership in Egypt and Syria, intensified superpower interest in the region and the failure of further diplomatic initiatives paved the way for the fourth Arab–Israeli war. The conditions for conflict resolution after the 1967 war had simply not been right: the Arab states were unable to make peace from the position of utter defeat, Israel was unwilling to make concessions after its spectacular victory, the international community was unable to create an appropriate environment for negotiations and the superpowers lacked the will and ability to impose peace (Yapp, 1991). It was in this context that the change of political leadership in Egypt provided a window of opportunity for a departure from entrenched positions.

The War of Attrition

In March 1969, Israel and Egypt had become involved in a prolonged low-intensity war known as the War of Attrition. In many ways it was a continuation of the 1967 war, and the Egyptian decision to launch this war can be seen as an attempt to break the deadlock. It was a conflict characterized by sporadic bombardment, commando raids and fire and counter-fire against strongholds along the Suez Canal. Egypt's principal aim was to keep the superpowers' interest alive – without that, the reclaiming of the Suez Canal seemed impossible (Peretz, 1996). Nasser wanted to create sufficient instability to provoke superpower involvement and pressure the Soviet Union into supplying the Egyptian army with arms (Bailey, 1990). In that sense, Nasser's strategy was successful. Egypt received Soviet arms, technicians and combat personnel. In April 1970, Soviet pilots were detected flying Egyptian planes over the Suez Canal (Hopwood, 1991). A further aim of Nasser was the destruction of the Israeli **Bar Lev Line** fortification (Ovendale, 1992). He sought to inflict such a heavy toll on Israel that it would be forced to withdraw. Between June 1967 and July 1970, more than 1,000 Israeli soldiers were killed (Peretz, 1996).

Israel responded with bombardments of both military and civilian targets along the canal. By the middle of 1970 Egypt was sustaining considerable losses, and on 23 July Nasser accepted US Secretary of State Rogers' cease-fire proposal. On 8 August 1970 the War of Attrition came to an end. Nasser stated that he agreed to the ceasefire on the understanding that the United States would pressure Israel to accept Resolution 242 and withdraw from the Occupied Territories (Hopwood, 1991).

The Palestinian revival and Black September

On the Palestinian front, the 1967 war had made it clear that the Arab states were not able or willing to 'liberate' Palestine. Israel had gained control over more Palestinian land and a population of 665,000 Palestinians; an additional 350,000 to 400,000 Palestinians had become refugees.

> No one, least of all Israel, could dodge the problem of this new Palestinian actuality. The word 'Arab' no longer served to describe everyone who was not Jewish. There were the 'old' Arabs in Israel, the new West Bank–Gaza set, the militant fighters, and the various communities scattered in Lebanon, Jordan, Syria, and the Arabian Gulf.
>
> (Said, 1992: 38)

Yet Resolution 242 failed seriously to address the situation of the Palestinian people and their political aspirations. As a result of the Arab defeat and international disregard of the Palestinian problem, the Palestinians became more independent politically, with Arafat emerging as the decisive voice among Palestinian leaders. It had become clear that the Palestinians could 'rely on no one but themselves' (Tessler, 1994).

In winter 1967 Fatah started working underground in the West Bank, and the Arab–Israeli conflict, for the first time in 20 years, started to include an element of distinct Israeli–Palestinian confrontation, as exemplified by the battle of Karameh on 21 March 1968, which restored Palestinian morale. The ranks of the *fedayeen* of Fatah, as well as other organizations such as the Popular Front for the Liberation of Palestine (**PFLP**), swelled through an influx of volunteers.

Attempts at instigating an uprising in the West Bank were quickly crushed by the Israelis. The emerging Palestinian National Movement (**PNM**) consequently had no choice but to operate from Jordan. In 1968 and 1969 Fatah established a network of proto-state institutions within Jordan, including a political department, newspapers, grassroots committees and clinics which served politically to mobilize the population. Yasser Arafat was elected chairman of the executive committee, as well as becoming the head of the PLO's political department. He set out to unify the resistance groups and to transform the PLO into a cohesive and comprehensive political front. The process of unification was completed in 1970, and the PLO was able to draw upon a fighting force of 5,000 to 10,000. Supported by states such as Saudi Arabia and Libya, the PLO stepped up its armed struggle against Israel.

The process of institutionalization, structural and political development and operational independence increasingly set the PLO on a collision course with the Lebanese and Jordanian governments. Palestinian attacks from Jordanian and Lebanese territory made Lebanon and Jordan the target of Israeli retaliatory strikes. There were an estimated 560 incidents initiated from the Lebanese side of the border in 1969–70 (Tessler, 1994: 451).

Even more destabilizing than Palestinian–Lebanese relations, were Palestinian–Jordanian relations. By 1970 the PLO had established a 'state within a state' in Jordan and had become a clear challenge to King Hussein's authority. Two unsuccessful assassination attempts on King Hussein by PFLP agents in early September and four spectacular airline hijackings were the final straw. On 17 September 1970, the Jordanian army moved against Palestinian positions. The *fedayeen* were unable to mount a credible defence. The fighting ended 10 days later, on 27 September, when Nasser called a peace conference in Cairo. The Jordanian estimate of Palestinian fatalities was 1,500, while some Palestinian sources claimed the number to be as high as 30,000. Inter-Arab relations had suffered a serious blow, which was further compounded when Nasser died of a heart attack the following day. Over the next year the PLO was ousted from Jordan, leaving Lebanon as the sole base for free operations against Israel.

Syro–Egyptian plans for war

Sadat succeeded Nasser upon the latter's death on 28 September 1970. In an attempt to dissociate his leadership from Nasser's, Sadat initiated some crucial changes to Egypt's domestic and foreign policy, which had direct repercussions on the Arab–Israeli conflict. Nasser, according to Sadat, had reduced 'the revolution to a huge, dark and terrible pit, inspiring fear and hatred, but allowing no escape' and Nasser's economic legacy was 'in even poorer shape than the political' (Hopwood, 1991: 103). As a result Sadat set out to de-Nasserize Egyptian politics and to improve the country's failing economy. Among the changes Sadat pursued was Egypt's relationship with the Soviet Union. Sadat had become increasingly disillusioned with Moscow's delayed arms supplies and consequently, on 18 July 1972, expelled 15,000 Russian military advisors. Although this expulsion was a way to speed up Soviet arms shipments, to gain US favour, and to dissociate the Soviet Union from the upcoming war, Israel saw in this move an indication of Egyptian weakness. Indeed, 'at the beginning of 1973, Israel felt that American support and military aid, the decline in international pressure following the Munich Olympic massacre and Egypt's weakening links with Russia made an Arab attack unlikely' (Ovendale, 1992: 216).

At the same time Sadat started to pursue diplomatic initiatives to resolve the 'no war, no peace' status quo. US Assistant Secretary of State Joseph Sisco recalls Israel's reaction to Sadat's 1971 proposals as follows:

> We met in the cabinet room around a huge conference table. Golda Meir, [Moshe] Dayan, [Abba] Eban, [Yitzhak] Rabin, [Yigal] Allon – the whole galaxy of Israeli high-level officials – were present. After two days of in-depth discussions, it was clear we weren't making much progress. I said, 'But, Prime Minister, Sadat only wants a symbolic 500 riflemen across the Canal.' But Golda Meir wouldn't budge.
>
> (Bregman, 1998: 108–9)

Sadat had offered to open the Suez Canal if Israel drew back from the canal and to declare a ceasefire and sign a peace treaty with Israel based on UN Resolution 242 (Peretz, 1996). Israel, however, refused to withdraw to the pre-1967 armistice lines, believing that its new boundaries were vital for its national security. These diplomatic efforts not only failed to produce peace, they also contributed to the Israeli estimates that Egypt was not in a position to fight another war.

Yet despite the fact that Sadat knew that Egypt could not defeat Israel militarily, he opted to go to war in order to persuade Israel to make peace on terms acceptable to the Arabs. He had never intended the war to be more than a limited military operation, aimed at furthering his political and diplomatic objectives (Tessler, 1994). An attack on Israel would break the defeatist attitude of the population. It would boost his regional standing, and, if Egypt held its own, Sadat could use this more equal position as a basis for future negotiations with Israel. Talks with Israel were necessary as Sadat wanted to reclaim Sinai and the Suez Canal for Egypt, especially as, three years after coming to power, he was still competing with Nasser's popular image. As Nasser had lost Sinai in 1967, Sadat saw the recapture of Sinai as the key to finally distinguishing himself from Nasser. Further, an agreement with Israel would reduce the defence burden on the state. The Egyptian economy had virtually collapsed as a result of Nasser's state control, the cost of the Aswan Dam, the Yemen war and the re-equipment of the Egyptian military after the 1967 war. And finally, an end of war between Egypt and Israel would create the stability required to attract foreign investment and would pave the way towards US economic aid.

On 30 November 1972, Sadat and Defence Minister General **Ahmad Ismail Ali** decided to go to war on the assumption that the superpowers would prevent a complete military victory by either side (Ovendale, 1992). Sadat initiated private meetings with **Hafez al-Asad** in order to initiate a double front against Israel. On 31 January 1973, Syria's and Egypt's armed forces were placed under joint command. In an attempt to gain Arab backing for his plans, Sadat also consulted Saudi King Feisal and Algerian President Boumedienne, as well as accepting a substantial financial contribution from Libya (Ovendale, 1992). Detailed planning of the war began in March.

Figure 5.1 Syrian President Hafez al-Assad and Egyptian President Anwar Sadat
 shaking hands in the airport in Cairo, October 7, 1972. © Keystone-
 France\Gamma-Rapho via Getty Images

Syria's motivations in joining the war to some extent mirrored those of
Egypt. Asad had manoeuvred himself into the presidency in 1970 and also
saw a war as a way to consolidate his leadership. Asad's war aims, however,
were mainly territorial. As he was the defence minister when the Golan
Heights had been lost, he was determined to reclaim this territory from
Israel. Unlike Sadat, Asad neither saw the war as a step towards a future
agreement, nor did he want an end to the conflict with Israel.

A surprise attack was to catch Israel off-guard and leave it vulnerable, as
the United States was paralyzed by Watergate, was still suffering from its
extrication from Vietnam and Vice-President Spiro Agnew was facing tax
charges.

The 'surprise' attack

On 6 October 1973, at 2 p.m., Egypt and Syria attacked Israel, launching
the fourth Arab–Israeli war, referred to by Israelis as the Yom Kippur War
and by Arabs as the Ramadan War. The war came as a surprise to Israel,

to the extent that Israeli intelligence had failed to predict the confrontation despite evidence to the contrary. Israel had underestimated the frustration of the Arab governments over Israel's occupation of the Golan Heights, Sinai, West Bank and the Gaza Strip. It had also perceived the Arabs as weak, especially since Egypt had just expelled its Soviet military advisors. Sadat's repeated announcements that 1971 was the year of decision, without following through with action, further convinced Israel that Sadat's pronouncements were empty threats (Peretz, 1996). Indeed, Israeli military and political decision makers had grown complacent, convinced of their own invincibility, and mobilization of the Egyptian army had been interpreted as annual manoeuvres.

The commander of the Armed Corps, General Avraham Adan, gives an insightful account into Israeli thinking at that time:

> My colleagues and I were certainly surprised. The underlying assessment of Israeli Intelligence was that the armed forces of the Arab nations were still unprepared for war; hence the probability of war seemed very low. For the past ten days, the Director of Military Intelligence had stuck to this evaluation, offering reasonable explanations about the build-up of forces. Moreover, the evening before, when he had briefed us about the evacuation of families of Soviet technicians from Egypt and Syria, he explained it as just the result of the widening gap between the Arabs and the Soviets. Now suddenly, without any signs of emotion or embarrassment, the DMI was predicting that war would erupt within hours.
>
> (Adan, 1986: 5)

At 4 a.m. on 6 October, Defence Minister Dayan was informed that Egypt and Syria were going to attack, and Israeli reserves were partially mobilized. A pre-emptive strike was ruled out, however, for fear that Israel would be seen as the aggressor and thereby alienate the United States. Israeli Prime Minister **Golda Meir**, in her autobiography, justified her position as follows:

> I know all the arguments in favour of a pre-emptive strike, but I am against it. We don't know now, any of us, what the future will hold, but there is always the possibility that we will need help, and if we strike first, we will get nothing from anyone.
>
> (Meir, 1975: 359)

Underlying her decision was the US concern about drawing the Soviet Union into the conflict, alienating Egypt, the possibility of an oil embargo and involvement in yet another foreign war. Full mobilization was also ruled out at that point. Israeli mobilization earlier in the year had already placed a heavy burden on the economy and, being in the midst of a general election, the government could not risk further costs, should the attack not occur after all.

Egypt launched a massive airstrike and artillery assault on Israel, and Syria invaded the Golan Heights. Egyptian forces crossed the Suez Canal and pushed back Israeli troops. In the north, while Israel was still mobilizing, Syria took Mount Hermon. In fact, the IDF was outnumbered 12 to 1 when the fighting began (Peretz, 1996). Mobilizing Israel's forces was easy, as it was **Yom Kippur**, the Jewish Day of Atonement, and most reservists were either at home or at the synagogue. In the first few days Israel came close to defeat and had been forced to withdraw from a number of positions. Although these Arab military accomplishments were unparalleled, the IDF managed to contain the threat (Tessler, 1994). A massive American airlift of military equipment combined with Israeli counter-offensives turned the tide [**Map 3, p. xxviii**]. Washington had been reluctant to send arms during the first week of the conflict, fearing it might antagonize the Arabs, while also hoping that Israel might become more accommodating (Goldschmidt, 1996). American reluctance was further influenced by the fact that US Secretary of State **Henry Kissinger** had received a message from Sadat stating that this war was only a limited operation aimed at forcing an Israeli withdrawal from the territories occupied in 1967, which would be followed by a peace settlement (Fraser, 1995).

Syrian forces were repelled by 11 October, and Israeli forces had crossed the Suez Canal by 18 October. Israeli forces were driving back the Arab armies (Ovendale, 1992). It was at this point that the United States and the Soviet Union decided to impose a ceasefire. On 20 October, Kissinger flew to Moscow and drafted a ceasefire agreement with Communist Party Chairman **Leonid Breznev**. The ceasefire was accepted by all sides on 22 October. The last of the fighting ended on 24 October, but not before the Soviet Union had put its own troops on alert and threatened intervention in order to relieve the Egyptian Third Army, which had been trapped. This has led some analysts to assert that a superpower confrontation had been a distinct possibility. Others, however, have claimed that the Soviet Union had no intention of sending troops, but wished only to put pressure on the United States to restrain Israel. The United States also only went on red alert in order to disguise its compliance with this demand (Yapp, 1991). On 25 October, the Egyptian Third Army was resupplied; Arab dignity was saved, and the United States was able to gain influence in Egypt, while Israel still emerged victorious.

One final element of the war was the so-called oil weapon. Following the outbreak of the war, the Arab member-states of **OPEC** stopped oil exports to the United States and the Netherlands and reduced overall exports by 25 per cent. The embargo, which lasted until 1974, was designed to punish those states that were seen as overtly supportive of Israel and served to boost Arab confidence further. Ultimately, however, it was the fact that the Arabs for the first time had not been militarily defeated, and the political gains from the war, which created conditions that were much more conducive to negotiations than at any time since 1948.

Consequences of the war

Politically, the Arabs had won the war. Egyptian confidence had grown dramatically as a result. From an Egyptian perspective, Israel had only been saved by the United States. The belief in Israel's invincibility had been destroyed. Moreover, Sadat had acquired the international reputation of an accomplished political strategist. 'Sadat emerged from the war a world statesman, something Nasser aspired to but never achieved' (Ovendale, 1992: 221). He was hailed as the 'hero of the crossing'.

Despite the Israeli victory, confidence had been seriously shaken, resulting in public anger directed at Prime Minister Golda Meir and Defence Minister Moshe Dayan and leading to a full investigation of the intelligence failure under the Agranat Commission. The commission's report was highly critical of military intelligence, discipline and training, but failed to address the responsibility of political leaders for Israel's losses (Tessler, 1994).

At the same time, human losses and a general feeling of uncertainty strengthened the search for a settlement. An estimated 3,000 Israeli and 8,500 Egyptian and Syrian soldiers were killed and 8,000 Israelis and almost 20,000 Syrians wounded (Peretz, 1996: 74). It was the first Arab–Israeli war in which Israel suffered a high casualty rate, had men missing in action and had prisoners taken by the enemy (Adan, 1986). These traumatic effects led to the emergence of an Israeli peace movement.

Ironically, the insecurity created by the war also gave rise to Israel's religious right. Thus it was not the victorious 1967 June War which led to a government-backed settlement policy for ideological rather than security reasons, but the despair of the Yom Kippur War which resulted in reviving the notion of a greater '**Eretz Yisrael**' (Land of Israel) (Drezon-Tepler, 1990). Consequently, groups such as **Gush Emunim** started to gain prominence.

Above all, Sadat had made it clear that Egypt was ready for a settlement with Israel, and Syria was willing now to accept UN Resolution 242. US Secretary of State and President Richard Nixon's national security advisor Henry Kissinger was convinced that both Egypt and Syria were ready for compromise. Israel, too, being in economic and political turmoil, was believed to be more flexible.

The United Nations was at the forefront of attempts to restart negotiations with UN Resolution 338 [**Doc. 15, p. 147**], which was passed when the ceasefire was ordered on 22 October 1973. The resolution called for the immediate termination of all military activity and implementation of UN Resolution 242. In December, Soviet and American foreign ministers convened a Middle East peace conference in Geneva. However, this initiative accomplished little. In fact, it has been argued that Kissinger only backed the Geneva conference in order to give the Soviets the impression of cooperation before he pursued direct talks with the Sadat and Meir governments (Smith, 1996). Nevertheless, the groundwork for Kissinger's famous shuttle diplomacy had been laid.

6   The Egyptian–Israeli peace process

The shift from conflict to negotiation, or from war to peace, has proved a particularly difficult one in the context of protracted conflict. Indeed, continuing a war can be the most comfortable option as it represents an almost predictable certainty in the face of the uncertainties of peace and change. In most cases the decision to engage in a peace process has been motivated by a stalemate which makes it clear that neither side can completely defeat the other, the presence of spokespersons for both sides and the availability of a formula for the way out (Zartman, 1989). The 1973 October War presented the possibility for all of these. Renewed military confrontation made it clear, on the one hand, that Egypt could not defeat Israel despite the element of surprise and acquisition of Soviet arms and, on the other hand, that Israel, despite being victorious in all Arab–Israeli wars, was not protected from Arab attacks. Further, US Secretary of State Henry Kissinger's determination to find a settlement provided both sides with a formula which made it easy to move beyond a disengagement agreement. And finally, the determination of President Anwar Sadat and the willingness of Israeli Prime Minister **Menachem Begin** to take the risks of peace made successful Israeli–Egyptian negotiations possible.

Disengagement

Attempts at restarting negotiations began with the ceasefire on 22 October and UN resolution 338 [Doc. 15, p. 147]. On 11 November 1973 the first agreement between Israel and Egypt was reached at kilometre 101 on the Cairo–Suez road. It provided for relief for the Egyptian Third Army trapped behind Israeli lines, the replacement of Israeli checkpoints by UN checkpoints and the exchange of prisoners (Fraser, 1995). Equally, or even more important, it marked a change in Egyptian–Israeli relations exemplified by Egyptian Chief of Staff General Abdel Ghani Gamasy, who said to Israeli Deputy Chief of Staff Israel Tal:

> Look, this is the first time that a war has ended between us in equality. We can say we won and can say it's a tie. From this position we can negotiate. This time we want to end the conflict.
>
> (Bregman and el-Tahiri, 1998: 126)

In December 1973, the United Nations, the United States and the Soviet Union convened a Middle East Peace Conference in Geneva. According to Kissinger, 'The Geneva Conference was a way to get all parties into harness for one symbolic act, thereby to enable each to pursue a separate course' (Kissinger, 1982: 747). However, the conference failed to reconvene after the opening speeches. It accomplished little, apart from providing the professional diplomats with a 'testing ground for all the arcane knowledge acquired in a lifetime of study about procedures, about abstruse points of protocol, about "auspices" and "chairmanship"' (Kissinger, 1982: 755).

Behind the scenes Kissinger continued to work towards disengagement along the Suez Canal in order to stabilize the situation. In principle, Kissinger was still operating within the framework of the United Nations. In practice, however, he had bypassed both the United Nations and the Russians when he embarked upon his shuttle diplomacy following the collapse of the Geneva conference (Smith, 1996). He was convinced that he could achieve at least partial agreements, based upon a step-by-step approach and a land-for-peace basis. So 'the US diplomat tirelessly shuttled back and forth between Jerusalem, Cairo, and Damascus' (Tessler, 1994: 481). He told Israel that the conclusion of an agreement would reduce pressure for further concessions, while, at the same time, he told the Arabs that partial Israeli withdrawal would ultimately lead to complete Israeli withdrawal. Kissinger's persistence and negotiating skills were successful. On 18 January 1974, the Disengagement of Forces Agreement, or Sinai I, between Egypt and Israel was signed. It provided for the withdrawal of Israeli forces from the west bank of the canal. A second Israeli accord with Egypt, known as the Sinai II Accord, was signed on 1 September 1975, enabling Cairo to regain more control over the Sinai Peninsula, including the oilfields. US President **Gerald Ford**, who had succeeded Nixon upon his resignation in August 1974, had been disappointed with the Israeli unwillingness to make concessions in Sinai II; the Israeli approach 'frustrated the Egyptians and made me mad as hell' while 'Kissinger's exasperation with [Yitzhak] Rabin knew no bounds' (Ball, 1984: 346; Ford, 1979: 249).

The disengagement agreement with Syria had been even more difficult than the Israeli–Egyptian one. Damascus had adopted a hardline view, and border clashes continued for months after the ceasefire (Peretz, 1996). These tensions between Syria and Israel made it difficult to pursue settlement beyond disengagement. Hafez al-Asad had little interest in negotiations with Israel unless the Arabs formed a united front and consequently viewed Sadat's willingness to pursue an agreement with deep suspicion. On the one hand, he feared that Egypt's willingness to compromise would undermine his own efforts to regain all the territory of the Golan Heights. On the other, he saw this as an opportunity to make his bid for Arab leadership. The realignment of regional powers consequently saw a decline in Syrian–Egyptian relations, while Syria realigned itself with Iraq, Algeria, Libya, South Yemen and the PLO (Peretz, 1996).

Israeli–Syrian negotiations took place against the backdrop of Israeli domestic problems. Prime Minister Golda Meir resigned in April 1974 and was succeeded by former Chief of Staff General **Yitzhak Rabin**. For Israel an agreement with Syria proved more difficult as the Golan Heights had posed a close threat. Indeed, neither side had much territory to spare. The Israeli agreement to withdraw from just beyond Quneitra on the Golan Heights was finally secured on 31 May 1974. 'What really persuaded the Israelis was Kissinger's clever mixture of threats and secret assurances' (Fraser, 1995: 110). It had also, however, become clear that Syrian–Israeli negotiations would go no further. Kissinger's assessment of this situation was that 'to Sadat, disengagement was the first step in what he suspected, given Syrian ambivalence, would have to be a separate Egyptian peace; Asad probably rationalised that it was the last phase prior to a renewed confrontation with Israel' (Kissinger, 1982: 748).

The 1977 Likud victory

In June 1977 Menachem Begin became prime minister of the first Likud government since the establishment of the State of Israel. The shift within the Israeli electorate was the result of voter dissatisfaction with the Labour Alignment, which had been racked by rivalries and scandals (Tessler, 1994). It also marked the political coming of age of the second generation of Jews of Afro-Asian origin. Having originated from Muslim countries, they were more likely to regard the Arabs as untrustworthy and to oppose territorial concessions. Indeed, it has been claimed that their ideological contribution has been 'populist chauvinism and crude anti-Arab sentiment' (Sprinzak, 1991: 15). Their experience with Labour leaders during the 1950s and 1960s was one of being treated as culturally inferior and being housed in transition camps for prolonged periods. This further contributed to the election victory of the Likud.

The election signalled a change in Israeli domestic policy. The general expectation was that this would be a change towards intransigence and militancy. Indeed, with 'Begin in power, it was feared, the chances of a political settlement of the Arab–Israeli conflict had been ruined, and the probability of a new war had grown' (Bar Siman Tov, 1994: 19). This perception was based on the fact that Likud policy marked a significant departure from previous Labour governments with its commitment to Judea and Samaria (the West Bank). As heir of the Jewish underground organization Irgun during the time of the British mandate, and indebted to Vladimir Jabotinsky's revisionist philosophy, the party emphasized national security and contained an anti-Arab element. Its ideological platform advocated an aggressive settlement policy of the West Bank on the grounds that this territory was an integral part of Israel. Arabs in this territory, and even those within the pre-1967 boundaries, the so-called **Green Line**, were regarded as alien to the country. Likud's approach was one of **territorial maximalism** combined with a strong reliance on military power based on the beliefs of the indivisibility of the Land of Israel, hostility towards Arabs, never-ending war against the PLO and 'a constant siege mentality along with enthusiastic utterances about religious redemption' (Sprinzak, 1991: 16). Accordingly, Begin made it clear that Israel was going to retain the Golan Heights, hold on to the West Bank and exclude the Palestinians from negotiations. It is therefore not surprising that observers at the time of Begin's election regarded the defeat of Labour as a major setback for peace in the region. Yet, at the same time, Begin, while still prime minister elect, approached US Ambassador to Israel Samuel Lewis and told him that his first aim as prime minister would be negotiations with Egypt (Bar Siman Tov, 1994). Thus Sadat's belief that the time was 'ripe' for peace was not unfounded.

On 9 November 1977, following several months of painfully slow, secret Israeli–Egyptian negotiations through the mediation of King Hassan II of Morocco, Sadat announced to the Egyptian National Assembly that he was willing to go to Israel and address the Israeli Knesset [**Doc. 16, p. 147**] in order to get the ball rolling again. It has been claimed that US President **Jimmy Carter's** insistence on including the Russians through the Geneva conference pushed Sadat into going to Jerusalem in order to pre-empt Soviet involvement. Another motivation cited for Sadat's decision to make this unprecedented move is Israeli intelligence information about a Libyan plot against his life, which was passed to him through King Hassan (Ovendale, 1992). Now that the ball was in Israel's court, Begin, in a sense, had no choice but to accept. Israeli Defence Minister Ezer Weizman pointed out the irony in his memoirs.

> The first offer [for peace] had come and met with a response under Begin's leadership. . . . Begin's reputation was that of a superhawk, a right-wing extremist, and Herut was perceived as a party of war. As it turned out, it was only because Begin was such a blatantly self-declared hawk that he could get away with taking chances.
>
> (Weizman, 1981: 23–4)

On 19 November, Sadat arrived in Jerusalem to discuss peace. It was the first official, direct and public contact between an Arab state and Israel, breaking down some of the psychological barriers which had existed since 1948. Yet the American government remained dubious that Sadat and Begin could reach an agreement without third-party mediation, especially since it had become obvious that Sadat liked neither Begin nor Foreign Minister Moshe Dayan, preferring Defence Minister Ezer Weizman instead.

Of particular interest within the emerging negotiations are the different – and to some degree conflicting – visions of the outcome of the talks. When US President Jimmy Carter took office in 1976, it was clear that he intended to play a more active role in the Middle East and to introduce some of his own ideas into US policy. Carter's conception of a settlement included the

resolution of the Palestinian problem, substantive Israeli territorial concessions, Arab recognition of Israel and Soviet involvement as a mediator. Carter's ideas differed significantly from those previously held by Kissinger, who
had neither considered the PLO a factor in the peace process nor believed
that the Soviet Union had a role to play. Carter tried to provide the peace
process with new direction, a direction which was to some extent at odds
with Egypt and Israel.

A change in Israeli views had also taken place over the period of negotiations. Yitzhak Rabin, who was the Israeli prime minister during the first
stages of the US mediation beginning in January 1977, declared that he
could compromise on the territory of the Sinai, but there would be no concessions on the Golan Heights. The issues of Palestinian inclusion into talks,
and the West Bank, were kept vague. Once Begin took office in June 1977,
the status of the West Bank was clarified. Begin had run on an electoral platform which considered the West Bank to be an integral part of the Land of
Israel. He also opposed the inclusion of the PLO in negotiations, equating
Yasser Arafat with Hitler.

Sadat outlined his idea of a settlement in his speech to the Knesset. He
wanted neither a separate or partial peace nor a third disengagement agreement. Instead, he wanted a 'durable peace based on justice'. Such a settlement would require the Israeli withdrawal from the territories captured in
the 1967 June War and the Palestinian right to self-determination. Despite
the historic connotations, Begin was determined not to be 'swayed by the
emotion of the moment into making concessions he would later regret'
(Fraser, 1995: 122).

Sadat's visit to Jerusalem in November 1977, which has been described
as one of the most remarkable events of the post-war era (Bailey, 1990),
sparked another round of intense Israeli–Egyptian–US diplomacy, including
a visit by Begin to Ismailia on Christmas Day 1977. The Ismailia conference,
however, ended in failure.

> It had also highlighted the glaring differences between the leaders on
> either side. Sadat had hoped the conference would bring about an
> understanding in principle. He'd offered Israel full peace – in return
> for withdrawal from the Sinai and an understanding over the Palestin-
> ians. . . . As for Begin, he had ignored principles, plunging into details
> instead, most of which scarcely interested the Egyptian president.
>
> (Weizman, 1981: 136)

In early 1978, it became clear that Israeli–Egyptian talks had become
deadlocked over the issue of the West Bank and Palestinian rights to self-
rule, proving American fears correct. In an attempt to break this deadlock,
Carter decided to convene a summit at Camp David in September 1978 in
order 'to save the peace'.

The Camp David Accords

The Carter administration, with all its faults in other areas of policy making, was able to provide the environment that made Egyptian–Israeli peace negotiations possible. It displayed an almost unprecedented degree of consensus between the president, Secretary of State **Cyrus Vance** and National Security Advisor Zbigniew Brzezinski.

The potential for stalemate had become clear soon after Sadat's visit to Jerusalem. Israel, in an attempt to retain the West Bank, blocked any proposed clauses which could be interpreted in favour of an independent Palestinian entity, while Egypt demanded Israeli recognition of the Palestinian right to self-rule (Smith, 1996). Begin was only willing to concede administrative autonomy: in essence, control over health, welfare and education (Peretz, 1996). In a move to break the impasse, Carter called a summit at Camp David, which Israel and Egypt were unable to refuse as the invitation had been from the US president personally (Victor, 1995). The diplomatic exchanges, which lasted from 5 to 17 September, were intense, and the atmosphere was not always the most cordial. Indeed, two days before the end of the negotiations Sadat threatened to withdraw.

Nevertheless, two agreements were concluded and signed in 'an emotional ceremony in the East Room of the White House late on 17 September 1978' (Bailey, 1990: 357). The first comprised the principles for an Egyptian–Israeli peace treaty and normalization of relations [Doc. 17, p. 148]. Israel would give up Sinai, including settlements and airfields. The second provided a 'Framework for Peace in the Middle East', based on Resolutions 242 and 338, the resolution of the Palestinian problem, good neighbourly relations and Palestinian autonomy in the West Bank (excluding Jerusalem) and the Gaza Strip [Doc. 17, p. 148].

According to Carter's and Sadat's interpretation of Palestinian autonomy, a Palestinian self-governing authority, freely elected by the inhabitants of the West Bank and Gaza Strip, should replace the Israeli military administration. During a five-year transition period the final status of the territories should be negotiated (Ovendale, 1992). Carter genuinely believed that he had obtained a major concession on the West Bank, but Begin interpreted Palestinian autonomy as no more than 'personal autonomy' (Fraser, 1995).

Both Begin and Sadat had difficulties convincing the public that the concessions made were justified. Sadat had cut Egypt off from the rest of the Arab world, while Begin was faced with the emergence of a new radical right consisting of the newly established **Tehiya** party, Gush Emunim, the **Land of Israel Movement,** and **Kach** who were determined to fight against Camp David. Despite these obstacles, Sadat and Begin were able to achieve legitimacy in the eyes of most Egyptians and most Israelis, respectively.

On 26 March 1979 the Egyptian–Israeli peace treaty was signed. Israel returned Sinai to Egypt in return for peace, full diplomatic relations and

Figure 6.1 President Jimmy Carter of the United States (centre), Egyptian President Anwar Sadat (left), and Israeli Prime Minister Menacham Begin (right) join hands after the Egypt–Israeli peace treaty is signed. © Frank Johnston/Washington Post/Getty Images

shipping through the Suez Canal and Gulf of Aqaba. In the months following the treaty, it became clear that Begin had no intention of relinquishing Israeli control over the West Bank and Gaza Strip. The continuation and indeed increase of Israeli settlement activity confirmed this. It is thus not surprising that the negotiations on the autonomy scheme only continued for a short period and were suspended by the end of 1979. The Carter administration was unable to put pressure on Israel, because it became caught up in the emerging Iranian Revolution, the US hostage crisis in November 1979, the Soviet invasion of Afghanistan in December and upcoming presidential elections.

Implications of peace

Arab leaders were caught between a rock and a hard place. They had to decide whether it was better to be left out of negotiations or to participate in them. In the end only Egypt proceeded, and the general Arab reaction to the Israeli–Egyptian peace turned into one of open hostility. The exclusion of the Palestinians, in particular, provided a rallying point. While Arab leaders now sought to fill the regional leadership vacuum by declaring sympathy with the Palestinians, the PLO became more determined in its quest for Palestinian self-determination. Prominent Palestinian scholar Edward Said's assessment of the autonomy provisions of the Camp David Accords reflects popular Palestinian feelings at that time: 'You cannot expect millions of Arab Palestinians to go away, or to be content with occupation, or to acquiesce to an Israeli, or an Egyptian, or an American, idea for their destiny, their "autonomy", or their physical location.' For the West Bank Palestinians, the Egyptian–Israeli agreement seemed to confirm continued Israeli rule over them, declared openly by Begin himself, whatever the expectations of Carter and Sadat (Smith, 1996).

The implications of peace for Egypt were both positive and negative. The Arab League imposed a political and economic boycott on Egypt and moved its headquarters from Cairo to Tunis. Egypt's membership in the Arab League was suspended, and Egypt became ostracized. The suspension of negotiations on the West Bank led to the charge that Sadat 'had abandoned the Palestinian cause in order to recover the Sinai' (Tessler, 1994: 514). The lack of rapid economic growth which had been promised to the Egyptian population left him open to further criticism. In the end, Sadat paid the ultimate price for peace with Israel. He was assassinated on 6 October 1981 by members of the Islamist organization Al-Jihad as he reviewed a parade to commemorate the crossing of the Suez Canal.

Yet despite Sadat's assassination and the pervading disaffection of Egyptians and hostility of most other Arabs, Sadat's successor **Hosni Mubarak** upheld the peace agreement with Israel. Egypt thus became the first Arab state to make peace with Israel. The Egyptian boycott against Israel was lifted, embassies were opened, regular airline flights began in March 1980 and Egypt started selling oil to Israel. Both Egypt and Israel benefited from the peace in terms of US aid and support. And as early as 1974, after the first disengagement agreement had been concluded, US President Richard Nixon had offered both Egypt and Israel help with civil nuclear power (Bailey, 1990). Finally, in the long run, Sadat's peace initiative also made it possible for Egypt to emerge as the key Arab mediator in the 1991 Middle East peace process.

Peace had less equivocal benefits for Israel. The Knesset's massive support for the treaty with Egypt vindicated Begin's decision to return Sinai. It provided Israel with security and stability along its southern border and thereby freed up the country's limited resources. The peace agreement had removed the Arab country with the largest military force from the Arab–Israeli conflict and precluded a two-front option against Israel.

Normalization became the most important Israeli aim after the treaty had been signed. The main stumbling block on this front remained Israeli–Egyptian friction over Palestinian autonomy. Israel's continued settlement policy, the 1981 annexation of the Golan Heights and the stalemate in the autonomy talks, as well as Israel's 1982 invasion of Lebanon, soon turned the two states' relations into a cold peace.

7 The 1982 Lebanon War

After 1970, peace and stability along Israel's border with Lebanon became paramount for Israel's security. The expulsion of the PLO from Jordan to Lebanon after **Black September** increasingly became a threat to Israeli interests. The Lebanese civil war which erupted in 1975 further heightened Israeli concerns. The war raised the distinct possibility that Lebanon could fall to the PLO, end up under Syrian control or that civil unrest could contaminate the region as a whole. It is therefore not surprising that when Lebanon's Maronite Christians appealed for aid from Israel, Israel seized upon the opportunity to influence events in Lebanon. The initially cautious approach of the Rabin government was soon replaced by the committed stance of the Begin government. Peace with Egypt, moreover, freed Israel to focus on the north. As a result, what had started as a spate of retaliatory raids against Palestinian *fedayeen* developed into a grand strategy through which Israel sought to change the geo-strategic make-up of the Middle East. Israel's 1982 invasion of Lebanon was the means to this end.

The Lebanese civil war

In 1975, yet another Lebanese political crisis was unleashed during a strike of Sidon fishermen. Soldiers trying to remove a roadblock were ambushed. Tensions spread north when Maronite **Kataib** party leader Pierre Gemayel was fired at by Palestinians on 13 April. In retaliation, the Kataib attacked a Palestinian bus passing through the Beirut suburb Ain al-Rummana. This incident sparked off further clashes between Palestinians and Christians; the Lebanese civil war had begun.

At the heart of the conflict was the political and socio-economic power imbalance between Christian and Muslim communities. One of the main problems which had led to the unrest was that of minority-majority integration. Instead of the political leaders balancing the interests of the different communities in the true sense of Lebanon's consociational democracy, and thereby creating a basis for a wider Lebanese identity, they pursued their own limited agendas, resulting in communal distrust. The other key issue was the still-unresolved question of Lebanon's identity as an Arab, Mediterranean or Christian state.

Constructed upon a system in which government offices were allocated on communal grounds based on a census conducted in 1932, Maronite Christians traditionally held the presidency, Sunni Muslims the premiership and Shi'a Muslims the position of the speaker of the house. Since 1932 the demographic realities, however, had not only shifted in favour of Lebanon's economically disadvantaged Shi'as, but the inter-communal balance had also been tipped by the influx of an estimated 270,000 Palestinian refugees (Peretz, 1996). Lebanon's Christians feared political changes which would denigrate them to the second-class position Christians occupied in other Muslim-majority states. They saw the status quo as the only guarantee for their religious and cultural freedom. At the same time Lebanon's Muslims – Sunni, Shi'a and Druze – were pushing for political reform.

The state started to disintegrate when the different ethno-religious communities lost trust in the formal institutions, which they no longer believed to be powerful or impartial enough to protect their respective interests (Schiff, 1987). Sectarian allegiances emerged as the primary affiliation even before the 1975–76 war when the political system was suffering from the strains of rapid development. Increasing pressure for fairer representation and equitable distribution of wealth and status came to be supported by sectarian militias.

In an effort to stop the sectarian conflict from both destroying Lebanon and spilling over into neighbouring Syria, Asad sent Syrian troops into Lebanon in 1976. For Asad, Lebanon's troubles provided the perfect opportunity not only to prevent the possibility of future Lebanese military rule, but also to assert control over Palestinian forces and to deter Israel from filling the power vacuum. In addition, Asad's shrewd move brought Syria one step closer to fulfilling its territorial claims, as well as once again demonstrating that he himself was the most effective Arab leader in the region. Thus in the context of regional dynamics, Lebanon became a key factor in the Syrian–Israeli deterrence dialogue. It also became a surrogate battlefield for the Israeli–Palestinian conflict after the PLO's move to Beirut.

Limited Israeli intervention

Border clashes between Palestinian *fedayeen* and Israelis had steadily increased from the early 1970s onwards. The resulting instability led the Christian population in South Lebanon to appeal for Israeli aid. This was provided in the form of weapons, food and medication known as the 'Good Fence' policy, which was a strategic response to the Lebanese government's lack of control over the south. In March 1976, Lebanese army officer Saad Haddad started to establish the so-called South Lebanese Army (SLA), approved of and later supported by Israel (Evron, 1987).

The first large-scale Israeli military intervention was Operation Litani. It was launched in response to a Palestinian attack on an Israeli bus on the Haifa–Tel Aviv road on 11 March 1978. This incident in the heart of the country, in which 37 Israelis died and another 78 were wounded, resulted in a new direction in Israel's Lebanon policy. The main objectives of Operation Litani were the punishment of the PLO and the destruction of the PLO infrastructure south of the Litani River. A further objective added during the operation was the creation of a security zone in cooperation with Haddad's forces.

Parallel to the developments in South Lebanon, Israel's relationship with Beirut politician **Bashir Gemayel**, son of Kataib leader Pierre Gemayel, began to solidify in 1977. Bashir Gemayel's aims were to build a free Lebanon – free of Syrian troops, free of Palestinian *fedayeen* and free of stifling feudal traditions. His first two aims coincided with Israel's security interests, providing a basis for increased collaboration. In practical terms this meant weapons, training and military advisors for Bashir's forces. This stronger Israeli commitment was also reflected in Prime Minister Begin's statements. He publicly announced, 'we shall not, under any circumstances, abandon the Christians into the hands of their tormentors' (Medzini, 1984: 287).

Bashir Gemayel proceeded with unifying all Christian militias into the Lebanese Front. For the first time optimism and a determined strategy were visible in the Christian camp.

> If a unified Lebanon could be maintained, which would preserve the ethos and power structure of the traditional Lebanese entity, then the Front should strive for it. If that were not the case, the 'smaller Lebanon' strategy should be resorted to.
>
> (Rabinovich, 1985: 114)

Israeli–Maronite relations from 1977 to 1980 developed from covert connections into an overt alliance aided by the unification of the Maronite forces and the Likud government's interventionist approach, as well as the consolidation of the PLO in Lebanon. Maronite and Israeli interests started to converge around common aims and enemies. Syrian and Palestinian forces needed to be ejected from Lebanon, and a stable Maronite-dominated state needed to be re-established.

Operation Peace for Galilee

Regional and domestic Israeli changes in 1981 and 1982 paved the way for Israel's invasion of Lebanon. In 1981 Israel's government was reshuffled. Foreign Minister Moshe Dayan was succeeded by Itzhak Shamir, and Defence Minister Ezer Weizman by **Ariel Sharon**. Both Dayan and Weizman had served as a restraining force, while Shamir and Sharon had the opposite effect, thus increasing the preference for a military option (Schulze, 1998). The second factor increasing the likelihood for an Israeli invasion was a two-week war of attrition between Palestinian guerrillas firing rockets at Israel's north and the IDF and SLA shelling Palestinian positions. An estimated 5,000 Israeli families fled the area, revealing Israel's vulnerability.

This two-week war in June 1981 was followed by a US-mediated cease-fire, which in Israeli eyes had deprived the IDF of the option to take puni-tive action (Schiff and Ya'ari, 1984). Moreover, the ability of the PLO to maintain this ceasefire increased Arafat's international standing and thus increased the Palestinian political threat. It was at this point that the deci-sion to launch another ground operation was taken.

The regional and international environments were also conducive to Israeli military action. The last stage of Egyptian–Israeli peace negotiations had finally been concluded, so Israel could focus on its northern border. War with Syria was also considered to be on the cards in the near future, so why not engage the Syrians on Israel's terms? And finally, the US administration, in particular Secretary of State **Alexander Haig,** had not openly opposed Israeli invasion plans when Israel's ambassador to Washington tested US reaction. Indeed, in a meeting between Haig and Sharon on 25 May 1982 when Sharon briefed the secretary of state on the possibility of an Israeli ground operation, Haig only told Sharon that nothing should be done with-out clear provocation (Bregman, 1998: 166). Sharon did not have to wait long. On 3 June, Israeli Ambassador Shlomo Argov was shot outside the Dorchester Hotel in London. The assassination attempt was traced to Abu Nidal's Palestinian faction, but as Begin considered the PLO to be ultimately responsible for all Palestinian actions and Sharon could not let this 'clear provocation' pass, the ball for Israel's invasion of Lebanon was set rolling.

Plans for the invasion had already been coordinated between Sharon and Bashir Gemayel in January 1982 when they had discussed linking up Bashir's quest for the presidency with a large-scale Israeli operation. Indeed, Sharon had proposed to eliminate the PLO from Lebanon with the aid of the Lebanese Forces, after which a political solution would be possible (Schulze, 1998). So using the 3 June assassination attempt on Israel's ambassador in London as a pretext, Israel invaded Lebanon on 6 June 1982. 'Operation Peace for Galilee' was announced as a 48-hour limited operation similar to the 1978 'Operation Litani'. Defence Minister Ariel Sharon declared the goal to be the elimination of the PLO in South Lebanon (Peretz, 1996), but by the time the first ceasefire was called Israeli troops were already on the outskirts of Beirut [**Map 4, p. xxix**]. It soon became clear that Operation Peace for Galilee had much broader aims. The first aim was to establish a new political order in Lebanon by securing the election of a Maronite Chris-tian government under Lebanese Forces Commander Bashir Gemayel. This new government would then sign a full peace treaty with Israel. In terms of security, this would establish a more comprehensive security arrangement than the limited version in South Lebanon with the SLA. In a way it was like substituting a proxy-militia with a proxy-government so that a new order could be created. Attaining such a basic change in the politico-strategic situ-ation in Lebanon required the destruction or neutralization of all military elements, which might inhibit the election of a Lebanese president who was allied with Israel (Yaniv, 1987). Thus the second aim was the wholesale expulsion of the Palestinians from Lebanon. This would remove the military threat from Palestinian guerrillas to both Israel and Lebanon, would remove the demographic threat to Lebanon's Christians and would set back the PLO's state-building efforts. Closely related was the third aim, the destruction of Palestinian nationalism in the West Bank and Gaza Strip. This was based on the belief that it was the PLO that fostered Palestinian nationalism rather nationalism being a genuine expression by the Palestinian people. Thus the blow struck to the PLO would halt the growth in Palestinian nationalism. The fourth aim was the defeat and expulsion of Syrian troops which had been in Lebanon since 1976. The Syrian role was no longer perceived as convenient to Israeli security interests, and therefore the Syrian military presence needed to be removed. Indeed, a review of Israel's security status ordered by Sharon in 1981 had indicated that Syria would probably attack Israel in late 1983 or early 1984. Thus Syria's military capacity had to be reduced. It was hoped that this would even set in motion the domestic disintegration of that state as well (Evron, 1987). And the fifth and final aim was freeing Israel from past traumas such as the 1973 war (Eban, 1992; Peleg, 1987; Rabinovich, 1985). Clearly, peace for Galilee was not the main objective; rather, it was a basic change in Israel's regional position.

As the IDF advanced towards Beirut, it engaged both Palestinian and Syrian forces on its way to linking up with the Lebanese Forces. On June 9 the IDF attacked Syrian troops and maintained the offensive for four days (Gabriel, 1984: 67). On 12 June, Israeli troops reached the outskirts of Beirut. At this point Sharon's 'grand strategy' started to disintegrate. The plan had envisaged that the Lebanese Forces would deal with Muslim West Beirut and 'clear out' the PLO. This would make it unnecessary for Israeli forces to enter the city, and Israel could avoid being seen as occupying an Arab capital. However, when Israeli and Maronite troops joined up at Ba'abda, Bashir made it clear to Sharon that he had no intention of fulfilling his side of the bargain (Benziman, 1987). He was willing to aid the IDF, but not to engage in combat, in order not to jeopardize his election. After all, he wanted to become president of *all* of Lebanon. As a result, Israel had to deal with the PLO in West Beirut itself.

On 1 July, Israeli troops laid siege to the city, despite the fact that a ceasefire had technically been in place for six days. The siege was aimed at striking a mortal blow to an estimated 12,000 to 14,000 PLO fighters (Gabriel, 1984). It started with a concerted campaign of psychological warfare consisting of leaflets and mock bomb-runs to convince the PLO that an attack was imminent. US mediator Philip Habib, who had been sent in to defuse the crisis, had achieved little. The PLO was determined to stay in Beirut, while the IDF was equally determined to evict it. On 3 July, the IDF sealed off West Beirut and opened tank and artillery fire on Palestinian positions. As the siege continued, Israel cut off water, food supplies and fuel. Gunboats began to shell West Beirut, and rocket exchanges broke out between the PLO and the IDF. As the fighting increased, Habib continued to press for an agreement behind the scenes. On 6 August, a commitment to PLO

Figure 7.1 Bashir Gemayel gets into his car after being elected president of Lebanon on 23 August, 1982. © AFP/Getty Images

withdrawal was finally secured. But it was not until 22 August that the first PLO contingent of 379 men departed from Beirut (Gabriel, 1984). In total, 11,000 guerrillas left for Tunisia, Algeria, Yemen and Syria, and PLO head-quarters were relocated to Tunis.

While the Israeli army was 'liberating' Lebanon in order to restore Maronite hegemony, Bashir Gemayel denounced Israel and entered the pres-idential race on a platform of cross-community cooperation, tolerance and national reconciliation. His success was short lived. Having been elected on 23 August, he was killed in the bombing of the Kataib headquarters on 14 September 1982, a week before he was due to take office.

The failures of Operation Peace for Galilee

The death of Bashir Gemayel was also the death knell for Israel's Leba-non plans. The IDF immediately moved towards the Green Line, while Sha-ron proceeded with his plans to get rid of an estimated 2,000 PLO fighters 'who had gone civilian' (Kimche, 1991). On 15 September, Israeli Chief of

Staff Rafael Eitan and General Amir Drori met with the general staff of the Kataib militia and agreed that the latter would enter the Palestinian camps (MacBride, 1983). The next day, on 16 September, after a meeting with Elie Hobeika and Fadi Frem of the Lebanese Forces, 150 Kataib militiamen entered Sabra and Shatilla under IDF supervision (Black and Morris, 1991). In Eitan's words they were 'eager to take revenge [for Bashir's death] and there may be rivers of blood' (Peleg, 1987: 162). Yet at the same time, he publicly maintained that the 'IDF had no knowledge until Saturday morning of what was going on' (MacBride, 1983: 168). This statement was contradicted by Israeli and foreign journalists who heard about the massacre on the Friday morning. Estimates of the dead vary widely. The Israeli Kahan Commission claimed that 700 to 800 civilians died, while others place the number as high as 1,500 to 2,000 (Jansen, 1982). Israeli journalists Zeev Schiff and Ehud Ya'ari described the massacres as the 'wholesale slaughter of families', including 'hanging live grenades around their victims' necks', infants being trampled to death, and rape (Schiff and Ya'ari, 1984: 264). Far from 'guerrillas gone civilian', the majority of the victims were women and children, and almost half of them Shi'a Lebanese (Harris, 1997: 176).

Bashir Gemayel's death was a crucial turning point. No other Maronite leader combined the ability to govern Lebanon with a political orientation acceptable to Israel. His brother Amin, who succeeded him, not only had a different political vision, he also did not want an alliance with Israel, courted good relations with the Arab world and preferred to rely on US mediation.

The failure of Operation Peace for Galilee, however, was ultimately the result of Israeli misconceptions (Schulze, 1998). Israel had based its plans on the illusion of Bashir Gemayel's power in the Maronite community and the power of the Maronites in Lebanon. Further, Israeli decision makers failed to understand Maronite goals. Maronite non-cooperation, once Israel had entered Lebanon, compounded by Bashir Gemayel's death and the lack of contingency plans, placed Israel in an unenviable position.

The 1983 May 17th agreement

Through US mediation, official negotiations between Israel and Lebanon began on 28 December 1982. To Israel's chagrin, Amin Gemayel not only insisted upon including Shi'a and Sunni representatives in the negotiations, he also refused to agree to a single word without first having the approval of the Sunni prime minister (Kimche, 1991: 159).

The domestic outcry over the Sabra and Shatilla massacres made it imperative for Israel to produce a treaty in order to justify the war. But differences in the Lebanese and Israeli positions soon became apparent. Israel wanted security for its northern border, full diplomatic relations and normalization. Lebanon, in contrast, wanted to minimize contact with Israel and, above all, wanted Israeli withdrawal. The agreement [**Doc. 20, p. 151**] that was signed on 17 May 1983 fell short of both Israel's security and Lebanon's political requirements. The treaty terminated the war without installing peace, but guaranteed respect for territorial sovereignty and political independence. The secret annex dealt more specifically with the security arrangements. The southern boundary of the security zone was defined as the international border between Israel and Lebanon, the northern boundary as the Awali River. For Israel it was no more than a glorified armistice agreement, which it felt compelled to ratify in light of the economic and political burden of the occupation and mounting casualties.

Lebanon was in an equally difficult position. Amin Gemayel had sought US mediation in order to achieve not only Israeli but ultimately also Syrian withdrawal from the country. But as Israeli withdrawal had been made contingent upon Syrian withdrawal, neither seemed likely. Moreover, Syria threatened the renewal of civil strife should Lebanon ratify the treaty (Yaniv, 1987). From Damascus's perspective, Israel had achieved what it wanted – a political deal with Beirut, an enfeebled PLO and a broad band of Lebanese territory under direct control. On 5 March 1984, following talks between Asad and Gemayel, Lebanon unilaterally abrogated the agreement.

Repercussions of the invasion

In the summer of 1985 Israel decided to withdraw its troops to the security zone. Having had its fingers badly burnt, security for the northern border became the focus of Israel's Lebanon policy. The Lebanon war had tarnished the standing of the Israeli defence establishment and had split Israeli society. Israel had taken six days to reach Beirut in June 1982, laid siege to the city for three months, occupied the Shouf Mountains for a year and the western Bekaa and south for three years (Picard, 1996). Israel's gains were a defunct peace agreement and the evacuation of the PLO, both of which were incommensurate with the heavy Israeli casualties, international condemnation after Sabra and Shatilla, the economic costs of an estimated $1 million a day and the resumption of attacks against Israel from southern Lebanon. Palestinian nationalism in the West Bank and Gaza Strip also increased. Military gains had clearly not translated into political ones.

The costs of the Lebanon war had severe repercussions on Israeli society. Horrified by massacres of civilians, questionable military results and strategy and having been 'sold' a limited operation while, all the time, a 'grand plan' had been in the minds of decision makers caused outcry in the Israeli population. This clear 'war of choice' rekindled debates in the military establishment on the limits of military force, it questioned the notion of 'purity of arms' and resulted in Israel's first conscientious objectors. The war also provided the peace movement with new life. Peace Now and other groups gained momentous support as well as considerable criticism from a now deeply divided Israeli society. From the Lebanon war onwards, Israel remained split over the issue of negotiations, territorial concessions and security policy.

Within journalistic and academic circles Israel's Lebanon war sparked a debate on the underlying reasons and, ultimately, responsibility. The conventional view holds Defence Minister Ariel Sharon responsible to a large degree and Prime Minister Begin to a more limited degree (Schiff and Ya'ari, 1984). The war is seen as the result of Sharon's personal ambitions, thereby absolving the rest of the Israeli decision-making elite. The conventional perspective further maintains that the invasion of Lebanon is an aberration in Israeli foreign and defence policy. This view has been challenged on a number of grounds. First, Sharon, while bearing a significant amount of responsibility, was not solely responsible. Instead the decision-making elite as a whole was responsible, and the hawkish direction can be explained through the common phenomenon of 'groupthink'. Second, Israel's Lebanon war was not an aberration but the culmination of a long-standing Lebanon policy since the 1920s, which was based on false premises. Returning to earlier discussions of interventionism or non-interventionism in Israeli foreign policy, Israel's Lebanon policy from the creation of the states of Lebanon and Israel onwards is a clear example of Israeli interventionism (Schulze, 1998).

While the war sparked intense debate in Israel, it was used as a stick by Lebanese Muslims to beat the Maronites with. As a result of collaboration with Israel, the Maronites lost their preferential standing. Instead of ruling Lebanon, they now had to defend their very existence (Sofer, 1988). By the end of the civil war in 1990 a sizeable segment of the Christian community had found refuge abroad. Lebanon's dependence upon Syria was formalized through the 1989 Taif Accord and the 1990 Treaty of Brotherhood and Friendship. Syria had emerged in a stronger position than ever before, becoming the arbiter over Lebanon's future.

For the Palestinians changes were no less dramatic. The PLO lost its last border access to Israel with its evacuation to Tunis in 1982. This had the effect of shifting PLO strategy towards a more diplomatic level, while in the long run returning the struggle to those Palestinians under Israeli occupation in the West Bank and Gaza Strip. So rather than eliminating the influence of the PLO, Palestinian nationalism became stronger, while at the same time, through the shift in strategy, the PLO gained increased international recognition. The link between the two made it unequivocally clear that, ultimately, Israel would have no choice but to negotiate with the PLO.

8 The *intifada*

The aims of Israel's invasion of Lebanon included destroying not only the PLO's military basis but its political one as well. Operation Peace for Galilee was intended to strike a severe blow at the PLO's international standing and to weaken the budding resistance and nationalism in the West Bank and Gaza Strip. With the evacuation of the PLO from Beirut to Tunis, Israel seemed to have achieved at least one aim of the 1982 invasion. The Palestinian guerrilla movement had lost access to Israel's border. Yet it was exactly the PLO's Lebanon experience which laid the foundation for the 1987 *intifada* uprising in the Israeli-Occupied Territories as well as the PLO's decision to declare an independent Palestinian state with a government in exile. The abandonment by Arab politicians, the Sabra and Shatila massacres and the move of the PLO to Tunis shifted the focus to the West Bank and Gaza Strip, encouraging local politicians. At the same time, the marginalization of the PLO, now in Tunis, also led to a tactical shift from guerrilla warfare to a diplomatic offensive. Both the PLO's international standing and Palestinian nationalism increased as a result. Thus in the long run, Israel's determination to remove the Palestinian presence from Lebanon achieved the opposite effect.

The PLO after 1982

The military defeat of the Palestinian resistance in Lebanon after the siege of Beirut revealed the shortcomings of the PLO's strategy. The notion of armed struggle as the foundation for the establishment of a Palestinian state was called into question (Gresh, 1988). The guerrilla struggle after 1967 and the semi-regularized army developed in South Lebanon in the late 1970s had been ineffective in liberating Palestine. With the dispersion of PLO forces in nine Arab countries, a plausible military option no longer existed.

The lack of a 'battlefield', however, was not the only problem faced by the resistance movement. Factionalization and friction dominated Palestinian politics. Arafat's opponents, with Syrian encouragement, condemned him for the defeat and were highly critical of his decision to consider a diplomatic option (Smith, 1996). The move to Tunis had physically cut off the Palestinian leadership from the bulk of the Palestinian people. The PLO's isolation was further compounded by the lack of support from its Arab brothers, most of whom had been unwilling to accept the PLO after its evacuation from Beirut. 'Having suffered a profound blow as a result of its military defeat in Lebanon, with its cadres and fighters now scattered over a dozen countries, the PLO ran the risk of permanent fragmentation' (Tessler, 1994: 610). Palestinian strategy needed to be reassessed.

The debate within the PLO focused on the future of the resistance movement; the 1982 Reagan peace plan [Doc. 18, p. 150], which called for Palestinian autonomy as outlined in the Camp David Accords; the Fez plan [Doc. 19, p. 150] drawn up at an Arab summit meeting on 9 September 1982, calling for Israeli withdrawal, the dismantling of settlements, a PLO government, compensation for refugees and a two-state solution; and the possibility of Jordanian–PLO rapprochement. Playing his cards cautiously, Arafat embarked upon separate negotiations with the United States and Jordan. 'The initial positions of the Palestinian leader were: yes to the establishment of a Jordanian–Palestinian confederation; but after the establishment of a Palestinian state; no to any delegation of power during the negotiations' (Gresh, 1988: 231).

Yet Arafat received little encouragement for his diplomatic initiative. Opposition within his own ranks was fuelled by Syria, Iraq and Libya. Official Israeli policy remained that the PLO should have no role whatsoever in any negotiations. This position was supported by the Reagan administration, leaving little room for the PLO to manoeuvre. At the same time, the United States pushed for a Jordanian solution for the West Bank, which envisaged Israel giving up territory as well as accepting Palestinian negotiators from the West Bank and Gaza Strip (Smith, 1996). It was in this context that at the 16th PNC in February 1993, the PLO accepted the Arab Fez plan and officially refused the Reagan plan, but not the process initiated by the United States. Beyond finding an acceptable negotiating position, 'the true leitmotif of the Council was the affirmation of national unity and the independence of Palestinian decision-making *vis-à-vis* the Arab regimes' (Gresh, 1988: 233). It was clear that survival had become the most important objective of the PLO post-Lebanon.

While the PLO was searching for a unified position and diplomatic avenues, Israel under its new National Unity Government under the premiership of **Shimon Peres** sought a settlement with Jordan, to the exclusion of the PLO. The prospects for an Israeli–Jordanian agreement, however, were undermined by Likud encouragement of settlements in the West Bank as well as by Arafat's decision actively to pursue PLO–Jordanian rapprochement. Jordan, too, pushed its own interests in the search for an acceptable agreement. 'As the central Arab player in the American design, as well as a pivotal member of the emerging bloc of mainstream Arab states, Jordan would see its political fortunes improve should the peace process go forward' (Tessler, 1994: 618).

On 11 February 1985, an agreement between Jordan and the PLO was signed. The Amman Agreement, or Hussein–Arafat Accord, [Doc. 21, p. 152] called for the establishment of a Palestinian state on the West Bank in confederation with Jordan. It envisaged a complete Israeli withdrawal from the territory, including East Jerusalem, in return for peace. Implicitly this meant the recognition of Israel's right to exist.

This agreement opened the way for negotiations between the Palestinian resistance and the US administration, but fell short of genuine Jordanian–PLO reconciliation. Both Jordan and the PLO saw American approval of their overtures as a way to stop Israeli settlement policy (Smith, 1996). King Hussein further saw the agreement as a way to protect himself against the challenge from Arab radicalism, as well as a possibility of further extending his influence over the West Bank and Gaza Strip (Tessler, 1994).

While the PLO and Jordan were discussing the composition of a future joint Palestinian–Jordanian team for eventual peace negotiations, Palestinian radicals attempted completely to derail any possible talks by attacking Israel. This triggered yet another round of Israeli–Palestinian violence. On 25 September 1985, three Israelis were killed in Cyprus. On 1 October, Israel bombed PLO headquarters in Tunis, killing 56 Palestinians and 15 Tunisians. On 7 October, PFLP leader Abu Abbas instigated the hijacking of the Italian liner, the *Achille Lauro*. International outrage over the murder of crippled American Jew Leon Kinghoffer brought all cautious advances towards the PLO to an immediate standstill (Ovendale, 1992).

These problems were further compounded by the US administration's support of direct Jordanian–Israeli talks, with the result that the US administration displayed a clear lack of interest in the PLO–Jordan initiative. Israel, too, remained obstinate. It was not going to negotiate with the PLO in any form.

By February 1986, the situation had deteriorated to such an extent that when Arafat offered to accept UNSC Resolutions 242 and 338 in return for American recognition of the Palestinians' right to self-determination, US President Ronald Reagan refused point-blank. The United States was 'not in favour of an independent Palestinian state'. Reports that King Hussein was secretly making arrangements with Israel for joint control of the West Bank added to the tension. Then, on 19 February, in the face of the PLO's refusal to endorse UNSC 242, King Hussein decided to abrogate the Jordanian–PLO agreement (Tessler, 1994). Arafat, however, remained determined to pursue a political solution. On 5 September 1986 at the non-aligned summit in Harare, he declared:

> The PLO has done everything in its power to reach a just and equitable solution, preserving the inalienable rights of the Palestinian people as defined in international law, including their right to return, to self-determination and to build their own independent state, with Jerusalem as its capital. We demand that an international conference be held to establish peace in the region as a whole.
>
> (Gresh, 1988: 241)

The PLO remained in an unenviably weak position during 1986 and 1987. Four years of diplomacy had achieved nothing, while Israeli settlement policy continued and Israeli–Palestinian clashes in the territories increased steadily. The outbreak of the *intifada* in December 1987, however, changed the situation irreversibly. The Jordan option favoured by both Israel and the United States became untenable.

The *intifada*

On 8 December 1987, an Israeli army transport crashed into a line of Arab cars carrying labourers in Gaza. Four Palestinians were killed and seven injured. Rumours that the accident had in fact been an act of retaliation for an Israeli stabbed to death the previous day in Gaza's main market spread rapidly, and demonstrations erupted during the funerals of the victims. The demonstrations spread from the Gaza Strip to the West Bank; a Palestinian popular uprising had begun. It provided the Palestinians with an outlet for frustration and anger at Israel's occupation, operations conducted in the name of security, Israel's expanding settlement policy, Israel's control of water resources and the growing aggressiveness of Jewish settlers. Palestinian men, women and children stood up to Israeli soldiers with a determination not seen before. Israeli politicians, however, refused to accept the source of Palestinian discontent, instead blaming Iran, Syria and the PLO for the uprising which became known as the *intifada* (shaking off) (Ovendale, 1992).

Contrary to Israeli perception, the *intifada* had not been instigated by outside powers, but was a spontaneous uprising. It started as a rebellion of the forsaken and forgotten at the bottom of the social heap (Schiff and Ya'ari, 1989). 'At its heart, the *intifada* was a rebellion of the poor and the youth, the less-advantaged sectors of the population who organized popular committees that PLO representatives then sought to co-opt under their direction' (Smith, 1996: 297). The strategy was one of civil disobedience, restricting itself to stone throwing, demonstrations and protests. It was aimed at showing the injustice of life under military occupation.

> Palestinians felt they had reached a dead end: they were not living as free human beings and they had no hope for the future. That sense of total blockage internally combined with the sense that no help could be expected from the outside. The PLO was too fragmented and distant, and the Arab states had lost interest. Europe and the Soviet Union lacked leverage and the US was too committed to Israel to comprehend the Palestinian situation, much less broker a satisfactory accord.
>
> (Lesch, 1988–89: 4)

When the *intifada* erupted, the PLO was no less surprised than Israel and the PLO leadership at first was uncertain how to react (McDowell, 1989). Consequently, a political agenda from the PLO leadership in Tunis did not appear until January 1988, after the local Unified National Command (**UNC**) had issued its 14-point plan.

> The fourteen points were divided between demands for Israeli concessions regarding self-determination; directives for the population on how to retain the pressure through strikes and demonstrations; and a request – directed to the PLO – to include Palestinians from inside the Occupied Territories in the structure of the PNC.
>
> (Bregman, 1998: 192)

In response to the local leadership and in an attempt to exert its control over events, the PLO called for the establishment of an independent Palestinian state that would co-exist with Israel. The uprising, it claimed, would continue until the basis for 'real peace' had been reached. The strategy for resistance on the ground was one of widespread civil disobedience. The Palestinian population was urged to sever all connections with the Israeli occupiers by boycotting Israeli goods, by refusing to pay taxes and by refusing to work for Israelis. This was augmented by general strikes, demonstrations and flying the prohibited Palestinian flag. Committees were organized and forces were coordinated through the UNC, which comprised elements from Fatah, the PFLP, the **DFLP** and the **PCP**. These committees were not only responsible for the *intifada* but also for social services ranging from supplying villages under curfew with food and establishing education programmes, to arranging for the care of wounded Palestinians. Islamist parties such as Islamic Jihad and **Hamas**, which were only starting to become political players, became progressively involved. Steadfastness, or *sumud*, had become central to the Palestinian strategy (Tamari, 1991), and for the first time in history the Palestinian people were unified.

The question is sometimes asked why it took so long for the *intifada* to erupt. When Israel occupied the West Bank and Gaza Strip in 1967, the Palestinians in the territories were exchanging one form of foreign control for another. Initially, they seemed even to have benefited. In the 1970s Palestinians under Israeli rule received higher wages than those under Jordanian rule. Jewish settlements were also small in number and isolated from Arab villages at that time. And at that time the PLO still had a credible military strategy. This situation changed in the 1980s. Israel's settlement policy intensified. Between 1977 and 1987 the number of Israeli settlers increased from fewer than 5,000 to more than 60,000, and the number of settlements from 36 to 100 (Peretz, 1996). Israel under the Likud government was 'creating facts on the ground', through a policy of creeping annexation. Not only did the overall number of settlements increase, but they also started to appear right next to Arab villages. The message was unequivocal. In addition, economic recession in Israel led to a decline in the Palestinian standard of living, the situation being particularly bad in the over-populated camps in

Figure 8.1 Palestinian demonstrators throw rocks at Israeli soldiers in Nablus during violent protests against the Israeli occupation. © Esaias Baitel/AFP/ Getty Images

the Gaza Strip. The PLO was defeated in Lebanon. And, finally, a younger generation of Palestinians had come of age. They lacked the comparative experience of Jordanian rule which their parents had endured and no longer looked towards Jordan for a solution. They had known nothing but the occupation, with its frustrations and humiliations (Fraser, 1995). Daily contact with Israeli soldiers had ensured that the 'fear factor' was minimal. It was time for the Palestinians to take their future into their own hands.

The emergence of a local leadership within the framework of the *intifada* provided both challenges and opportunities for the PLO (Tessler, 1994). The biggest challenge, by far, however, was the high economic price paid by the population. Many Palestinians who had previously been employed in Israel lost their jobs, and unemployment reached over 50 per cent at times. Small businesses collapsed under the burden of curfews and general strikes. Farmers were unable to reach markets to sell their produce and were often cut off from their fields because of military restrictions.

Israeli reaction

Israeli decision makers initially expected the protests to die down. Defence Minister Rabin, believing the disturbances were nothing more than 'normal unrest', departed on a trip to the United States. Indeed, it took a month for everyone to realize that the continuing incidents could not be suppressed in routine fashion (Peretz, 1996). Nevertheless, Israeli decision makers still treated the *intifada* in light of existing policy on Arab protest. The uprising was just another form of 'terrorism' and was accordingly approached by the use of force. New measures were instituted with Rabin's policy of 'might, power, and beatings' as an alternative to live ammunition. This was accompanied by the use of teargas, mass arrests, torture under detention and curfews. But none of these measures was able to bring the uprising under control. Rather, it fuelled Palestinian determination, started to stir criticism within Israel and aroused international outrage. Israel's international and domestic image declined further when, in April 1988, the Israeli Cabinet approved the assassination of **Khalil al-Wazir (Abu Jihad)** in his Tunis home, believing him to be the instigator of the uprising (Smith, 1996). On 15 April, an Israeli taskforce of four boats and a submarine set out for Tunis. In the early hours of 16 April, two commandos went ashore, entered Abu Jihad's villa and shot him in front of his wife. The Israeli raid, which had taken no longer than five minutes, succeeded only in stopping the latest set of directives to the UNC (Bregman and el-Tahri, 1998: 194). It failed to stop the *intifada* and, much to Israel's chagrin, Abu Jihad's death led to a rapprochement between Arafat and Syria (Ovendale, 1992).

Despite stepping up its security measures, it was noticeable that Israel did not have an effective overall strategy. The IDF was unable to end the uprising, and its operations turned into damage-limitation exercises. Israeli forces were unable to occupy 500 Arab villages simultaneously (Peretz, 1996). In addition to military measures, Israel employed administrative measures in an effort to contain the *intifada*. Universities were closed, primary and secondary schools were suspended for lengthy periods, dozens of houses were blown up, entire communities were placed under curfew, suspected activists were deported, Arabic-language newspapers were censored, charities were closed and the transfer of currency into the territories was restricted (Tessler, 1994). The military and financial costs of keeping the territories under Israeli control rose dramatically and with them the economic burden on the state. But it was the political costs that really left Israeli decision makers gasping for breath.

While the uprising did not lead to immediate Palestinian statehood, it had effectively restored the Green Line, threatening Israel's 'historic' claims to the West Bank and Gaza Strip. The notion of Palestinian docility under occupation had been shattered. The separation of the territories was further underscored when, on 31 July 1988, King Hussein relinquished Jordan's claim to the West Bank [**Doc. 22, p. 153**]. In the wake of Jordan's move, Israeli decision makers were unsure about their next move. Labour, which had advocated the Jordan option, saw Likud's position strengthened in the run-up to the November general elections.

In the meantime, the PLO and the local Palestinian leadership were making preparations for statehood. Against the background of mounting international and domestic criticism of Israeli efforts to contain the *intifada*, the PNC proclaimed the state of Palestine with Jerusalem as its capital in November 1988 [Doc. 24, p. 155]. By 1989 it had been recognized by more than 100 countries. The PNC also announced its readiness to negotiate with Israel on the basis of UNSC Resolutions 242 and 338. This was followed by Arafat's renunciation of terrorism and recognition of Israel in December, opening the way for US–PLO dialogue. Israel, however, conceded little. The Shamir government offered 'elections for autonomy' over unspecified daily affairs, and the Palestinians, as predicted, rejected the offer. Violence continued: US State Department statistics estimated that 366 Palestinians had died and more than 20,000 were wounded in the *intifada* by February 1989 (Ovendale, 1992). By the end of 1989, 626 Palestinians and 43 Israelis had been killed, 37,439 Palestinians wounded and an estimated 40,000 arrested (Hunter, 1993).

In April 1989, Arafat was elected as the first Palestinian president. Israel, whose international standing was severely damaged by media coverage of armed soldiers beating unarmed women and children, had to act. The role of policing the territories also had a demoralizing effect upon Israeli soldiers. A number of new peace groups emerged, and for the first time the Israeli army was faced with a significant number of conscientious objectors to service in the West Bank and Gaza Strip. The left-wing Peace Now movement gained increasing support for its demonstrations (Lockman and Beinin, 1989; McDowell, 1989), while, at the same time, the extreme right was becoming more popular. Israeli proposals for resolving the situation were no less polarized, ranging from full Israeli withdrawal to the expulsion of all Palestinians. Israeli Prime Minister Shamir's 1989 peace plan emerged in this context as a response to the PLO peace initiative. It called for a halt to the *intifada* and for elections to be held in the territories. The aim of the elections was to select a Palestinian delegation with which Israel would negotiate in order to establish a self-governing authority in the West Bank and Gaza Strip during an interim period, to be followed by additional negotiations to determine the final status of these territories (Tessler, 1994). The Shamir plan received cautious approval from the United States, but the plan collapsed only weeks later, when US Secretary of State James Baker pushed the notion of land for peace. The Palestinians, too, did not feel the plan offered enough, especially as it did not give a role to the PLO.

Shamir's position of a 'greater Israel' improved briefly with the sudden influx of Russian Jews after the collapse of the Soviet Union. He spoke of settling the Russians in the territories. His ambition, though, ran up against US determination to stop such settlement plans, if necessary through cuts in US aid. While US–Israeli relations were tense over Israel's settlement policy, US–PLO relations faltered over the definition of terrorism and the notion of legitimate targets. US President George Bush finally suspended the dialogue with the PLO on 20 June 1990, after a Palestinian raid on a beach near Tel Aviv.

Despite the lack of progress towards a diplomatic solution, and despite the fact that the official position of the Israeli government had not changed, the *intifada* had a clear impact on political thinking in the Jewish state. Israeli politicians and the public alike started to realize that the Palestinian problem was at the core of the Arab–Israeli conflict and that negotiations would, therefore, ultimately have to be with the PLO (Tessler, 1994). The uprising made it clear to the United States and Israel that the Jordan option was dead. At the same time the PLO was forced to abandon its policy of 'constructive ambiguity' (Peretz, 1996: 95). Above all, the *intifada* put the Palestinian issue back on the international agenda and empowered the Palestinian people.

The creation of Hamas

The final development within the context of the *intifada* to be discussed here is the emergence of an Islamist alternative. Israeli intelligence officials had advocated the encouragement of religious groups in the Gaza Strip as a means of counterbalancing the influence of the PLO in the 1970s. 'For the better part of a decade, the Israelis had allowed fundamentalist Muslims to move into positions of power in the religious establishment' (Schiff and Ya'ari, 1989: 223). Although no serious rift developed between the PLO and the Islamists, the decline of the PLO after 1982 created a void, and Islamic politics had found a foothold in Gaza.

On 14 December 1987, a new organization, Hamas (Islamic Resistance Movement), appeared on the political scene. Its first communiqué described itself as a branch of the Muslim Brotherhood and linked itself to a 'chain of *jihad*' through Arab Revolt leader Izz al-Din al-Qassim (Lockman and Beinin, 1989; Ovendale, 1992). Its newly established leadership, including Sheikh Ahmed Yassin and Dr Abd al-Aziz al-Rantisi from the Islamic University of Gaza, reflected its broader social appeal.

With its emergence Hamas not only swallowed up the Muslim Brotherhood, it also became an Islamic alternative to the secular PLO. The movement advocated an Islamist–nationalist doctrine, challenging the PLO's claim to be the sole legitimate representative of the Palestinian people through its religious vision, political and social goals, as well as its communal action (Mishal and Sela, 1997). Hamas's goals were the creation of a Palestinian state in all of Palestine based on Islamic principles and Shari'a law, as set out in the Hamas Charter [Doc. 23, p. 153] in August 1988. Article 6, for example, defines the struggle against Israel as one to be 'waged over every inch of Palestine', which it considers to be an inalienable Muslim endowment, or *waqf*, while Articles 12 and 15 address the sacred duty of every individual Muslim to fight the enemy threatening Muslim land.

The *intifada* brought to the surface both the primacy and urgency of Palestinian activism. Islamist organizations existing prior to the uprising had focused on communal activities. The *intifada* shifted this focus towards political activism and violence against Israel in pursuit of an Islamic state in all of territorial Palestine (Mishal and Sela, 1997).

Hamas called upon the Palestinian population to cooperate in both violent and non-violent actions.

> The controlled civil revolt, like the continuous decline in the number of directives calling for severance of economic ties with Israel, was evidence that from the very beginning of the *intifada*, Hamas had calculated its strategy on the basis of cost–benefit considerations.
>
> (Mishal and Sela, 1997: 20)

The PLO's initial response to the emergence of an Islamist alternative was conciliatory, praising its historical record of armed struggle. At the same time, Hamas declared its willingness to work with the PLO on an agreed-upon agenda for the liberation of Palestine, while remaining beyond the authority of the UNC. Indeed, throughout the *intifada* as a whole, Hamas capably demonstrated its flexibility by differentiating between the short-term goal of establishing a Palestinian state in the West Bank and Gaza, and the long-term goal of establishing a Palestinian Islamic state that would replace Israel (Mishal and Sela, 1997). The PLO's conciliatory position had been influenced by the belief that an outright clash with Hamas would destroy the *intifada* (Schiff and Ya'ari, 1989). Yet rivalry between the two organizations was evident in the struggles over who would control the strikes.

In spring 1990, the control of the UNC and the PLO's influence were clearly slipping away, and there were armed clashes between Fatah and Hamas. Dissatisfaction with the lack of progress of the uprising led Palestinians to turn towards more radical solutions, including Hamas and the PFLP, despite the PLO's argument that Israel had supported the establishment of Hamas in order to weaken the *intifada* (Schiff and Ya'ari, 1989). In an attempt to recapture control, Arafat moved closer to the last 'pan-Arab' leader, Saddam Hussein, a move which placed him on the wrong side of the international community only months later when Iraq invaded Kuwait.

Part III
The Middle East
peace process

9 From Madrid to the second *intifada*

Israeli–Palestinian negotiations, 1990–2005

The collapse of the Soviet Union in 1989 and consequent end of the Cold War changed the old bipolar world order to a new unipolar, US-led international system. Former Soviet clients in the Middle East, who could no longer rely on Soviet military and economic aid, cautiously reoriented themselves towards the United States and Europe. At the same time, staunch US allies in the region came under closer scrutiny, often resulting in less uncritical support. These changes were accompanied by a reassessment of US–Israeli relations, as well as a US–Arab realignment. This process was further hastened by the 1990–91 Gulf War. Indeed, Iraq's invasion of Kuwait on 2 August 1990 brought former Soviet clients such as Syria into an uneasy alliance with the West, while Israel turned from a long-standing strategic asset into a political liability. And, above all, the Gulf War made it clear that regional stability had to be put at the top of the international agenda. It is therefore not surprising that by the end of the war two issues needed to be addressed: Iraq's potential to threaten the region, and the instability caused by the Arab–Israeli conflict. This paved the way for the first multilateral Middle East peace conference since 1948.

The Madrid Conference and framework for peace

The peace process in the Middle East was officially initiated with a letter of invitation [Doc. 25, p. 156] to the US–Russian co-sponsored Madrid Conference. It followed US Secretary of State James Baker's extensive shuttles to the Middle East between March and October, in which he put his peace plan to Arab and Israeli leaders. According to Baker, 'the idea was to give both the Arabs and the Israelis what they needed. The Arabs wanted an international conference supervised by other countries, the Israelis wanted face-to-face negotiations with their Arab neighbours' (Bregman, 1998: 206). So on 30 October, Israel, for the first time, was sitting down with Syria, Lebanon and Jordan, the latter's delegation being a joint Palestinian–Jordanian one. 'The tacit understanding between all the Arab participants had been that the accord with Israel would be achieved by them as a group' (Victor, 1995: 4).

While the parties invited to the conference did not engage with each other on a substantive level, a framework for negotiations was, nevertheless, constructed. The Madrid framework divided the talks into a bilateral and a multilateral track. The bilateral track aimed at achieving separate peace treaties between Israel and its Arab neighbours Syria, Lebanon, Jordan and the Palestinians. The multilateral track was designed to resolve issues affecting the region as a whole, promoting peace, stability, and cooperation. The working groups on water, the environment, arms control, refugees and economic development, which were set up within this track, included delegates not only from the Middle East but also representatives from the international community.

After the opening conference the negotiations moved to Washington where they soon reached a stalemate. The problems already became evident when the Israeli delegation failed to turn up for the negotiations during the first week in the belief that 'the safest way to avoid concessions was to stay at home' (King, 1994: 85). Once the delegation did arrive, Israel remained steadfast in its stipulation not to include the PLO. At the same time Palestinian representatives of the Jordanian delegation had their hands bound by the PLO refusal to give them decision-making powers (Victor, 1995). The backdrop of continued Israeli settlement policy in the Occupied Territories and the deterioration of Israeli Prime Minister Itzhak Shamir's relations with the US made progress virtually impossible.

The Oslo process, 1992–99

The June 1992 election victory of Labour in Israel provided a new environment for the Middle East peace process (Flamhaft, 1996). This environment was further aided by the unintended 'benign neglect' shown during the first months of the Clinton administration, which created the space for Norwegian mediation (Wells, 1996). Unofficial Israeli–Palestinian talks started on two separate avenues: Oslo and London. They, in essence, provided both sides with the possibility of exploring each other's positions without recognition, commitment or indeed violating Israeli law under which meetings with the PLO were illegal. The Oslo process began to crystallize toward the end of year, when the Knesset passed a bill lifting restrictions on contacts with the PLO for private individuals. The first round of pre-negotiations in Norway followed on 20–22 January 1993. Norway considered itself to be an appropriate facilitator for Israeli–Palestinian talks as it did not have any major interests in the Middle East and was on good terms with both Israel and the Palestinians. Three main ideas were agreed upon by PLO negotiator Abu Alaa and Israeli academic Yair Hirschfeld. There would be an Israeli withdrawal from Gaza, gradual devolution of economic power to the Palestinians, and international economic assistance.

Unofficial talks were further helped by the fact that both Israelis and Palestinians had agreed to avoid delving into historic grievances. At the same time, Israeli–Palestinian negotiations in Washington moved at a snail's pace. Even setting an agenda for the negotiations proved to be a nightmare. Talks broke down completely in December 1992, when Israel deported 415 Palestinian Islamists to South Lebanon. While the PLO may have secretly approved of the removal of some of its rivals, it had to publicly condemn Israeli action and felt compelled to boycott the negotiations. The stalemate in Washington focused minds in Oslo and, ultimately, resulted in Rabin's decision to upgrade the Oslo process and replace Israeli academics with government negotiators. The Declaration of Principles (**DOP**) [Doc. 26, p. 157] was drafted, redrafted and amended throughout spring and summer 1993. Aspects of jurisdiction, security and Jerusalem remained sticking points, as did the issue of mutual recognition.

On 30 August 1993, Rabin presented the DOP to the Cabinet for approval. On 9 September, under the auspices of Norwegian Foreign Minister Johann Jorgen Holst, Arafat and Rabin exchanged letters of mutual recognition (Fraser, 1995). On 13 September 1993, the Israeli–Palestinian DOP was signed on the White House lawn in Washington. The declaration outlined the arrangements for interim self-government, early empowerment for Palestinians in the West Bank and elections of a Palestinian council. Permanent-status negotiations were scheduled to begin no later than three years following the DOP, with agreement to take effect after the fifth year of the interim period. The DOP did not, however, find approval from all Palestinians. For example, Palestinian negotiator **Hanan Ashrawi** pointed out that

> it was obvious that the people who wrote the document didn't live under occupation because a freeze on all settlements wasn't included nor was the release of prisoners, which are the two main issues that would have given the document credibility throughout the Occupied Territories.
>
> (Victor, 1995: 245)

The agreement, nevertheless, was of historic significance. It gave each party the recognition it had sought from the other and confirmed before the world that there is nothing about the essence of either Zionism or Palestinian nationalism that makes conflict resolution impossible (Tessler, 1994).

The DOP was followed by the Cairo Agreement on 4 May 1994, which included provisions for Israeli military withdrawal, the transfer of authority from the Israeli Civil Administration to the Palestinian National Authority (**PNA** or **PA**), a Palestinian police force and relations between Israel and the PA (Peretz, 1996). Further progress was made on 28 September 1995, with the Israeli–Palestinian Interim Agreement on the West Bank and Gaza Strip, which aimed at broadening Palestinian autonomy, but also addressed security, elections, economic relations and the release of prisoners.

Palestinian elections were scheduled for 20 January 1996. Arafat received more than 90 per cent of the vote on a voter turnout of 68.46 per cent in the West Bank and 80 per cent in Gaza. The elections provided the PA with the required legitimacy. The stability provided by the elections, however, was not able to counter-balance the instability the assassination of Israeli Prime Minister Rabin on 4 November 1995 had caused. A shocked and deeply divided Israeli society took a collective step back from the peace process. The subsequent election campaign was characterized by insecurity and Hamas violence, which had been on the increase since the 25 February 1994 Ibrahimi mosque massacre in Hebron. Both were reflected in the election of a more hardline Likud government headed by **Benjamin Netanyahu**. Thus the assassination of Rabin proved to be a turning point, marked by a degree of Israeli disengagement from the peace process.

Against this background of months of stagnation, the Hebron Agreement of January 1997 was hailed as a crucial breakthrough for the deadlocked Israeli–Palestinian negotiations. The agreement called for the Israeli redeployment from Hebron within 10 days and the assumption of responsibility by the Palestinian police henceforth. Both sides further committed themselves to the prevention of terrorism with a number of specific provisions of joint security measures. Civil powers and responsibilities with the exception of those relating to Israelis and their property were also to be transferred to the Palestinian side. Israeli responsibilities consisted of further redeployment and the release of Palestinian prisoners. Palestinian responsibilities were the revising of the Palestinian National Charter and preventing violence. The Hebron Agreement was the only movement on the peace process under Netanyahu, who was then voted out of office in the first direct Israeli prime ministerial elections in May 1999.

Palestinian institutions and society, 1996–99

Moving towards final status negotiations was not the only challenge. If the Palestinians were serious about a viable state of their own they had to establish the necessary institutions of governance. The first institution to be set up was the PA, which was established in 1994 as a five-year transitional acting Palestinian government until the conclusion of final status negotiations. It was to govern over the territory of the West Bank and Gaza Strip as and when it was handed over by the Israelis. In 1994 and 1995 the PA proceeded with establishing a bureaucratic support structure and a security apparatus. In January 1996 elections for the Palestinian Legislative Council (**PLC**) as well as head of the PA took place. The PLC had 88 seats with representatives from 16 districts in the West Bank and Gaza Strip and functioned as a parliament whose responsibilities included confirming the cabinet posts.

The emergence of the first governmental institutions was accompanied by a building boom, which gave the impression of greater economic prosperity. The sleepy West Bank town of Ramallah was turned into a temporary seat of governance. New hotels, cafés, restaurants, offices and foreign embassies appeared almost overnight. In Gaza a new international airport was built.

And Bethlehem received a complete facelift for the Jubilee 2000 year. However, this building boom, being aid driven, did not reflect the real state of the economy, which after 1993 saw a downturn. Indeed, by mid-2000 one in five Palestinians had slipped below the poverty line (Gunning, 2007).

The discontent resulting from financial hardship was further exacerbated by the lack of transparency and accountability with respect to the large amounts of money from foreign donors such as the EU. Palestinians started to openly charge the PA with corruption and pointed to the villas and cars of PA officials. They were also deeply disappointed with the increasing authoritarianism of their new government. The vision of Palestine they had fought for was that of a democratic, secular and inclusive state. That vision had virtually disappeared. It had become the victim of an institution-building process driven by Israeli security needs rather than democracy.

Palestinian society became fractured. The first split was that between the so-called 'insiders' and 'outsiders'. When the PA set up its offices it was the outsiders from Tunis, the old PLO leadership, who took up the cabinet posts. The insiders who had fought the 1987 *intifada*, the grassroots leaders, were marginalized (Hilal in Giacaman and Lønning, 1998: 129). As the PA started to lose credibility because of the increasing evidence of corruption and its failure to deliver on its peace process promises, the old revolutionary structures started to re-emerge with guerrilla organizations such as Fatah, DFLP and PFLP, as well as the Islamist groups such as Hamas and Islamic Jihad taking on a new life. This political fragmentation was accompanied by increasing militarization as all these groups were still armed. They now took on security functions in addition to the already factionalized security apparatus of the PA in which the General Intelligence Service, Preventive Security Force, Presidential Guard, Force 17 and Special Security Forces already competed with each other and served special interests rather than the PA as a whole (Usher in Giacaman and Lønning, 1998).

The main beneficiary from the disillusionment with the PA was Hamas, and in 1998 and 1999 Islamism was on the increase as evidenced by trade union and university elections. This resulted in further tensions not just between Hamas and Fatah supporters but also between religious and secular Muslims as well as Christians. With the political, economic and religious faultlines deepening, Palestinian society became a powder keg.

The 2000 Camp David summit

The defeat of Netanyahu and the election of **Ehud Barak** as Israeli prime minister in May 1999 raised hopes again that peace was in reach. Israelis and Palestinians re-entered formal negotiations in November 1999 with the aim of drawing up a Framework Agreement on Permanent Status (**FAPS**). In mid-April 2000 talks were shifted to what became known as the Stockholm track which focused on the political issues of FAPS: the end of the conflict, the finality of claims, the establishment of a Palestinian state, territorial issues, Jerusalem, refugees and security. However, by May the negotiations had become totally deadlocked, so much so that by June the negotiations were suspended in favour of a formal summit. It was hoped that the presence of the two leaders, Barak and Arafat, would lead to a historic compromise. Camp David, where Israel and Egypt had successfully negotiated peace in 1978, was chosen as the site. President **Clinton** himself was to take on the role of mediator.

The summit was convened on 11 July and initiated with the 4 September 1999 Sharm al-Shaykh Memorandum with the aim of concluding FAPS, which would then be followed by a Comprehensive Agreement on Permanent Status (**CAPS**), together constituting the Permanent Status Agreement (**PSA**). Barak's proposals for final settlement were a Palestinian state on most of the territory of the West Bank and Gaza, a safe passage connecting the West Bank and Gaza Strip, security arrangements in the Jordan valley with an Israeli military presence at agreed-upon spots, a land exchange, al-Quds as the capital of a Palestinian state including the Muslim and Christian quarters of the old city, Palestinian custodianship but Israeli sovereignty over the Temple Mount and the demilitarization of the future Palestinian state (Meital, 2006: 76).

This proposal fell short of the minimum requirements of what Arafat could agree to. First, Israel refused to withdraw to the 4 June 1967 line. As a result it was unclear exactly how much of the West Bank the Palestinians would receive. Several calculations were put forward at the summit by both Israelis and Palestinians. Some excluded East Jerusalem, others excluded no-man's land from 1948 and others were based on the whole territory captured in 1967. The percentage of West Bank territory for the future Palestinian state thus ranged from as little as 70 per cent to as much as 94 per cent. No consensus was reached. Second, Arafat regarded Israel's security demands as a threat to Palestinian sovereignty. These would geographically fragment any future Palestinian state not just into the West Bank and Gaza, but also split the West Bank into a northern and southern area with settlement 'pockets', making the establishment of a viable Palestinian state impossible. Third, Israel's position on refugees and the right of return was unacceptable. Israel unequivocally rejected the right of return and any moral responsibility for creating the refugee problem. Israel was only prepared to allow for the return of some Palestinians in the context of family reunification as well as contributing to an international compensation fund. Fourth, the Palestinians could not waiver sovereignty over the *Haram ash-Sharif* as the compound was holy to all Muslims.

Palestinian problems with the proposals were further compounded by the fact that the United States seemed to endorse Israel's ideas and that neither the United States nor Israel regarded the Palestinian domestic arena as relevant or indeed showed any sympathy with Arafat's position (Meital, 2006: 82). Not surprisingly, Arafat believed that he had been 'summoned'

Figure 9.1 US President Bill Clinton looks on while Palestinian leader Yasser Arafat and Israeli Prime Minister Ehud Barak shake hands at Camp David on the opening day of the Middle East peace talks, 11 July, 2000. © White House Photo/Newsmakers

to Camp David to suit the US agenda of securing an agreement before President Clinton's term in office expired and before Barak fell victim to a vote of no confidence. Thus, the summit only reinforced Arafat's perception of his own weakness. He found himself trapped between accepting a deal that was far from the minimum that the Palestinian national consensus could accept and thereby lose Palestinian, Arab and Muslim legitimacy, or rejecting the proposals and thereby alienate Israel and the United States (Schulze, 2001). Moreover, Barak's abrupt personal style, giving orders and expecting them to be followed without question rather than negotiating as equals, had the effect that Arafat simply rejected the proposals without putting forward counter-proposals. This was Arafat's biggest mistake. It left the international community with the impression that Israel's proposals had been generous and unprecedented, as Barak was willing to offer shared administration of parts of Jerusalem, while Arafat had not even been willing to consider the proposals as a basis for negotiation. Thus Arafat was quickly blamed for the failure of the summit.

The second *intifada*

The second *intifada*, or *al-Aqsa intifada*, was triggered by the visit of Likud leader Ariel Sharon to the Temple Mount/*Haram ash-Sharif* on 28 September 2000. Sharon's visit aimed at shoring up Israel's claim to a united Jerusalem as well as undermining Barak. The widespread violence that followed was the result of anger at Sharon's presence but also of long-term pent-up Palestinian frustration with a peace process perceived as supporting Israeli hegemonic ambitions, of discontent with the lack of change in the everyday life of the average Palestinian, of dissatisfaction with their own leadership and of rage particularly by a younger, profoundly alienated, generation. The extent of the violence took both Israel and the PA by surprise. The latter quickly moved toward harnessing the uprising in order to use it as leverage against Barak. Indeed, Arafat embraced it as the core of his post–Camp David strategy. Harnessing the *intifada*, however, proved impossible as there were too many disparate armed groups involved, many of which originated from the rejectionist camp and thus had no interest in cooperating with the PA. While the first days of the second *intifada* were reminiscent of the 1987 uprising, the nature of the protest quickly changed as firearms appeared on the street. What had been popular demonstrations turned into a volatile mixture of riots and attacks carried out, amongst others, by the PFLP, DFLP, Fatah Tanzim, Hamas and Islamic Jihad loosely organized into the 'Nationalist and Islamic Forces of Palestine'. The Israeli security forces and settlers became the prime targets in a strategy inspired by the one **Hizbollah** had successfully used to compel Israel to pull out of southern Lebanon in May 2000.

Arafat's decision to embrace violence at this stage in the peace process was a strategic gambit, serving multiple purposes. First, the uprising aimed at putting pressure on Israel to make more concessions in the negotiations with respect to the two crucial elements required by Arafat in any final status agreement: Jerusalem and refugees. Second, the uprising directly challenged Israel's settlement policy and, in particular, the viability and defensibility of outlying settlements. Third, it provided a window of opportunity to reshape the negotiating framework to one more favourable to the Palestinians by broadening or internationalizing the process to also include the UN and the European Union (EU). This shift away from Oslo became evident at the October Arab summit, which called for the implementation of UN Security Council Resolutions 242 and 338 and UN General Assembly Resolution 194 on Palestinian refugees. This was a clear rejection of the essentially bilateral Israeli–Palestinian Oslo structure with US mediation and a return to the multilateral Madrid framework and full Israeli withdrawal to the 4 June 1967 boundaries. Fourth, the violence served to empower the Palestinians who suffered from asymmetry and lack of parity ever since the beginning of the negotiations. The *intifada* had domestic benefits as well. It provided an outlet for an increasingly alienated population, frustrated by the broken promises and corruption of their leadership. It refashioned Palestinian consensus behind Arafat's position and provided the Palestinian police, which to some extent had been perceived as Israel's proxy, with new-found credibility (Schulze, 2001).

All these gains, however, were short lived as Arafat struggled to control the uprising. Hamas upped the ante with Qassam rockets, and its suicide bombings proved so effective that they were not just copied by other Islamists but also by secular Palestinian groups. With violence ruling the day, the earlier revival of the revolutionary structures was further reinforced and the opportunity arose for the re-emergence of the 'insiders', the local leadership of 1987–92. The rejectionists were also strengthened and Hamas, in particular, started to mount a credible challenge to Fatah. This led to battlefield competition between Hamas' Izz al-Din al-Qassam Brigades with Fatah's Al-Aqsa Martyr Brigades, increasing the militancy of all Palestinian armed groups.

As the *intifada* progressed Palestinian popular opinion started to shift away from supporting an ineffective, internationally isolated PA toward supporting Hamas, which was seen as doing something about the Israeli occupation and which had not agreed to unacceptable compromises with Israel. This became clear with the death of Arafat in November 2004. The United States and Israel hoped that his successor, **Mahmoud Abbas** (Abu Mazen), who was elected president of the PA on 9 January 2005, would be able to bring the violence under control, reform the PA and resume negotiations. However, despite the fact that he received agreement by Hamas in March 2005 to honour a 'period of calm', he was perceived as weak by Israel and the United States as well as by the Palestinian population. Only a year later, on 25 January 2006 Hamas won the legislative elections, taking 74 out of 132 seats. The Hamas victory was not necessarily the result of popular desire for an Islamic state, but a reflection of how disillusioned the people were with Fatah.

Israel's response to the *intifada*

Israel's initial response to the uprising was reactive, amounting to political crisis management. While Barak's overarching aim was the eventual resumption of the negotiations in order to achieve a final status agreement and consequently an end to the conflict, Israeli decision making focused on the achievement of short-term security-oriented goals: containing the violence in the Palestinian territories, bringing about an end to the fighting, limiting Israeli casualties and preventing the erosion of Israeli positions on the ground. Achieving some of these aims, however, needed almost opposite approaches. While containment of a popular uprising necessitated a moderate security response amounting to policing and total restraint in order not to escalate the situation further, ending the violence required credible deterrence and a show of force. This posed a dilemma, particularly in the early days of the *intifada* in which civilian demonstrations set the tone. Here the mistakes of the early months of the first *intifada* were repeated. Indeed, the scenes of stone-throwing youths facing IDF soldiers in September/October 2000 were remarkably reminiscent of 1987–88, as was criticism of Israel for excessive use of force (Schulze, 2001).

Once Palestinian tactics changed from riots to low-intensity conflict and targeting Israeli civilians, Israel's response changed. Israeli decision makers had little choice but to opt for decisive action in order to limit Israeli casualties and to protect Israeli territory. The decision to draw upon heavy and long-range military equipment, however, sat uncomfortably with the political aims of an eventual resumption of negotiations. It also, in combination with attempts to get Arafat to end or quell the uprising based on the belief that he could stop the violence by simply issuing clear operational directives, undermined Arafat's control and strengthened the dissenting elements within Fatah. The continuation and escalation of the Palestinian attacks, moreover, challenged both Israel's deterrence capability and its containment policy (Schulze, 2001). Barak's handling of the second *intifada* lost him the confidence of the population and ultimately the premiership. He was succeeded by Ariel Sharon in a special election in February 2001.

Sharon changed Israel's approach toward the second *intifada* from short-term responses to a longer-term strategy of unilateral disengagement. Underlying this strategy was his belief that Arafat was not a partner, that the Oslo process was finished and that there would not be an immediate resumption of negotiations. Any future talks would be based on new parameters and only with a completely reformed PA headed by a Palestinian acceptable to Israel. When the **Roadmap [Doc. 28, p. 160]** was put forward by the United States, EU, UN and Russia in mid-2002 and initiated in April 2003, Sharon endorsed it as a new approach. At the same time he remained committed to unilateral disengagement. Sharon's separation strategy comprised four key elements. First, to isolate Arafat and the PA politically in order to force the former to resign and the latter to reform. Second, to target the PA structures militarily in order to weaken Arafat's power base and to punish it for participating in the violence against Israel. Third, to 'decapitate' Hamas and Islamic Jihad by arresting or killing their leaders as well as destroying their command structures and support bases in order to reduce their military capacity and threat against Israel. And fourth, to separate Israeli and Palestinian territory physically in order to make Israel's border more defensible. This territorial separation started with the building of a fence along the West Bank. Work on this barrier began at the end of 2002 and upon completion it would be 703 km long. Some 90 per cent would consist of fences with vehicle-barrier trenches and 10 per cent of 8-metre-high concrete walls. The purpose of this barrier was to keep suicide bombers out, and in this respect it was very successful. However, it was a highly contentious project as in some areas it cut deep into the West Bank rather than following the Green Line, as well as raising images of apartheid. The **West Bank Barrier** was followed by disengagement from Gaza and the northern West Bank in August 2005.

Peace initiatives, 2000–05

While violence clearly dominated Israeli–Palestinian relations since the outbreak of the second *intifada*, that did not mean that there were no attempts at restarting the negotiations. Indeed the first such attempt came only months after the collapse of the Camp David Summit. On 21 January 2001 talks opened in Taba, Egypt. These were not as high profile as the previous summit. Barak, Arafat and the Americans were not present. It was a last-ditch attempt to conclude a permanent status agreement as Israeli elections were only two weeks away. The negotiations themselves made substantial progress on the issues. After a week both sides stated that they 'had never been closer to reaching an agreement'. The gaps on the scale of withdrawal, the settlements and security arrangements were reduced. In an unprecedented move the Palestinian delegation for the first time presented a map showing their acceptance of Israel's annexation of Jewish neighbourhoods in East Jerusalem (Meital, 2006: 88). Israeli Minister **Yossi Beilin**, in a reciprocate move, put forward a proposal for Israel to take in a quota of refugees over a number of years. This proposal, however, was not supported by the Israeli negotiating team. In the end, no agreement was concluded as the timing was simply not right. The Israeli public did not want its government to make such important commitments right before the elections. Palestinians feared that even if commitments were made they would not be upheld by a new Israeli government. And in any case, what was on offer at Taba, while significantly closer, still fell short of the minimum that the Palestinians could accept.

The next peace initiative came in spring 2002 and was proposed by Saudi Crown Prince Abdullah at the Arab League meeting in Beirut and was adopted by the Arab League on 28 March. The **Arab Peace Plan** called for a full normalization between the Arab states and Israel in the context of a final settlement. The Arab peace message, however, was lost when on the same day a Palestinian suicide bomber killed 30 people celebrating Passover in the Park Hotel in Netanya. Five more bombings followed this one over the next five days. The Arab Peace Plan did not stand a chance. There have been a number of attempts to revive the plan since 2002. None have so far been successful.

In July 2002 the Quartet of the United States, EU, UN and Russia picked up the tattered pieces of the Arab Peace Plan and put together the so-called Roadmap. However, it was not until the appointment of Mahmoud Abbas as Palestinian prime minister in April 2003 that the Roadmap was officially initiated so that neither the United States nor Israel had to deal with Arafat. The Roadmap was a performance-based plan in three phases, which ultimately envisaged a safe and secure Israel coexisting with a viable, sovereign and democratic Palestine. The first phase focused on ending the violence on both sides followed by a normalization of Palestinian life, the building and rebuilding of Palestinian institutions and civil society and the dismantling of settlements since March 2001. The second phase saw democratic Palestinian elections, a new democratic Palestinian constitution, comprehensive security performance and the creation of a Palestinian state with provisional borders and sovereignty as a way station to a permanent status settlement. The third phase would produce a permanent status agreement and result in the end of the Israeli–Palestinian conflict. This would come in the context of an international conference and would be based on UNSC Resolutions 242, 338 and 1397, including a just and fair solution to the Palestinian refugee situation, the status of Jerusalem and full normalization. The Roadmap was endorsed by both Israeli and Palestinian leaders as a way forward, but it has so far not been implemented. Moreover, with the election of Hamas it has been questioned whether the Palestinians are still committed. Nevertheless it remains the only game in town as far as the international community is concerned.

Two additional proposals have come from the Israeli left and right, respectively, mainly in response to Sharon's disengagement plan. The former was put forward by Yossi Beilin, who, together with Yasser Abed Rabbo, both veterans of the Oslo process, drafted the so-called **Geneva Accord** on 1 December 2003. Unlike the Roadmap it was not a phased solution but a detailed draft permanent status agreement, drawing the borders close to the 1967 boundary, giving the Palestinians most of the Gaza Strip, West Bank and parts of Jerusalem. Most Israeli settlements would be removed, some such as Gush Etzion and Maale Adumim would be annexed to Israel and the Palestinians would agree to limit their right of return to a number acceptable to Israel. The second proposal was put forward by Binyamin Elon, whose **Elon Peace Plan** proposed the annexation of the West Bank and Gaza Strip with Palestinians either becoming Jordanian citizens or permanent residents in Israel. Neither the first nor the second proposal was adopted by the Israeli government.

Assessing the Israeli–Palestinian negotiations, 1993–2005

From the outset of the Israeli–Palestinian negotiations there were a number of obstacles: the fate of Jewish settlements in the West Bank and Gaza Strip, the status of Jerusalem, the release of prisoners, violence by extremists, refugees and their right of return, the different perceptions of the timeframe for negotiations and the scale of concessions.

Militant nationalists, both Israeli and Palestinian, opposed the peace process from the beginning. As signs of progress became evident, their determination to sabotage the negotiations also increased. Ultra-nationalist Jewish settlers vowed never to abandon their homes in the West Bank and to fight anyone who tried to move them (Peretz, 1996). They staged demonstrations, blocked roads, assaulted Palestinians and destroyed Arab property.

Palestinian attempts to disrupt the process originated from the rejectionist PFLP and DFLP, as well as Hamas and Islamic Jihad. The latter two were particularly successful at creating an atmosphere of terror, which made negotiations difficult, if not impossible. Attacks on Israeli soldiers and civilians increased, culminating in suicide bombings in the heart of Israel from 1994 onwards. Not surprisingly the outbreak of the second *intifada* spelled the end for the Oslo process, and the violence on the ground became one of the largest stumbling blocks for a resumption of negotiations.

Israeli settlement policy was also an obstacle and, despite perception to the contrary, there was little difference between Labour and Likud governments. Indeed, the settlement expansion rate increased post-1993 with the Rabin administration. As to be expected, it was a cornerstone of Likud's expansionist agenda following the 1996 elections. The government's decision to proceed with the Har Homa/Abu Ghneim settlement following the 1997 **Hebron Agreement** was a clear attempt to stall the impending final status talks, while also signalling a no compromise position on Jerusalem, Jewish settlement policy and Palestinian statehood. This pointed to the much larger problem that Israel continued to believe that it could 'deal with a Palestinian entity, which will somehow be drawn into a political and economic framework' with Israel and Jordan, but that this entity would not be a state (King, 1994). And last but not least, Barak used settlements to shore up Israel's position on an undivided capital city but also to keep as many coalition partners on board as possible. Indeed, during the first half of the year 2000, the construction of settlements increased by 96 per cent.

Another obstacle was the conflicting perceptions of the timeframe of the peace process. In simple terms much of Israel's actions were directed at buying time. In Israel, the peace process was generally perceived as proceeding at too fast a pace. Territory was being given away while no tangible improvement in the security of Israeli citizens was gained in return. The electorate's seesawing between Labour and Likud reflected this insecurity at an electoral level. Conversely, for the PA and the Palestinian people, the negotiations were progressing too slowly. Several accords and protocols after Madrid, Arafat was still unable to point to more than limited autonomy, forced to tread a fine line between Israeli demands and challenge from within. Timing was also an issue at the Camp David summit and the Taba talks. With respect to the former, the Palestinians did not believe that the timing was right for a summit as the Stockholm track had not brought the sides close enough together to reach an agreement. Arafat felt that he was being forced into an Israeli agenda dictated by a possible no-confidence vote and an American agenda determined by the presidential elections. With respect to Taba, the imminent Israeli elections were a clear obstacle to either side making a commitment.

Further problems underlying the process stemmed from the status of the respective leaders within their own electorates. Yitzhak Rabin's assassination in November 1995 revealed the deep divisions in Israeli society, which revolved around the issues of security and territory. Rabin had been able to overcome these cleavages through his strong leadership personality. His successor, Shimon Peres, in comparison, could not carry a popular vote in an atmosphere of public fear and anger resulting from the Hamas suicide bombings in early 1996. Netanyahu and his campaign to stop further concessions to the Palestinians, however, only got marginally more popular support. Thus, the backing for Netanyahu's initial anti-peace process platform was as tenuous as the backing for Peres's pro-peace process platform, and Netanyahu was as much constrained by the opinion of the Israeli people as Peres had been. Not surprisingly, Netanyahu lost the confidence of the electorate like Peres had done. New hopes were placed in Barak, who was likened to Rabin but in the end was not able to fill the latter's shoes. The election of Sharon brought renewed hopes for security, which was indeed achieved with the West Bank Barrier. However, real peace remained elusive. And last but not least, Israeli confidence plummeted again with Olmert who, after the 2006 Lebanon war, was seen as simply incompetent.

While the Palestinian leadership was less volatile, Palestinian President Yasser Arafat's position was not a strong one, with challenges from the Islamist opposition. Palestinian elections in January 1996 had legitimized his leadership, but the delays in the Palestinian–Israeli negotiations and Arafat's consequent inability to deliver tangible results to the Palestinian people undermined his position. Following the outbreak of the second *intifada* Arafat was no longer seen as a partner by either Israel or the Americans, which put any negotiations on hold until he was replaced. The appointment of Abbas as prime minister raised hopes, but he was weak compared to both Arafat and the Islamist opposition. He could not hold all factions within the PA together. Moreover, his election as president after Arafat's death showed how few real alternatives there were within the PA.

10 Israel, Jordan, Syria and Lebanon, 1994–2015

The signing of the DOP in September 1993 made it possible for Israel and its Arab neighbours to move ahead bilaterally. Jordan's King Hussein saw the DOP as a great achievement not only because it looked like a two-state solution was in reach but also because the PLO was now able to negotiate directly with Israel. This ended decades of Jordan being either compelled to speak for the Palestinians or being seen as a solution to the Palestinian problem. It now allowed Jordan to follow its own national interests. In comparison, Syria's President Asad saw the DOP as a disaster as it undermined Arab unity and the pursuit of a comprehensive peace. He believed that the Palestinians would have received a better deal if Israel had been required to negotiate multilaterally, especially with respect to refugees and the right of return. However, at the same time, Asad saw the DOP as freeing Syria from its pan-Arab obligations and, like Jordan, placing it in the position to pursue its own agenda. Whether the DOP was a good or bad deal for the Palestinians was now Arafat's problem. Syria had to focus on the return of the Golan Heights. Thus, shortly after the signing of the DOP both Jordan and Syria started to negotiate bilaterally with Israel. The Jordanian–Israeli talks quickly ended in a full peace treaty. In fact they were the most amicable and least contentious negotiations of the whole Middle East peace process. The opposite was true for the Syrian–Israeli talks. Twice they came close to an agreement; twice they collapsed in accusations and counter-accusations.

Peace with Jordan

The obvious success story was the 1994 Jordanian–Israeli peace agreement. This agreement was concluded without any of the problems plaguing the Israeli–Palestinian negotiations. For one, Israel and Jordan did not have a significant territorial dispute; with a few minor adjustments the border between the two states was upheld and recognized. Moreover, there had always been rather amicable but unofficial relations between the two states dating back to the mandate period. While the Israeli–Palestinian relationship may be described as one of extreme distrust and insecurity, trust and a comparative absence of violence had existed in Israeli–Jordanian relations since 1967. Thus, in essence, the Jordanian–Israeli agreement was an official recognition of an already existing situation of non-belligerence – a legal sanction for an inevitable process of normalization.

The common agenda for the peace treaty was agreed to on 14 September 1993 and consisted of the issues of security, water, refugees and borders. On 25 July 1994, King Hussein and Prime Minister Rabin had their first public meeting, which resulted in the Washington Declaration. The declaration stated that the 'state of belligerency between Jordan and Israel was terminated', that both states agreed to pursue peace on the basis of UNSC Resolutions 242 and 338 and that Israel would respect 'the special role of the Hashemite Kingdom over Muslim holy shrines'. Direct telephone links, joint electricity grids, new border crossings and cooperation on combating crime and drug smuggling followed. On 26 October 1994 the Jordanian–Israeli Peace Treaty [Doc. 27, p. 158] was signed.

The process of normalization of relations between Israel and Jordan focused on additional bilateral agreements in the areas of tourism, environmental cooperation, trade, police cooperation and agriculture. Joint projects on energy and water further cemented relations. At the same time an anti-normalization campaign emerged spearheaded by trade unions, professional bodies, Palestinians living in Jordan and the Muslim Brotherhood. Not surprisingly this campaign was strengthened with the outbreak of the second *intifada*. Full normalization will remain elusive until a viable Palestinian state is established and the Israeli–Palestinian conflict is over. Even then psychological barriers within the Israeli, Palestinian and Jordanian populations still need to be dismantled in order for 'normal' to assume its true meaning.

Negotiations with Syria, 1994–95

While the Jordanian–Israeli negotiations proceeded smoothly, with little disagreement and rapidly resulted in a full peace treaty, Syrian–Israeli, and by extension Lebanese, negotiations were difficult and required painful concessions. There were two periods of Syrian–Israeli negotiations in which an agreement was almost in reach. The first followed the DOP until the assassination of Rabin in November 1995. The second followed the election of Ehud Barak as Israeli prime minister in May 1999 until the collapse of the talks in March 2000. During both periods the key issue was the Golan Heights and the line to which Israel should withdraw in return for full peace. During the 1999–2000 period two further questions were added: namely what commitments had Rabin made to Asad through the United States during the 1994–95 talks? And to what extent were they binding upon subsequent Israeli prime ministers?

At the 1991 Madrid peace conference the Syrian government laid out its position as follows. The Golan Heights are Syrian. International law as embodied in UNSC Resolution 242 does not permit the acquisition of territory by war. Therefore Israel should withdraw to the 4 June 1967 lines, and only then can negotiations on peace begin. Any negotiations would aim at a comprehensive peace. There would be no bilateral negotiations. Israel, at the time under the Shamir government, was not interested in negotiating with Syria, which it saw as a state sponsoring terrorism. It was also not interested in relinquishing the Golan Heights because these were vital to Israel's security. Thus, although a Syrian–Israeli track existed on paper, there were no negotiations. This changed with the election of Rabin, who based the new Israeli negotiating position on Labour's traditional formula of land for peace – in short, exchanging an Israeli withdrawal from the Golan Heights for a full peace treaty.

The Rabin years brought Syria and Israel closer to an agreement than ever before, and many have speculated that if Rabin had not been assassinated in November 1995, a peace treaty would have been concluded. During this period both Israel and Syria kept their cards very close to their chests. Only after the talks collapsed in January 1996 with Acting Prime Minister Shimon Peres's call for early elections, did details about the talks start to emerge, followed by allegations and counter-allegations. According to Syrian chief negotiator **Walid al-Moualem** Rabin had committed himself to withdraw to the 4 June 1967 lines and 'he was representing Israel, not himself personally. After Rabin was assassinated, Peres informed us in November through the Americans that he wanted to continue the talks, and he repeated the commitment' (al-Moualem, 1997: 82). However, Israeli chief negotiator Itamar Rabinovich claimed that although Israel had committed itself to the principle of withdrawal there was no agreement or commitment to either the United States or Syria regarding the extent, depth and duration of the withdrawal from the Golan Heights. Moreover, Rabin wanted to make withdrawal conditional not only on normalization but also on an Israeli referendum. What was on offer, according to Rabinovich, was a three-phased 'package'. The first phase, nine months after the signing of an agreement, would involve a limited Israeli withdrawal. Israeli settlements would not be affected, and Syria would have to offer normalization. A second phase of further withdrawal would then take place after 18 or 24 months, followed by a third phase which would complete the withdrawal to a line agreed upon (Rabinovich, 1998: 140).

The exact line of withdrawal was not the only issue of contention. Security arrangements were another. Rabin saw the Golan above all as a security issue. He was concerned with the prospect of several Syrian armoured and mechanized divisions stationed in Syria's southwestern corner and in Lebanon launching a surprise attack against Israel. So Israel devised a 'security regime' comprising five integrated elements: first, the depth of the demilitarized area and area of limited employment; second, the size and deployment of the Syrian armed forces; third, at least one Israeli early-warning station on the Golan; fourth, monitoring by a non-UN international force with US participation; and fifth, a system of verification and transparency (Rabinovich, 1998: 170). Not surprisingly Syria saw Israel's 'security regime' as a major stumbling block to reaching an agreement. As al-Moualem pointed out,

> the Israelis have military superiority over any combination of Arab states. They have nuclear bombs, the most advanced arms and technology. American arms and supplies and technology are completely open to them. Israel manufactures 60 per cent of its needs in military equipment and is the fifth arms exporter in the world. Yet despite all this, they used to tell us they are afraid of Syria?
>
> (al-Moualem, 1997: 86)

The ramifications of this disagreement only became clear when Peres lost the elections. The new Israeli Prime Minister Benyamin Netanyahu proceeded to denounce Rabin's policy toward Syria and stated that talks would only be resumed without prior conditions. Nothing of a binding nature had been agreed to between the two countries in previous talks. He also stated that the Golan Heights were non-negotiable as they were strategically vital for Israel. So the only formula on offer was peace for peace rather than land for peace. This effectively collapsed the Syrian–Israeli track.

Lebanon First, 1996–99

Netanyahu's lack of interest in the Israeli–Syrian or indeed the Israeli–Palestinian track was due to his belief that they would ultimately require territorial compromise, which he and his party were not willing to make. He thus shifted towards trying to find an accommodation with Lebanon where Israel's concern was security rather than land. Netanyahu reiterated Israel's position as already outlined at the 1991 Madrid conference – namely that Israel was prepared to withdraw its troops from the security zone if the Lebanese army deployed north of the security zone and, for a period of six months, was able to prevent any terrorist activities against the security zone and Israel. Three months following that period Israel would be prepared to sign a peace agreement with Lebanon. Moreover, prior to any changes in its redeployment on the Lebanese front, Israel had to be convinced that the military organs of all terrorist groups operating out of Lebanon had been irreversibly disbanded. And finally, the government of Israel wanted practical and valid guarantees that no harm would be inflicted upon Lebanese citizens and South Lebanon Army personnel residing in the security zone and that they would be absorbed into the governmental and societal fabric of Lebanon.

Netanyahu's decision to focus on a deal with Lebanon while letting Syria and the Palestinians stew became known as the **Lebanon First** option. Netanyahu made several attempts to reach out to the Lebanese government during his time in office but none were successful. 'Lebanon First' failed for three key reasons. First, it did not meet Lebanon's requirements for an agreement. Lebanon had a Palestinian refugee population of 350,000 to 400,000 that were seen as a political liability and economic burden. Thus Lebanon made a deal contingent upon the right of return for these Palestinians. Second, 'Lebanon First' ignored the existing power balance. De facto Lebanon was not a sovereign state but controlled by Syria. Lebanon could not objectively deliver what Israel wanted. It was not in a position to take on Hizbollah, demobilize the movement and guarantee Israel's security. And it was not in a position to pursue bilateral negotiations even if it had wanted to. That is why Lebanon's negotiating position centred on the implementation of UN Resolutions 425, 508 and 509, which called for the complete and unconditional withdrawal of Israel from Lebanese territory, with the assistance of UN forces, under the sovereignty of the Lebanese government. And third, the whole notion of 'Lebanon First' was a psychological non-starter for the Lebanese in light of the highly contentious and still recent history of the 1982 Israeli invasion of Lebanon and the aborted 1983 peace treaty resulting from it (Schulze, 2002).

Israeli–Syrian negotiations, 1999–2000

Israel shifted its attention back to negotiations with Syria after yet another change in government. In May 1999, retired general Ehud Barak was elected prime minister. During his election campaign he promised an Israeli withdrawal from southern Lebanon within a year. Then, in his inaugural speech on 6 July, Barak promised to work simultaneously on peace with all Israel's neighbours – Syria, Lebanon and the Palestinians. This was followed by an unprecedented public exchange of compliments between Hafez al-Asad and Barak. Then Syria ordered the Palestinian rejectionists and Hizbollah to cease military activity against Israel. And in December 1999 Israeli–Syrian negotiations were formally reopened in Washington, followed by substantive talks in January–February 2000 in Shepherdstown.

The Shepherdstown talks were divided into four parallel committees: one on security, one on boundaries, one on normalization and one on water. The idea was for all committees to proceed in parallel and in secret. However, a couple of days later newspaper stories appeared in the Arab and Israeli press that Syria had agreed to a normalization of relations with Israel. This leak, which had come from the Israeli negotiating team, not only broke the rule of secrecy, it also came at one of the most delicate moments in the negotiations. Progress had been made in some but not all committees. With respect to normalization Israel and Syria had decided to start with an exchange of ambassadors. With respect to security they agreed to two monitoring stations. There was no agreement on water and boundaries. According to Syria, Israel had to withdraw to the 4 June 1967 lines, and this included shorefront and therefore rights to the water of the Sea of Galilee. Israel not only stated that Syria had had no access to water on 4 June 1967 but that Israel would only have to withdraw to the 1923 international boundary. The disagreement was further compounded by delays on the boundary committee, which, according to the Syrians, were caused by Israeli stalling tactics. So when the details of agreement on normalization were leaked, it looked like Israel had achieved normalization without territorial concessions. Syria was not able to say that Israel had agreed to return the Golan Heights. Moreover, the manner in which the negotiations had been conducted and leaked suggested to Syria that Israel was not serious and not ready to make the necessary concessions. Not surprisingly, the Syrian negotiating team withdrew from the talks. Clinton later placed the blame for the collapse of the talks on Barak. In his memoirs he wrote that 'Syria had shown flexibility on what Israel wanted, providing its needs were met; Israel had not responded in kind' (Clinton, 2004: 887).

On 26 March, Clinton made a final attempt to bridge the gap between Israel and Syria. He invited Asad to meet him in Geneva. Under the impression that Israel was now willing to withdraw to the 4 June 1967 line and allow Syria access to the Sea of Galilee, Asad flew to Switzerland. However, Clinton was not able to deliver Israel, and Asad returned to Syria empty handed and disillusioned. This left Barak, who still had to fulfil his election promise, with no choice but to opt for a unilateral withdrawal from Lebanon without any security guarantees. On 24 May, in the dark of night, the IDF pulled out of the security zone. Some 6,500 SLA members and their families, fearing for their safety, followed them into Israel. Less than a month later, on 10 June 2000, Hafez al-Asad died. He was succeeded by his son **Bashar al-Asad**.

Assessing the Syrian–Israeli negotiations, 1991–2005

Israeli–Syrian negotiations and, by extension, Lebanon were always going to be difficult. Israel considered Syria to be a significant strategic threat, not just because of Syria's military strength but because of the fact that Syria controlled Lebanon, supported Hizbollah, provided a safe haven for Palestinian rejectionists and had close relations with Iran. Added to these security concerns were concerns about water, as Syria insisted on access to the Sea of Galilee. Moreover, Israeli distrust of Syria was tremendous, creating psychological obstacles not just within military and political circles but also at a popular level. That is why even Rabin, who came closest to peace with Syria, had decided to make an agreement contingent upon a referendum. The collapse of the Israeli–Syrian track in March 2000 and Hafez al-Asad's subsequent death made Israel even more uneasy. Ehud Barak and his successor, Ariel Sharon, saw Bashar al-Asad as a poor replacement of his father – weak and not really in control of the military and the so-called 'old guard'. So despite the fact that Bashar reiterated his father's desire to conclude a peace treaty along the 4 June 1967 line, Israel did not believe that he was in a position to deliver any deal, never mind delivering a better deal. The Israeli–Syrian relationship deteriorated further with the outbreak of the second Palestinian *intifada* in September 2000. This was, on the one hand, the result of Israel's shift in focus from Syria to the West Bank and Gaza Strip, followed by increased unilateralism under Sharon. On the other hand, it was also the result of Israel no longer just seeing Bashar as an ineffective leader to make peace with but as actively trying to encourage violence against Israel. He refused to close down the offices of the Hamas external leadership, the DFLP and PFLP in Damascus, and he gave Hizbollah free rein to step up its activity in the Shebaa farming area and ultimately against Israel. Israel and the United States further alleged that he had aided Saddam Hussein's regime and was providing a safe haven not only for Iraqi Ba'athists but also for *jihadis* with possible links to Al-Qaeda. And last but not least, he was seen as supportive of Iran's nuclear ambitions, which Israel deemed a direct existential threat.

Syria's position was no less complicated. Hafez al-Asad had built his career upon placing Syria at the heart of the Arab–Israeli conflict. Syria's military capabilities were the crucial factor, which made this economically and politically weak country into a regional power. He feared that a move from conflict to normalization of relations would lead to a marginalization of Syria. Indeed, this marginalization was already evident with the opening of Israeli–Jordanian relations, the Clinton administration's mobilization of international opinion against terrorism with the 1995 Sharm al-Shaykh summit, the new Israeli–Turkish strategic relationship announced in February 1996 and Israel's May 1996 Operation Grapes of Wrath for which the United States is believed to have given the 'green light'. The post-9/11 global **War on Terror** further exacerbated these developments with Syria being included in the so-called **Axis of Evil**, and allegations that Syria had not only aided Saddam Hussein's efforts to smuggle out oil, but also suspicions that it may have helped to relocate Iraq's weapons of mass destruction.

Syria's marginalization was underlined by Asad's belief that Syria was being taken for granted, as was his strategic decision to make peace with Israel and his concessions to peace, which included allowing Syrian Jews to leave the country, cleaning up the drug traffic in the Beqaa Valley and an appearance of the Syrian foreign minister Faruq al-Shara' on Israeli television. Similarly Asad's unprecedented step of publicly praising Barak after the latter's election, followed by a quick, unconditional resumption of negotiations, was never appreciated. Instead, Israeli negotiators started playing games when the time for game playing had long ceased.

At the same time, neither Hafez al-Asad nor Bashar felt the need to rush into an agreement with Israel. Even months before his death and although Asad wanted to see the return of the Golan in his lifetime, he was unwilling to agree to something less than a full withdrawal to the 4 June 1967 line. Moreover, until 2005, the Syrian troop presence in Lebanon ensured that Lebanon would stay out of the peace process until Asad and later Bashar were ready for accommodation. With Syria being the only credible military power that could effectively disarm and dissolve Hizbollah, Syria was able to use its non-interference with Hizbollah activity against Israel as a leverage over the peace process. Even after the Syrian withdrawal Bashar made it repeatedly clear that although he was interested in an agreement with Israel, he also had other options.

The 2006 Lebanon War

Instead of a return to the negotiating table, the Israeli–Lebanese–Syrian dynamic returned to one of conflict with Israel's second Lebanon War. When Israel pulled out of southern Lebanon in 2000 Hizbollah, Lebanon and indeed the Arab world as a whole had seen this as an Arab victory. Israeli fears that Hizbollah would pursue the retreating troops across the border and would target Israel did not materialize. Instead the Israeli–Hizbollah battleground shifted to the area known as the Shebaa farms. While Israel maintained that it had fully withdrawn from Lebanon as the Shebaa farms, according to UN maps, were part of Syria, Hizbollah argued that it was Lebanese land as the farmers were Lebanese and thus Israel's withdrawal remained incomplete. Hizbollah's position was largely determined by its domestic position. It needed a continuing area of conflict with Israel in order to resist pressures to disarm and dissolve its military wing. And Syria supported Hizbollah in its interpretation of land ownership, as Syria, too, needed an area from where pressure could be exerted on Israel. Hizbollah also saw continuing military action against Israel as an act of solidarity with the Palestinians following the outbreak of the second *intifada*. However, until 2006 the Hizbollah–Israeli battle was sporadic, remained confined to this area and had 'rules'. Hizbollah knew how Israel would respond to a strike against its forces and vice versa. This changed in July 2006.

On 12 July 2006 Hizbollah launched an ambush on an Israeli patrol, in which Hizbollah captured two Israeli soldiers and killed three others. In the IDF rescue mission another five Israeli soldiers were killed and one Merkava tank was destroyed. Hizbollah was ecstatic as its operation had exceeded expectations. Hizbollah's attack aimed at opening a second front to take the pressure off Hamas, which was at that point on the receiving end of a fully fledged Israeli offensive. Hizbollah also saw their ambush as an opportunity to demonstrate its own offensive capacities and to boost popular admiration, which had been fading since May 2000. Its leaders further believed that Israel's Prime Minister **Ehud Olmert**, who had taken over after Sharon suffered a stroke and went into coma, was weak, inexperienced and too preoccupied with Hamas to strike back. Hizbollah's assessment could not have been more wrong. Israeli leaders since late 2005 were almost itching for a fight with Hizbollah. They were tired of the constant taunting over Shebaa, and they perceived Hizbollah's position as having been weakened during 2005 as a result of the pro-Western and pro-democracy **Cedar Revolution** following the car bomb assassination of Lebanese Prime Minister Rafiq al-Hariri on 14 February, Syria's implications in the Hariri assassination,

Syria's forced withdrawal from Lebanon in April and the victory of the anti-Syrian camp led by Hariri's son Saad al-Din in May. In addition to Hizbollah's perceived weakness, there were fears that Hizbollah was developing a first-strike capacity (Gambill, 2006: 2). Moreover, 'Israel had monitored a series of communications between Hizbollah and Hamas in which Hizbollah urged Hamas to hang tough in negotiations with Israel over the return of an Israeli soldier captured in June 2006' (Norton 2007: 133), which had angered Israeli policy makers. And last, but certainly not least, there seems to have been American encouragement for a more extensive Israeli operation against Hizbollah, which suited the US War on Terror. Indeed, in early summer Israeli and US officials met in Washington and made plans for a crushing attack on Hizbollah (Hersh, 2006).

A day after Hizbollah's ambush, Israel's retaliatory offensive began. By 14 July Lebanon was blockaded from the sea, the Beirut airport was hit and shut down and Hizbollah leader Nasrallah's offices were bombed. Israeli strategy relied on air power and artillery bombardment from northern Israel into Lebanon. Israel's stated goal as articulated by Olmert was the return of the two Israeli soldiers, a complete ceasefire and the deployment of the Lebanese army all the way to the border with Israel. However, what emerged quickly was that its primary objective was to destroy Hizbollah's military capacity by destroying its rocket arsenal, cutting its supply lines, targeting its leaders and removing its support base. In the first few days Israel had moral superiority as it was the victim of an unprovoked attack. Even Arab states such as Saudi Arabia, Egypt, Jordan and the United Arab Emirates publicly criticized Hizbollah's action. However, sympathy for Israel disappeared quickly as it became clear that cutting off Hizbollah from its supply lines and support base meant targeting the civilian population in southern Lebanon and effectively emptying the area.

Hizbollah responded by firing rockets into Israel at a rate of around 150 per day. If Israel had thought that Hizbollah had been weakened during the previous year and would be easily subdued, it was mistaken. Not only was Hizbollah able to maintain its firing capacity, it had also acquired longer-range capabilities. It was no longer just Israeli towns and villages along the border that were coming under attack, but large coastal cities such as Haifa. Moreover, rather than undermining Hizbollah's support base, Israel's attacks on southern Lebanon bolstered it. This was the result of bombings such as the 30 July Qana bombing in which 28 civilians were killed, as well as Hizbollah's immediate pledges to compensate anyone losing their home with between $10,000 and $12,000 (Norton, 2007: 140). There was no doubt that the Shi'a population rallied around Hizbollah during this war. The reaction of the rest of the Lebanese population was mixed, with Christian voices denouncing Hizbollah and calling for its disarmament as years of post–civil war reconstruction fell victim to Israeli bombs.

In mid-August the UN finally managed to broker a ceasefire. The July War, as it is referred to in Lebanon, or the Second Lebanon War, as it is called in Israel, lasted 34 days. During this time 500,000 residents of northern Israel and 900,000 residents of southern Lebanon were displaced. Israel counted 43 and Lebanon 1,109 civilian deaths. Military casualties comprised 118 Israeli soldiers, 28 Lebanese soldiers and 200 Hizbollah fighters. Material losses amounted to $500 million in Israel and $4 billion in Lebanon. Hizbollah's 'victory' was celebrated across the Arab world and among Islamists. However, Hizbollah admitted it was a hollow victory and that had they known what Israel's response would be like, they never would have kidnapped those soldiers. For Israel it left the bitter taste of defeat, not because it had truly been defeated, but because it seemed that Israel had learned nothing from the 1982 Lebanon War.

The Syrian Jihad

A resumption of Israel–Syrian negotiations became even less likely with collapse of Syria into civil war in March 2011 when protests erupted in the context of what became known as the Arab Spring, a popular uprising against authoritarian regimes that spread from Tunisia across parts of the Middle East including Egypt, Libya and Syria. Bashar al-Asad responded to the demonstrators calling for democratization by sending in the army. The brutal suppression of these protests ensured that a bitter anti-regime battle soon turned into a civil war along patronage, kinship and, above all, sectarian lines.

The initial anti-Asad armed opposition was dominated by the Free Syrian Army (FSA), which was established in July 2011 following the defection of a significant number of Syrian soldiers who refused to shoot at unarmed demonstrators. While the FSA had secular-nationalist aims, it did not necessarily have a secular-nationalist membership. Indeed, as the conflict entered its second year there were clear indications that the Syrian opposition was undergoing Islamization as distinctly Islamist brigades emerged under FSA Division 19. New Syrian Islamist groups were also established to fight alongside the FSA, such as Jabhat al-Nusrah, which was formed in 2012 under the leadership of Muhammad al-Jawlani. Unlike the Islamist units of the FSA who were effectively Islamic nationalists, Jabhat al-Nusrah subscribed to Al-Qaeda's *salafi-jihadi* ideology and had goals that reached beyond avenging the deaths of innocent Syrians. External *salafi-jihadi* groups also joined the conflict, most notably the Islamic State of Iraq (ISI) which had evolved out of Al-Qaeda Iraq (AQI) and became the Islamic State of Iraq and the al-Sham (ISIS) in April 2013.

By the third year of the conflict the number of *jihadi* organizations had increased to more than 40 different groups. This resulted in mergers and the formation of alliances as well as conflict between some of the *jihadi* groups. This conflict was exacerbated by the expansion of ISIS at the expense of other member groups of the Syrian opposition, its repeated attempts to force *jihadis* of other groups to swear allegiance to its leader Abu Bakr Al-Baghdadi and its treatment of the population in areas under its control.

Muslim volunteers and foreign fighters also started joining the Syrian conflict from mid-2011 onwards, motivated not only by the desire to provide humanitarian aid and to defend the local population, but also by the desire to be part of what increasingly became viewed as an apocalyptic battle, as well as their desire for martyrdom. Between 2011 and early 2014 an estimated 3,400 to 11,000 foreign fighters had entered Syria from over 70 countries. By November 2015 this number had increased to 30,000, most of whom had joined ISIS, which in June 2014 had declared an Islamic caliphate and now called itself the Islamic State.

Since the eruption of the conflict in Syria, Israel has watched the unfolding developments with trepidation, but also with a degree of aloofness as it did not feel directly threatened. The FSA and Jabhat al-Nusra were preoccupied fighting Asad, while ISIS/IS was more interested in fighting Jabhat al-Nusra, Asad's forces and the Kurds. Thus Israel's main concern was to prevent weapons transfers to forces which were fighting Israel such as Hizbollah. Indeed, in December 2015 Israeli Prime Minister Netanyahu admitted that Israel operated 'in Syria from time to time to prevent Syria from becoming a front against us'. These operations included air strikes against weapons shipments on a number of occasions near the Syria–Lebanon border.

11 Gaza Wars, 2006–2015

Since 2006 the Israeli–Palestinian conflict has geographically shifted to the Gaza Strip. This was primarily the result of three factors: the 2005 unilateral Israeli withdrawal from Gaza, the 2006 ascendance of Hamas in intra-Palestinian politics and Hamas's subsequent determination to stay in power. Militarily, the conflict revolved around a series of wars of attrition fought between Israel and Hamas which were characterized, on the one hand, by the firing of rockets and mortars by Hamas as well as Palestinian Islamic Jihad (PIJ) into Israel and, on the other hand, by Israeli air and ground operations against Hamas positions in Gaza. Israeli operations, from 'Summer Rains' in June 2006 to 'Protective Edge' in July 2014, collectively aimed at reducing Hamas's military capacity by curtailing its ability to fire rockets into Israel, as well as the smuggling of weapons into the Gaza Strip. Politically, they aimed at maintaining the status quo rather than defeating or destroying Hamas. This served the broader Israeli goals of keeping the Palestinians divided and weak in order to prevent the emergence of a viable Palestinian state.

The 2005 unilateral withdrawal from Gaza

On 12 September 2005, the IDF completed its unilateral withdrawal from the Gaza Strip, 38 years after occupying this territory during the 1967 June War. This withdrawal saw the forcible evacuation of 21 Israeli settlements in the Gaza Strip as well as four isolated settlements in the West Bank. It was part of Sharon's broader vision of territorial separation between Israelis and Palestinians, which had already seen the construction of the West Bank Barrier. At the same time, the unilateral disengagement from Gaza was aimed at addressing very specific Israeli concerns. It was a direct response to the growing 'demographic threat', as demographic predictions saw the combined number of Palestinians in Israel, the West Bank and the Gaza Strip surpassing the number of Jews by 2010. The withdrawal from Gaza was thus a way to ensure a Jewish majority by reducing the number of Palestinians by 1,375,000. It was also a response to the Roadmap put forward by the Quartet in 2003.

At the time Sharon had publicly endorsed the Roadmap as it prioritized security and an interim agreement. However, not all of its provisions were seen as serving Israeli interests, such as the call for a cessation of all Israeli settlement activity and its stated goal of an independent, democratic and viable Palestinian state. Thus, it has been argued that the unilateral withdrawal was a tactical manoeuver to deflect international pressure for Israeli withdrawal from the West Bank, a counterplan to a diplomatic vacuum which could have dragged Israel 'into dangerous initiatives like the Geneva and Saudi initiatives' (Rynhold and Waxman, 2008: 28), or even that it was designed to neutralize the Roadmap itself (Strand, 2014: 7). It clearly intended to put further Israeli–Palestinian negotiations on ice. As explained by Sharon's aide Dov Weissglas:

> This disengagement is actually formaldehyde. It supplies the amount of formaldehyde that's necessary so that there will not be a political process with the Palestinians . . . The disengagement plan makes it possible for Israel to park conveniently in an interim situation that distances us as far as possible from political pressure.
>
> (Rynhold and Waxman, 2008: 11)

It signified a broader Israeli policy shift from seeking a comprehensive settlement of the conflict to a long-term interim agreement and the 'remote management' of the Gaza Strip.

Unilateral disengagement from Gaza also served domestic purposes. As it had considerable public support with 55 to 63 per cent of the Israelis favouring a withdrawal, not least because it would free up the disproportionate amount of resources committed to holding Gaza, this policy became a way for Sharon to consolidate the increasingly fragmented Israeli polity behind the goals which he wanted to prioritize: Jerusalem and maintaining Israel's Jewish character. This does not, however, mean that there was no opposition. Criticism initially came from two groups on the Israeli right: religious Zionists who opposed the withdrawal on ideological grounds and some members of the Likud who objected to its unilateral nature. Following the withdrawal, criticism also started to emerge from the Israeli left over the incomplete nature of the withdrawal and the continued, now remotely managed, occupation.

The 2006 ascendance of Hamas

On 25 January 2006, 10 years after the first elections to the Palestinian Legislative Council, the second legislative elections were held. It was hoped, mainly in international circles, that these would serve to strengthen the democratic base of the future Palestinian state and that they would breathe new life into the flagging negotiations. Neither of these hopes was fulfilled when Hamas under the banner of 'change and reform' won 74 out of the

132 seats, with only 45 going to the ruling party Fatah. Hamas's electoral victory was partially a negative vote against Fatah, which over the past decade had proven incapable of delivering an independent Palestinian state and whose record of governance had been marred by corruption and nepotism. Hamas, in contrast, promised clean government and justice based on Islamic principles. It was also able to recapture the spirit of the original Palestinian resistance. Its political manifesto reaffirmed the armed struggle to end the occupation, the right of return and the right to self-determination.

Hamas's victory triggered a debate in the Israeli government over whether one could or should negotiate with Hamas. Opponents argued that Hamas was a terrorist organization whose goal was the destruction of Israel. Thus there was no common ground for talks. Some even placed Hamas in the same category as Al-Qaeda. Others thought that labelling Hamas a terrorist organization was too simplistic. They saw an opportunity to draw Hamas further into a political process in which pragmatic rather than ideological decisions had to be made. They wanted Israel to explore the possibility of negotiations, but wanted the international community to hold off on engagement with Hamas until it had committed itself to a peace process. This debate quickly shifted in favour of the hardliners. Israel, backed by the United States, announced that there would be no resumption of talks as Israel did not negotiate with terrorists, and Israeli diplomats quickly and successfully began to lobby the international community to deny Hamas legitimacy.

Sharing many of Israel's concerns, the Quartet on 30 January announced that further international aid to the Palestinians would be contingent upon Hamas renouncing violence, recognizing the State of Israel and accepting all agreements previously negotiated by Israel and the PA, including the Roadmap provisions for disarmament, security reform and cooperation with Israel over security. When Hamas showed no signs of accepting these conditions, the Israeli government on 19 February imposed economic sanctions. It froze the transfer of tax revenues and customs duties to the PA. This was further exacerbated by the EU's suspension of direct financial aid to the Palestinians on 7 April, including the salaries of more than 150,000 civil servants, following the investiture of the Hamas government on 29 March.

Gaza Wars: Operations Summer Rains and Autumn Clouds, June–November 2006

The first post-disengagement Israeli operation against the Gaza Strip was launched on 28 June 2006. It came in the context of new leadership dynamics not only on the Palestinian but also on the Israeli side where Ehud Olmert had succeeded Sharon as prime minister when the latter suffered a stroke and fell into a coma on 4 January. Olmert's premiership was affirmed by his formal election on 14 April, marking continuity in policy as Olmert was committed to Sharon's strategy of unilateral separation. However, he lacked both Sharon's experience and strategic acumen. As a result he was propelled into military action by his desire to prove his security credentials as well as the fact that rockets were still sporadically being fired from the Gaza Strip into Israel, despite a Hamas ceasefire which had been in place since February 2005.

The descent into confrontation started on 8 June 2006, when Israel resumed its policy of extrajudicial killings with the IDF's assassination of Jamal Abu Samhadan, who was the founder of the Palestinian Resistance Committees which Israel held responsible for firing many of the rockets from Gaza. Samhadan was also the interior and national security minister in the new Hamas government. Hamas responded to his assassination with a barrage of rockets which, in turn was countered by Israeli retaliatory air strikes on 9 June, killing eight Palestinians belonging to the same family. Hamas then declared its 16-month ceasefire over.

The violence escalated further when on 24 June, the IDF conducted a raid on the house of the Muamar family in the Gaza Strip, abducting two brothers, Osama and Mustafa, who they believed were involved in the firing of the rockets. The following day, on 25 June a Hamas commando unit attacked an Israeli border post, killing two soldiers and abducting another – Gilad Shalit. The abduction of Shalit paved the way for a full-scale Israeli offensive, Operation Summer Rains.

The stated aim of Operation Summer Rains, which provided the framework for a number of military operations between 28 June and 1 November 2006, was freeing Shalit and stopping the firing of Qassam rockets into Israel. The former included search operations, negotiations with Hamas and even the arrest of 64 Hamas officials, including cabinet ministers and parliament members from both the West Bank and Gaza Strip, which some labelled 'abductions' for the purposes of using them as 'bargaining chips' (Levy, 2010: 135). The latter saw the targeting of Hamas and PIJ, their strongholds and their infrastructure. As Hamas was the government in Gaza, this resulted in the Israeli destruction of Palestinian ministry buildings and offices, even the sole electricity plant. Moreover, the targeting of the militants meant targeting residential areas as combatants and civilians occupied the same space in the overcrowded Gaza Strip. Operation Summer Rains, which turned into Operation Autumn Clouds on 1 November, effectively placed Gaza under siege with electricity blackouts, relentless aerial bombings, shelling from the sea and ground incursions in which whole neighbourhoods were destroyed. When this first Gaza War ended on 26 November 2006, some 400 Palestinians had been killed, many of them women and children. Much of Gaza's infrastructure had also been destroyed. Yet, Gilad Shalit had not been freed and Hamas' military capacity had not been significantly weakened, nor was deterrence re-established.

The battle of Gaza and the blockade of Gaza

Operations Summer Rains and Autumn Clouds paved the way for a power struggle between Hamas and Fatah in June 2007, often referred to as the

'Battle of Gaza', as well as a further tightening of the Israeli restrictions on the Gaza Strip after Hamas successfully ousted Fatah from Gaza, which became known as the 'Blockade of Gaza'.

The conflict between Hamas and Fatah started with the electoral victory of Hamas. This created an oppositional dynamic between (Hamas) prime minister **Ismail Haniyyeh** and (Fatah) president Mahmud Abbas, which was further underlined by competing ideologies and political visions for Palestine. While the international community, as well as Israel, urged Abbas 'to deal' with Hamas by using his presidential powers to dismiss Parliament and call for new elections, Abbas instead chose to circumvent Parliament through presidential decrees, which he used to assert his authority over key administrative positions.

The power struggle between Hamas and Abbas became most acute in the area of security. In a bid to undermine Abbas, Hamas pushed for security reforms which would have removed Fatah loyalists from the security apparatus. Abbas responded by placing the Palestinian security forces directly under him and building up the Presidential Guard. Hamas, in turn, established a rival Executive Force. On 7 January 2007, Abbas then ordered the incorporation of Hamas's paramilitary forces into the Palestinian security apparatus. The enforcement of this order exacerbated the clashes between Hamas and elements of Fatah which had characterized much of the latter half of 2006 and had left 33 dead in December.

Full-out conflict was held back by the formation of a Palestinian unity government in March 2007, following the Mecca Agreement in February. This, however, was unable to bridge the differences between Abbas and Haniyyeh as tensions continued between Hamas and Fatah on the ground. These culminated in open warfare between Hamas's Executive Force and Abbas's Presidential Guard from 10 June to 15 June in which 118 were killed and 550 wounded. During this period Hamas militants seized several Fatah members and threw one of them off the top of a 15-story building in Gaza City. Fatah retaliated by killing the imam of Gaza's Great Mosque. Hamas then proceeded to oust Fatah and the Presidential Guard from all parts of the Gaza Strip, seizing Fatah posts and taking over the headquarters of the Preventive Security Services on 14 June. At this point Abbas, who considered Hamas's actions tantamount to a military coup, dismissed Haniyyeh and replaced him with Salam Fayad as the new Palestinian prime minister. Haniyyeh, however, refused to accept his dismissal as he believed that Hamas was the victim of a CIA conspiracy to remove him. Hanniyeh's refusal not only meant that there were two competing prime ministers but, coupled with the ousting of Fatah from the Gaza Strip, it also meant that there were two competing Palestinian governments in control of two separate Palestinian 'states'.

The seizure of the Gaza Strip by Hamas triggered yet another debate in the Israeli government between those who advocated a complete closure of the Gaza Strip with the aim of bringing down Hamas and those who advocated somewhat less pressure on Hamas in order not to escalate the situation and thereby necessitate a reoccupation. On 19 September 2007, Israel formally declared Gaza a 'hostile territory'. This was followed by the imposition of economic sanctions. Electricity, water and fuel supplies to Gaza were cut off. As Israel controlled five of the six land crossings – excluding Rafah which was under Egyptian control – it was able to introduce tight controls on products permitted to enter Gaza. These excluded so-called dual-use goods which could be used both for civilian and military purposes such as construction materials. They also excluded what were now defined as luxury goods: chocolate, jam, children's clothing and A4 paper. Moreover, the Qarni crossing, Gaza's link to foreign markets, was completely closed down.

This had a devastating impact on the already impoverished population. By September 2008, some 98 per cent of businesses were forced to shut down, the agriculture sector collapsed and the poverty rate rose to 79 per cent (Strand, 2014: 15–16). An estimated 40,000 Gaza fishermen were deprived of their livelihood as Israel imposed a 6-mile limit, reducing the amount of fish caught from 3,000 tons a year to 500 tons as most fish were 10 miles off shore (Levy, 2010: 66). This was further compounded by attacks on fishermen, the difficulties of finding fuel for fishing boats and the pollution of the sea with 50 million litres of sewage every day after the collapse of the sewage infrastructure.

Gaza Wars: Operation Cast Lead, December 2008–January 2009

On 19 June 2008 Israel and Hamas agreed to a six-month ceasefire through Egyptian mediation. At the heart of this agreement was Israel's commitment to a gradual lifting of the blockade imposed upon Gaza in return for Hamas ceasing to fire rockets into southern Israel. It was the possibility of an extension of this truce that paved the way for the next Gaza War. Hamas charged Israel with not abiding by the terms of the agreement with respect to lifting the restrictions, and Israel accused Hamas of smuggling weapons into the Gaza Strip. On 4 November 2008, Israel launched a limited operation into the Gaza Strip in order to destroy a tunnel it saw as the central route for weapons coming in. Hamas responded to this with renewed rocket fire. Between the beginning of November and mid-December some 2,000 Qassam rockets landed in the Negev in what Hamas dubbed Operation Oil Stain. On 19 December, Hamas formally announced the end of its ceasefire as Israel had not lifted the blockade. A week later, on 27 December, Israel launched Operation Cast Lead with the stated objectives of putting an end to the firing of rockets into Israel, preventing smuggling into the Gaza Strip and restoring deterrence.

Operation Cast Lead had two stages. The first stage started with air attacks against Hamas's headquarters, government offices, police stations, tunnels and weapons caches. It also included so-called surgical strikes against Hamas leaders, commanders and explosives experts as well as their houses. These air strikes were supported by the Israeli navy blockading Gaza from the sea. Artillery was fired from Israeli ships against areas from where Hamas rockets were launched, Hamas outposts, command and control centres and the office of Ismail Haniyeh. Israel also bombed a Gaza police graduation ceremony and a police station. As the operation proceeded Israeli bombs destroyed university student dormitories and mosques.

The second stage saw the start of an Israeli ground operation on 3 January 2009. Some 9,000 Israeli soldiers accompanied by tanks and artillery deployed into the Gaza Strip. They moved into some of the most densely populated areas, which were also the areas from which Hamas fired many of its rockets. As the number of casualties grew with this second phase, so did international pressure on Israel. On 6 January Israel bombed three UN-managed schools, killing some 43 Palestinian civilians who had been sheltering there, and wounding another 100. On 9 January the UNSC called for a truce, but it was not until 17 January that Israel announced a unilateral ceasefire. Operation Cast Lead resulted in some 1,400 Palestinian deaths, including 430 children. Another 5,450 Palestinians were wounded, including 1,550 children. The Red Cross described the situation in Gaza as a 'humanitarian crisis' with 50,800 homeless, 60 per cent of the agriculture destroyed, 219 factories destroyed and 122 health facilities damaged or destroyed including 15 of Gaza's 27 hospitals. According to official Israeli figures 10 Israeli soldiers and 3 civilians were killed.

Israel was widely condemned for its disproportionate use of force, its use of white phosphate and its alleged use of depleted uranium shells and dense inert metal explosives which are both deemed to be carcinogenic. Hamas, too, came in for condemnation for firing rockets from residential areas, using human shields and storing weapons in civilian buildings including mosques. Indeed, the UN Special Mission looking into the 2008–09 Gaza War concluded that both the IDF and Palestinian militants had committed war crimes. The Israeli government was also criticized by the Israeli left as waging a war 'to satisfy the considerations of internal politics' (Levy, 2010: 118), a war designed to establish Olmert's security credentials and to boost the electability of prime ministerial candidates Ehud Barak and Tzipi Livni.

Despite the criticism, Israel saw Operation Cast Lead as a success. It had reduced Hamas's military capacity by killing several high-ranking Hamas commanders such as Nizar Rayan, Abu Zakaria al-Jamal and Jamal Mamduch, as well as Hamas ministers such as Said Seyam. It also decimated Hamas's 'Iranian unit' and destroyed a large number of weapons caches and tunnels. Above all, the number of rockets fired into Israel from the Gaza Strip fell from 3,716 in 2008 to 858 in 2009 and 365 in 2010.

These achievements, however, were only short term. Not only did Hamas still have an estimated 1,000 rockets left when the ceasefire was called, but the Israel domestic intelligence agency Shin Beth estimated that smuggling would be renewed within two months (Levy, 2010: 116). Hamas had also gained popular support, and Gaza had attracted considerable international attention. Indeed, the scale of destruction in Gaza gave rise to international relief efforts, including the 2010 Gaza Flotilla, a conglomeration of ships operated by activists from some 37 countries, which sought to break the Gaza Blockade. Moreover, Operation Cast Lead compelled Hamas to improve the quality of its weapons and to acquire new ones with even greater capacity and range. The 15 March 2011 Israeli seizure of the ship *Victoria*, which was carrying missiles from Iran, and the 48-hour attack in which 70 rockets were fired in April were the first indicators that Hamas was regaining its military capacity. Rocket fire from Gaza also continued to increase again, reaching 680 by the end of the year of 2011.

Gaza Wars: Operation Pillar of Defence, November 2012

The third Gaza War erupted in November 2012. Like previous Gaza Wars, it was the culmination of renewed tensions between Israel and Hamas, as well as an increasing number of rockets fired into southern Israel from the Gaza Strip. The descent into outright conflict began on 10 November when a Hamas rocket struck an IDF jeep near the Qarni crossing, wounding four Israeli soldiers. On the same day four Palestinian teenagers were killed in an Israeli air strike while playing football. Hamas stepped up its rocket fire with 100 rockets fired from Gaza within a 24-hour period; on 14 November Israel launched Operation Pillar of Defence.

Operation Pillar of Defence, like Operation Cast Lead in 2008, sought to curb rocket fire into Israel and to reduce Hamas's military capacity. At a broader level it sought to re-establish Israel's deterrence capacity. Thus, it is not surprising that one of the first targets was Ahmed Jabari, the head of Hamas's military wing in the Gaza Strip. Jabari was not only seen as directly responsible for the increase in rockets fired into southern Israel as well as the smuggling of weapons into the Gaza Strip, but he was also seen as responsible for the kidnapping of Gilad Shalit in 2006. Israel's other attacks during the first few days of Operation Pillar of Defence focused on Hamas's military infrastructure – underground rocket launchers, weapons depots, command centres and smuggling tunnels – and the militant leadership in the Gaza Strip in the form of senior Hamas and PIJ figures.

While Operation Pillar of Defence resembled previous Israeli operations, not least because it was part of the same protracted Gaza conflict, there were two notable differences. The first was that there was no ground operation. This was due to Israel's strategy of exhaustion whereby Hamas and the Gaza Strip were targeted in such a way that it provoked a maximum response in the early days, literally exhausting Hamas's military supplies. The second difference was the Iron Dome missile defence system, which was used for the first time. The Iron Dome computed the trajectory of rockets fired. It then intercepted and destroyed those rockets predicted to hit a target area while leaving those that would land in empty spaces unintercepted. During Operation Pillar of Defence the Iron Dome destroyed a total of 422 rockets.

Israel's Operation Pillar of Defence was countered by a joint Hamas–Palestinian Islamic Jihad operation named Stones of Baked Clay. This operation aimed at inflicting as much damage on Israel as possible in order to extract the highest price possible for Israeli military action and, more broadly, the highest price possible for Israel's blockade of Gaza and continued occupation of the West Bank. Operation Stones of Baked Clay revolved around the firing of rockets into Israel, including Russian-made Grad and Iranian-made Fajr rockets. Indeed, some 1,511 rockets and missiles were successfully launched at the Israeli cities of Rishon LeZion, Beersheba, Ashdod, Ashkelon and for the first time since the 1991 Gulf War, Tel Aviv and Jerusalem. Operation Stones of Baked Clay also included efforts to spark a Palestinian uprising on the West Bank. However, while there was some burning of tires, throwing of stones and blocking of roads, as well as a small number of clashes between Palestinians and the IDF and between Palestinians and Israeli settlers, Hamas's calls for another *intifada* went unheeded. This reflected the awkward position West Bank Palestinians and the Abbas government found themselves in, whereby they objected to the Israeli military's operation in terms of its impact on the population of the Gaza Strip, but did not necessarily object to Israel's attempts to reduce the capacity of Hamas. More support came from Egypt and Turkey who practically vied with each other for 'most ardent supporter' status. Indeed, Egyptian Prime Minister Hisham Qandil visited Gaza in a show of solidarity on 16 November, the third day of the conflict. Egypt also positioned itself successfully as mediator in the efforts to bring about a ceasefire.

The 2012 Gaza War ended with a ceasefire on 21 November but not before a remotely detonated bomb exploded on a crowded bus in Tel Aviv, injuring 28. The ceasefire, according to Egypt, included a commitment to future negotiations on easing the restrictions on Gaza, allowing Palestinian farmers to work the land near the Israeli border and increasing the fishing limit for Gaza fishermen.

Palestinian casualties numbered 174 killed and 1,222 wounded, including 10 members of the al-Dalu family who all died in the same Israeli air strike against the home of Mohamad Jamal al-Dalu, a member of the Gaza police, who had been the target. Israeli casualties numbered 6 dead and 240 injured. The damage to the infrastructure of the Gaza Strip was considerable. According to the UNHCR in its report, 52 places of worship, 25 non-governmental organization (NGO) premises, 97 schools, 15 health institutions, 15 journalists' premises, 8 police stations, 16 government buildings, 15 factories and 12 wells were destroyed. The report also criticized Israel's disproportionate use of force and the targeting of civilians, as well as Hamas's use of residential areas for military purposes and the summary execution of seven Palestinians who were seen as collaborators.

Both Hamas and Israel declared a victory. Hamas had not only remained in power but increased its foothold on the West Bank, while Israel had effectively restored the status quo *ante bellum*. In 2013 only 41 rockets were fired into Israel from the Gaza Strip. Israel's victory, however, was not wholeheartedly embraced by the Israeli population. Indeed, in the Israeli right there were those who saw this as no more than tactical victory as Hamas had not only 'gotten away' with firing at Tel Aviv and Jerusalem, but Israeli Prime Minister Netanyahu had also negotiated with Hamas after they had struck at the heart of Israel with the Tel Aviv bus bombing.

Gaza Wars: Operation Protective Edge, July 2014

Changes in the Palestinian political dynamics in April 2014 set the ball rolling for the fourth Gaza War. After a seven-year hiatus Hamas and Fatah agreed to a reconciliation deal on 23 April, resulting in the formation of a Palestinian national unity government on 2 June. Israel's Netanyahu government responded to this reconciliation by announcing that it would not be able to negotiate with this new Palestinian government, thereby scuppering on-going efforts by the United States to restart Israeli–Palestinian talks. To emphasize his point, Netanyahu also cancelled the planned release of Palestinian prisoners.

It was the cancellation of the prisoner release that triggered a highly emotive cycle of violence, which started with the abduction of three Israeli teenagers on 12 June. Naftali Fraenkel (16), Gilad Shaer (16) and Eyal Yifrah (19) got into the wrong car in the West Bank when they hitchhiked home. A rogue Hamas cell led by Marwan Qawasmeh and Amer Abu Aysha kidnapped the three Israeli youths as collateral in order to force the reinstatement of the cancelled prisoner exchange (Blumenthal, 2014: 16). However, when Gilad Shaer managed to phone the police, the teenagers were shot dead and buried in land belonging to Qawasmeh adjacent to the family home near Hebron.

The abduction of Fraenkel, Shaer and Yifrah resulted in an extensive search operation. On 17 June thousands of Israeli troops poured into the West Bank under Operation Brother's Keeper, rounding up hundreds of Hamas members, including prisoners previously released in 2011. These actions on the ground were accompanied by Netanyahu declaring that 'Hamas must pay' and Foreign Minister Avigdor Lieberman calling for a reoccupation of the Gaza Strip. When the bodies of the three youths were found on 30 June, even Israeli statesman Shimon Peres at the funerals of Fraenkel, Shaer and Yifrah urged the IDF to 'act with a heavy hand until terror is uprooted' (Blumenthal, 2014: 18).

On 2 July, a day after the funerals of the three Israeli teenagers, a Palestinian youth Mohamed Abu Khadir (16) was grabbed by three Israeli settlers in Arab East Jerusalem, thrown into their car and murdered in revenge. His body was found hours later in Jerusalem Forest, and the autopsy report stated that he had been beaten unconscious, doused in kerosene and then burnt alive.

On 7 July the trickle of rockets fired from Gaza into Israel, which had provided a steady backdrop to the murders of the youngsters, turned into a flood as Hamas sanctioned an increase in attacks on Israel, firing 134 rockets into southern Israel in one day. In response Israel changed its strategy from hunting launch teams to air attacks on the infrastructure in Gaza (Shamir and Hecht, 2014–15: 84). On 8 July, Hamas retaliated by firing M-75 rockets towards Tel Aviv and Jerusalem. Israel, in turn, launched Operation Protective Edge.

Operation Protective Edge, like previous Israeli operations, sought to reduce Hamas's military capacity, particularly its ability to fire rockets into Israel. It also sought to destroy the extensive system of tunnels Hamas had dug, through which weapons were smuggled into the Gaza Strip and through which Hamas operatives could enter Israel undetected. Indeed, the tunnels had become the main reason for launching a ground operation in addition to the air strikes on 17 July. The idea of tunnels being used for infiltrating into Israel in order to launch attacks terrified the Israelis, as it negated the sense of security provided by the security barrier as well as the Iron Dome. There was also an expectation that like in Operation Cast Lead in 2009, an Israeli ground operation would cause Hamas to flee. However, this proved not to be the case (Shamir and Hecht, 2014–15: 86).

Operation Protective Edge lasted for 50 days, ending in yet another ceasefire on 26 August. During the seven weeks of fighting Israel attacked 5,263 targets, including 34 tunnels in the Gaza Strip, while Hamas launched 4,564 rockets into Israel. Almost 2,200 Palestinians were killed, including some 600 children. Indeed, an estimated 75 per cent of the Palestinian casualties were civilians. Moreover, as many as 520,000 Palestinians were displaced. According to the UN more than 7,000 family homes were destroyed and 89,000 more were damaged. Gaza's electricity infrastructure, sewage pipes and agricultural land had taken a severe hit as well as 220 factories, 203 mosques, two of the three churches in Gaza, several TV stations and 10 hospitals which were badly damaged or destroyed. Israeli casualties amounted to 66 soldiers and 5 civilians killed, as well as 469 soldiers and 897 civilians wounded. Between 5,000 and 8,000 Israelis were temporarily displaced from their homes.

Like in Operation Pillar of Defence, the considerably lower number of Israeli casualties can be largely attributed to the Iron Dome defence system. Yet it is noticeable that both Israeli and Palestinian casualties were much higher than in previous Gaza Wars. A closer look at the aims and strategies of Hamas and Israel go a long way toward explaining this rise in casualties and destruction. Like in previous Gaza Wars, Israel pursued a strategy of disproportionate retaliation and Hamas pursued a strategy of psychological exhaustion (Shamir and Hecht, 2014–15: 85). Unlike in previous Gaza Wars, however, Hamas saw its aim of staying in power best served by an all-out war rather than a limited confrontation due to the dire financial situation Hamas found itself in following the reversal of fortunes with respect to its key ally, Egypt. Following the ousting of Muslim Brotherhood president Muhammad Mursi in July 2013, the Egyptian army quickly moved to destroy and close down the network of tunnels linking Gaza to Egypt. The drying up of Hamas's funding led Hamas to opt for a full-on war, which served two purposes. First, it would allow Hamas to compensate for its loss in political and financial legitimacy through military legitimacy. Second, Hamas hoped to create an international crisis and with it a need for international intervention, which in turn, would loosen the noose around Gaza's neck (Shamir and Hecht, 2014–15: 85).

Israel, too, had an interest in a more intense conflict with Hamas. This was partially driven by its increasing struggle to maintain the status quo as Hamas benefitted from new regional alliances and had increased its military capacity and rocket range following each of the Gaza Wars. It was also the result of its retaliatory strategy which aimed to 'educate' Hamas by targeting its assets in order to ultimately get Hamas to reduce its violence against Israel (Stahl, 2015: 23). And finally, it was propelled by domestic political needs which required Netanyahu to demonstrate his security credentials vis-à-vis an increasing challenge from the ultra-nationalist/religious Zionist right, as well as to respond to the popular desire for the punishment of Hamas for the murder of the three Israeli teenagers.

When Hamas and Israel agreed to the ceasefire on 26 August [Doc. 29, p. 166], only some of their aims had been achieved. With respect to Hamas's key aims of an international intervention, the lifting of the siege on Gaza and more broadly the liberation of Palestine, only the second was partially addressed by the ceasefire and has yet to be implemented. Israel succeeded in reducing Hamas's military capacity by destroying the key tunnels, getting Hamas to fire most of its rockets and killing an estimated 15 per cent of Hamas's military. It also succeeded in restoring the status quo ante. However, whether Hamas learned the correct lesson, namely that it needs to reduce the level of violence, is questionable, as is whether Netanyahu succeeded in fending off the ultra-nationalist/religious Zionist right. Indeed, with respect to the latter it has been argued that Israel's far right not only managed to outflank the right-wing establishment but also showed that it made considerable inroads into the hitherto secular-nationalist military establishment, as some IDF officers openly justified 'the brutality of their actions in the military battle zone with messianic pronouncements' (Blumenthal, 2014: 14). It also used this fourth Gaza War, like previous Gaza Wars, to continue their battle against the Israeli left. In Tel Aviv 'organised thugs' assaulted anti-war protesters while the police stood by and death threats were issued to Israeli journalists critical of the war (Blumenthal, 2014: 23–24)

Making sense of the Gaza Wars

In order to understand the Gaza Wars between 2006 and 2014 as a whole, they need to be looked at more broadly in military, political and economic terms. In military terms, Israel's repeated operations were an exercise in containment with the aim of restoring and maintaining the status quo. Here the dynamics of periodic high-intensity conflict interspersed by calm or low-intensity conflict were tied to the notion of a 'tolerable level of violence' emanating from the Gaza Strip after the Israeli withdrawal in 2005. In simple terms this was based on the number of rockets fired into Israel. Whenever the number of rockets increased beyond the 'tolerable level', Israel responded with a military operation. Other factors of 'intolerability' also included the import of weapons and dual-use material into the Gaza Strip.

While the IDF was able to restore the military status quo with respect to the number of rockets fired from Gaza with each Israeli operation, it is notable that this came at an increasingly higher cost. Indeed, the Gaza Wars between 2006 and 2014 showed both an escalation in the dynamics and means of violence as well as diminishing returns as the periods of reduced rocket attacks became shorter. This raises the question to what extent the IDF was able to restore Israel's deterrence capabilities. Indeed, it seems that Hamas became more rather than less willing to militarily engage with Israel and certainly was able to raise its military capacity after each confrontation. This is exemplified by the increase in the range of the rockets fired over this period from the 17.7-km range of the locally produced Qassam rocket to the 75-km range of the Iranian-imported Fajr rocket. This widened the threat to the Israeli population beyond the town of Sderot on Israel's border with the Gaza Strip to placing 40 per cent of the Israeli population within reach, including the cities of Tel Aviv and Beer Sheva and even the outskirts of Jerusalem.

Between 2006 and 2014 some 17,425 rockets, mortars and missiles were fired into Israeli territory. Thus there is no doubt that these attacks presented the greatest security challenge for Israel since the construction of the security barrier and played a key role in the dynamics of war. However, an overly narrow focus on rocket numbers obscures the political, ideological and economic dynamics driving the conflict, which provide a somewhat different understanding of the Gaza Wars.

There were four key drivers for Hamas's increasing willingness to both provoke Israel and to tolerate heavier casualties between 2006 and 2014: its political competition with the PA/Fatah, the impoverization of the Gaza Strip, the changing geo-political environment and Hamas's overarching goal to remain in power. These drivers were heavily interlinked, tying together grievances and opportunity as well as desperation and radicalization.

The electoral victory of Hamas in 2006 provided it with a popular endorsement to take on the PA/Fatah in a bid for Palestinian leadership and advance its own goals of an Islamic Palestine based on *sharia* legislation and based on the territory defined by *waqf*, replacing both Israel and the PA. However, Hamas's ability to govern, to successfully project its alternative vision and to remain in power was hampered by the Quartet's suspension of foreign aid following the elections and Israel's restrictions on movement and goods in September 2007. Cut off from foreign economic aid, the Hamas government relied heavily on the taxes collected on illegally imported goods through the growing underground tunnel system that connected it to Egypt. This source of income, however, was insecure as the tunnels were periodically targeted by Israel and Egypt. Indeed, both the 2008 Gaza War and the 2014 Gaza War were precipitated by the destruction of some of these tunnels.

With the election of Muslim Brotherhood candidate Mohamed Mursi as president of Egypt in 2012, Hamas experienced a brief economic respite as the restrictions along the Gaza-Egypt border virtually disappeared. Moreover, the emir of Qatar, Hamad bin Khalifa al-Thani, during a visit to Gaza in October 2012 pledged $400 million in aid as part of the new Sunni realignment triggered by the sectarian war in Syria. This saw Hamas back away from its Shi'a and Alawi allies of Hizbollah, Syria and Iran. While Iran's financial support consequently declined, this was outweighed by being part of an alliance with the more 'respectable' mainstream players of Egypt, Turkey and Qatar. This new alignment emboldened Hamas politically and militarily in its challenge to both the PA and Israel.

When Mursi was then overthrown in July 2013 by the Egyptian military and replaced by General Abdel Fattah as-Sisi, Hamas suddenly found itself squeezed even more tightly than before. As-Sisi declared Hamas a terrorist organization, associating it both with the Egyptian Muslim Brotherhood and the newly formed ISIS Sinai, which had already attacked Egyptian soldiers. So Egypt embarked upon the 'strangling of Hamas' financial windpipe' in retaliation (Shamir and Hecht, 2014–15: 83). More than 1,500 of an estimated 1,800 tunnels were destroyed. At the same time the United States pressured Qatar into stopping its aid money. By 2014 Gaza was in a severe economic crisis with 70 per cent of Gaza's population dependent on humanitarian aid, a poverty rate of 39 per cent, an unemployment rate of 41 per cent, an annual population growth rate of 3 per cent (50,000 people per year) and 50 per cent of the population under the age of 14 (Chorev 2014:12; Rivlin 2014: 2–5). Unable to pay the salaries of its government employees beyond April, Hamas sought reconciliation with the PA in the hope that the PA would pay them. This possibility, however, was scuppered by the abduction and murder of the three Israeli teenagers, which Mahmud Abbas saw as an attempt to undermine him.

The increasing economic crisis in Gaza between 2006 and 2014 posed a clear danger to Hamas's ability to remain in power and to make its bid for Palestinian leadership. Thus it is not surprising that Hamas's operations against Israel in the 2008, 2012 and 2014 Gaza Wars were all aimed at forcing a lifting of the economic restrictions. Hamas's failure to achieve this through diplomatic means, despite the fact that a gradual lifting of the sanctions was part of every ceasefire agreement, strengthened Hamas's resolve to use military means. This became particularly clear in 2014 when Hamas actively sought to draw Israel into renewed confrontation because another Gaza War 'would allow it to revisit agreements with Israel and Egypt and extricate itself from the crisis' (Chorev, 2014: 12). This financial desperation also drove Hamas to endure a much higher level of physical damage before agreeing to a ceasefire (Shamir and Hecht, 2014–15: 81). Indeed, despite the high cost to Palestinians in Gaza, it is clear that the Gaza Wars were both necessary and opportune for Hamas. They were necessary in order to challenge Israel's economic stranglehold on Gaza since the 2005 withdrawal, but they also presented an opportunity to marginalize the PA/Fatah and their secular nationalist Palestinian state project.

The Gaza Wars between 2006 and 2014 also played an interesting role with respect to Israel's broader aims, and in order to fully understand this, it is necessary to take a closer look at the implications of wanting to preserve the status quo. Maintaining the status quo has not just been about restoring the military balance to the 'tolerable level of violence' but also about maintaining the broader status quo in the Israeli–Palestinian conflict, which was a status quo in which Israel retained military superiority while the Palestinian body politic remained divided and stateless.

The Israeli aim of maintaining the broader status quo in the Israeli–Palestinian conflict directly affected the efforts at reviving Israeli–Palestinian negotiations which were made periodically during the periods of calm in the Gaza Wars. The first of these efforts came in June 2007, after an almost seven-year period without talks. Palestinian President Abbas started meeting with Israeli Prime Minister Olmert to discuss the possible resumption of the peace process. On 27 November, this culminated in the Annapolis Conference under the auspices of the United States and the Quartet with the aim of implementing the Roadmap for peace, concluding with a final status agreement by the end of 2008 and establishing a Palestinian state. The conference ended in a joint Israeli–Palestinian statement. However, when it became public that Olmert had indicated that he was willing to relinquish parts of Jerusalem, one of the parties in his coalition government, the Sephardi religious party Shas led by Ovadia Yosef, withdrew from the coalition, thereby ending the coalition's majority in the Knesset. This effectively scuppered the Annapolis process. As the deadline for concluding a final status agreement approached, it was Israel who broke the ceasefire with Hamas by blowing up one of the tunnels and triggering the descent into the 2008–09 Gaza War.

The second effort at trying to revive Israeli–Palestinian negotiations came with the Clinton initiative when US Secretary of State Hillary Rodham Clinton explored the possibility of reviving the peace process in September 2010. She spent months shuttling between the Israelis, Palestinians, Jordanians and Egyptians to get a framework for achieving a two-state solution within a year only to have her efforts undermined by Israeli Prime Minister

Netanyahu's insistence that first the Palestinians had to recognize Israel as a Jewish state and Hamas and Hizbollah, who objected to a resumption of negotiations, had to be dealt with. Not surprisingly, these efforts achieved little. The third attempt came with the 2013–14 Kerry initiative which saw nine months of shuttle diplomacy by US Secretary of State John Kerry. This initiative collapsed in April 2014 with Israel pointing at the formation of the Hamas–PA national unity government as the cause while US negotiator Martin Indyk publicly blamed Israel for sabotaging the negotiations (Blumenthal, 2014: 15).

All three initiatives suffered from a mismatch between the aims of the United States/Quartet and the aims of Israel with respect to the Israeli–Palestinian conflict. The United States/Quartet wanted a comprehensive and final agreement which included the establishment of a viable Palestinian state, while Israel had come to the conclusion that its interests were better served by a long-term interim arrangement that precluded the establishment of a Palestinian state. Israel preferred maintaining the status quo and the balance of power favourable to Israel over a possible historic reconciliation.

Israeli aims with respect to the broader Palestinian–Israeli conflict were partially the result of the collapse of the Camp David summit and the subsequent eruption of another Palestinian *intifada*. It was the speed with which the fruits of the peace process from 1993 to 2000 disappeared and violence reappeared that led Israel down the path of unilateralism in the belief that only Israel could ensure Israel's security. This was further underlined by the widespread Israeli view that they had withdrawn from Gaza only to be subjected to rockets in return.

Interestingly, Israel's pursuit of the status quo has produced a convergence of interests between Israel and Hamas whereby between 2006 and 2014 Israel's political and military behaviour has effectively amounted to an unofficial policy of keeping Hamas in power, despite Israel's rhetoric to the contrary and Hamas's Islamist ideology and aim to destroy Israel (Stahl, 2015: 22). Israel's policy has been driven by the weakness and unreliability of Fatah and the PA, on the one hand, and on the other by the fear that if Hamas is removed from power in Gaza, it will result in anarchy or Hamas will be succeeded by more radical Islamists such as PIJ or ISIS Palestine. Hamas was thus 'needed' to impose authority on any rogue elements. The decision not to remove Hamas also derived from the lack of enthusiasm for reoccupying Gaza. Preserving the rule of Hamas worked for Israel because Hamas could be 'managed' through periodic Gaza Wars which effectively kept its military capacity in check. It could also be 'managed' through political isolation and economic sanctions, turning 'the welfare of Gaza into the ultimate bargaining chip with which to pressure Hamas, exacerbate tension between Palestinian factions, and cement the West Bank-Gaza split' (Strand, 2014: 18). The Gaza Wars thus clearly served Israel's interests in maintaining the status quo of Israeli military superiority and a long-term interim arrangement that precluded the establishment of a Palestinian state.

Part IV

Assessment

12 Understanding the Arab–Israeli conflict

Patterns, dynamics, evolution and conflict resolution

The Arab–Israeli conflict emerged as one of competing nationalisms laying claim to the same territory: Palestine. Jewish immigration to Palestine beginning at the turn of the century placed Zionists and local Arabs in direct competition with each other. Increased Jewish immigration, land acquisition and institution building became the focus of the early part of the conflict. British mandate policy from 1922 to 1948 exacerbated inter-communal tensions further as it was perceived by both Jews and Arabs to be biased in favour of the other. Dissatisfaction with British rule, as well as mutual suspicion and fear, increasingly led to the use of violence for political ends, while **zero-sum** perceptions of the conflict resulted in the belief that coexistence was impossible.

From the turn of the century until the end of the British mandate the conflict was predominantly a Zionist–Palestinian one with a colonial, international and Arab dimension. The latter influenced the conflict through British and later US policy, Arab support during the Arab Revolt and against the UN partition resolution, but also Arab competition with regard to nation and state building. Upon the expiry of the British mandate, the declaration of the State of Israel and the subsequent attack by Egypt, Jordan, Syria, Lebanon and Iraq, the conflict turned from a civil war into an inter-state war.

The 1948 war set the parameters of the conflict for the next four decades. The Palestinians were displaced, dispersed, marginalized and denied self-determination. They were used as a rhetorical tool by Arab leaders in their competition for regional hegemony. They were controlled politically and militarily to prevent their presence from de-stabilizing states and the region. At the same time, the Arab solidarity with the Palestinians and the 'usefulness' of the Palestinian cause ensured that the Palestinian refugees and the Palestine situation remained at the top of the Arab negotiating agenda. This posed an obstacle to accommodation with Israel as, from an Israeli point of view, the price of peace was too high if it meant Palestinian repatriation.

The 1948 war also left the issues of territory and security unsatisfactorily resolved. Israel had increased its territory, on the one hand gaining relative security, while, on the other hand, confirming Arab suspicions of an Israeli expansionist agenda. In the absence of peace, however, Israel could not achieve real security and thus turned into a garrison state. The Arab refusal to recognize Israel's right to exist and the Arab boycott further increased Israel's perception of isolation.

The final issue raised by the 1948 war is that of the city of Jerusalem. Jerusalem was divided as a result of the war, with the western part falling under Israeli control and the eastern part under Jordanian control. The partitioning of the city and the fact that the main Jewish holy sites were inaccessible gave rise to the Israeli aspiration for a united Jerusalem as the capital of the Jewish State.

The next four Arab–Israeli wars did not change the parameters of the conflict significantly. The 1956 Suez crisis increased Israel's military standing and made it a force to reckon with. While the Arab leaders continued to withhold political recognition from Israel, militarily they acknowledged that Israel was there to stay. The Suez crisis also resulted in Egypt's emergence as leader of the Arab world as Nasser was credited with having expelled the British and French. However, the vacuum left by Britain and France accelerated a process that had already begun after the Second World War, namely the expansion of the Cold War into the Middle East. The introduction of the Cold War framework led to a polarization of the region. It enabled local actors to play the superpowers off against each other in order to extract maximum concessions either politically and economically or in terms of military support. Conversely, it allowed the superpowers to fight proxy wars. Its main impact on the Arab–Israeli conflict as a whole was that it prevented a resolution through military means by repeatedly imposing ceasefires in order to prevent a total victory by one side over the other while, at the same time, further complicating the search for peace.

The 1967 June War boosted the Israeli position through its resounding victory and territorial gains. This increased Israel's security as the added territory provided it with strategic depth. It also provided it with land which could be returned in exchange for a formal peace with full recognition. However, the resounding Arab defeat and loss of territory only resulted in a hardening of the Arab position. Israel's Arab neighbours did not feel that they could negotiate from such a weak position. Instead the West Bank, Gaza, Sinai and Golan Heights became 'Occupied Territories'. Israel's control over this additional territory, in turn, gave rise to a much stronger Israeli political right with a territorial maximalist agenda. It also led to the emergence of a 'religious right' as religious Zionists interpreted the victory as a sign from God that Israel should settle what they saw as 'liberated territory'. The impact of the 1967 June War on the Palestinians was equally considerable. It resulted in another wave of refugees, most of whom ended up in Jordan and Lebanon. The Arab defeat, moreover, allowed the PLO to emancipate itself from the Arab states, reinvigorating Palestinian nationalism and leading to the first post-1948 Palestinian–Israeli confrontations in the West Bank. The PLO's emancipation, its efforts to liberate Palestine and its institution building created challenges for its host states which culminated in the

1970 Black September confrontation with Jordan and contributed to the 1975 Lebanese civil war.

The 1973 October War resulted in one major change: the destruction of Israel's feelings of invincibility which had arisen from the 1967 June War through the successful Syro–Egyptian surprise attack. Egypt's early successes especially levelled the playing field to such an extent that Egypt felt it could enter negotiations and achieve a fair deal. The 1979 Israeli–Egyptian peace agreement removed the Egyptian front from the Arab–Israeli conflict, allowing Sadat to focus on domestic issues and to shift Egypt's Cold War alliance from one with the USSR to one with the United States. The Palestinian refugee situation, Israel's control over the West Bank and Gaza Strip and Israel's overall security, however, remained unresolved as it had never been Begin's intention to cede Israeli control of this territory. The 1973 October War also shifted the Arab–Israeli conflict northwards as Egypt embarked upon disengagement while Asad in Syria entered into an arms race with Israel with the aim of achieving strategic parity and embarked upon a struggle with Israel for hegemony in the Levant.

The 1982 Lebanon War was in many ways the product of this Israeli–Syrian hegemonic struggle. While it failed to achieve peace with Lebanon and remove Syrian influence from Lebanon, it set in motion a number of developments which, in the long run, served to create conditions conducive to negotiations 10 years later. The evacuation of the PLO from Beirut to Tunis deprived the Palestinian resistance of its last border with Israel, thereby 'forcing' it down the diplomatic road. For Israel, the failure to achieve their aims also signalled unequivocally that a resolution to the Arab–Israeli conflict and the Palestinian problem could not be achieved by military force.

The Arab–Israeli conflict as a whole set the parameters for negotiations. Like in many other conflicts, the issues that needed to be addressed were quite clear. For Israel this meant recognition, legitimacy and security, while the Arab states wanted a just solution to the Palestine refugee problem, return of territory and assurances that Israel would not dominate the region politically, militarily or economically. The Palestinians wanted self-determination and statehood. Underlying issues that further needed to be dealt with included Israeli settlements, political violence, prisoners, the status of Jerusalem and water. All of these issues were on the table during the peace negotiations from 1991 to 2000 and some, such as recognition of the State of Israel by the PA and by Jordan were dealt with, while others, such as Palestinian statehood, security for Israel and the Golan Heights, were not satisfactorily addressed.

While all parties to the conflict knew the broad parameters of negotiations, the obstacles to negotiations seemed insurmountable: seven decades of Jewish–Arab relations riddled with mistrust, broken promises, violence, hatred and almost mutually exclusive interpretations of history. The psychological gap between the parties led to an absence of official and direct negotiations during the conflict. This did not, however, mean that contact between the protagonists was absent. Evidence of secret yet unsuccessful negotiations riddles Arab–Israeli history, but Israel and its Arab neighbours were unable and unwilling to make the necessary concessions required for peace.

The search for Arab–Israeli peace since 1948 makes it clear that the conditions may not always have been conducive for negotiations. Suitable conditions for achieving a lasting peace and stability include symmetry between negotiating partners, the recognition that the conflict cannot be resolved through military means, acceptable mediators or facilitators and a window of opportunity often resulting from a change in the conflict environment.

Asymmetry of power and legitimacy between negotiating partners is particularly obvious when looking at Israel and the Palestinians. Having gained statehood in 1948, Israel proceeded to become a regional superpower with every Israeli military victory. The Palestinians as a non-state actor were dispersed, displaced and subject to Arab attempts to control them, as well as Israeli efforts to deny them self-determination. The weakness of the Palestinians defined its national liberation as 'a struggle for attention, redress, and legitimacy, inseparably interwoven with a struggle for the power to pursue those ends' (Zartman, 1989: 7). Recognition of the PLO as the sole legitimate representative became a central issue of the conflict, comprising one dimension against the Israeli state and another dimension against the regional and international environment of the conflict.

Asymmetry also existed on the inter-state Arab–Israeli level. For instance, after the 1967 June War Israel's victory was so resounding that the gap between Israel's power and the Arab states' powerlessness made the conditions unsuitable for negotiations. The Arab and especially Egyptian success during the first week of the 1973 October War, however, narrowed the gap to such an extent that it paved the way for the 1979 Israeli–Egyptian peace.

Yet, symmetry alone does not guarantee successful negotiations. The recognition that a conflict cannot be resolved through military means, effectively creating a stalemate, is also required as an incentive for negotiation and compromise. The Egyptian–Israeli peace was based on such premises. Both Israel and Egypt were aware that war would not lead to a complete destruction of the other, while an absence of war, under the right conditions, would lead to numerous benefits, many of which were indirectly related to the negotiations such as reducing the defence burden or receiving US aid.

Mediators have played a prominent role in bringing about all Arab–Israeli agreements, starting with the 1949 armistices. The lack of recognition of Israel by the Arab states and of the PLO by Israel posed an obstacle to direct negotiations. Third-party mediation served the function initially of communicator and later one of manipulator and formulator. Mediators such as the United States during the 1978 Camp David talks and the 1991–2000 Middle East peace process were thus in a position to put forward their own ideas about possible outcomes as well as to use their leverage over various negotiating partners to provide threats or incentives.

The importance of conducive conditions is obvious when looking at why negotiations were possible between 1993 and 2000 and why they have not been possible since. A window of opportunity emerged as a result of regional and international changes in 1990, most notably the Iraqi invasion of Kuwait and the end of the Cold War. The former created a sense of urgency to resolve the Arab–Israeli conflict as it was a 'festering wound' that fed other conflicts, while the latter removed the dynamic whereby the United States and USSR vetoed resolutions and undermined peace efforts simply because they were on opposing sides in the Cold War. This window of opportunity provided the space for the formal Madrid Conference and Washington talks from 1991 to 1992 and the secret backchannel negotiations in 1992 and 1993 which resulted in the DOP. The success of the backchannel negotiations was the result of four factors: first, they created a semblance of symmetry between Israelis and Palestinians. Second, Palestinian leaders saw violence as having achieved its limits as the 1987 *intifada* petered out. Third, the Norwegians were seen as a credible mediator by both sides. And fourth, the secrecy of these talks reduced the pressure on the negotiators and allowed them to think creatively. Similarly in the 1999–2000 Israeli–Syrian talks, symmetry appeared to have been achieved with the mutual accolades by Barak and Asad, furthered by the understanding that should an agreement be reached, Hizbollah would be contained. Clinton was also seen as a committed, if not honest, broker. Conditions since have changed, and the window of opportunity has disappeared. Both Palestinians and Syria had their fingers burnt in the negotiations; both have been ostracized and marginalized by the international community; the failure of previous talks has given renewed currency to the use of violence and the United States has lost any standing as a neutral facilitator as, since 11 September 2001, it has not just become a regional actor but is seen above all as an aggressor.

As a whole, both the Arab–Israeli conflict and the negotiating experience have been characterized by a refusal to scale back maximum demands, prioritize objectives and a lack of willingness to compromise. The zero-sum approach, however, does not necessarily reflect a genuine incompatibility of the two sides' goals but that their underlying aims often were something other than a negotiated settlement such as gaining US support. For instance, the 1983 Israeli–Lebanese negotiations made it very clear that Lebanon was not interested in peace with Israel but did want to improve its relations with the United States.

The pattern which emerges is one of entrenched positions, dubious motives, poor timing, uninspired leadership and psychological obstacles. It was first broken in 1978 with the Camp David Accords, suggesting that negotiations made under the right conditions could be successful. The 1993 DOP and the 1994 Jordanian–Israeli peace treaty, as well as the 2000 Shepherdstown Israeli–Syrian talks and 2001 Taba Israeli–Palestinian negotiations, show that the gap between the negotiating parties need not be that great and that accommodation can be reached.

At the same time, it must be emphasized that violence continued throughout the peace process and has indeed ruled the day since the outbreak of the second *intifada* in September 2000 as violence has been useful for both

Israelis and Palestinians. Palestinian violence against Israel, which initially provided an exit strategy from the failed Camp David summit in 2000, has been multilayered. It included elements of popular violence alongside organized violence by militants connected to Palestinian leaders Israel has relations with – the PA – and militants connected to Palestinian leaders who seek to destroy the Israeli state – Hamas and PIJ. Popular violence has generally been driven by frustration with the continued Israeli occupation, has been low tech in nature – car rammings, knives, axes, even scissors – and fairly random in nature, thus maximizing the terror effect. This contrasts starkly with the more organized nature, the guns used by Fatah Tanzim and the Hamas suicide bombings during the Al-Aqsa *intifada*, as well as the rockets fired by Hamas and PIJ since Israel's unilateral withdrawal from the Gaza Strip. Palestinian violence has been used to level the playing field with Israel and to erode Israel's will to continue the occupation. This is further complicated by violence against Israel being used for internal Palestinian consolidation interspersed with periods of intra-Palestinian violence for political hegemony such as the battles between Hamas and Fatah in 2007.

The Israeli use of force against the Palestinians since 2000 has been comparatively simpler. Conventional and disproportionate as exemplified by the Gaza Wars between 2006 and 2014 as well as the 2006 Lebanon War, it has been used largely for the containment of Islamist militant groups Israel has no interest in negotiating with: Hamas, PIJ and Hizbollah. It has also been used to manage a conflict and 'park it in an interim solution', thereby keeping the Palestinians divided and preventing the establishment of a viable Palestinian state. It is in this context that the wave of Palestinian violence, which erupted in September 2015 and which has been dubbed the '*intifada of the knives*' by the international media, takes on more strategic significance in the sense that it has succeeded in spreading a feeling of terror and caused a greater loss of life and injuries than the rockets fired from Gaza. Indeed between 13 September and 9 December 2015 alone, according to the Israeli Foreign Ministry, 22 Israelis were killed and another 215 wounded in 90 stabbings, 33 shootings and 14 car rammings. This type of violence has been far less manageable than the challenge by Hamas and, as its geographic focus has been in and around Jerusalem, it has not only shifted the locus of the conflict back to the West Bank, but also into the heart of Israel. At the same time this violence needs to be seen in the context of the PA's and Fatah's strategy, meaning that there is, at least in principle, a negotiating partner. The question then is, for those who see the ripe moment for negotiations starting with a mutually damaging stalemate, whether the pain inflicted on Israel is enough for the government to see negotiations in its interest or whether Israel will continue to pursue a policy of preventing the establishment of a viable Palestinian state, which is very much driven by Israel's ultranationalist and religious right, because it serves its security and indeed its ideological interests.

Part V
Documents

Document 1

From Theodor Herzl's 'The Jewish State'

The Viennese Jewish journalist wrote 'The Jewish State' in 1896 after experiencing the upsurge in anti-Semitism in France in the context of the trial of Alfred Dreyfus.

The Jewish question still exists. It would be foolish to deny it. It is a remnant of the Middle Ages, which civilized nations do not even yet seem able to shake off, try as they will. They certainly showed a generous desire to do so when they emancipated us. The Jewish question exists wherever Jews live in perceptible numbers. Where it does not exist, it is carried by Jews in the course of their migrations. We naturally move to those places where we are not persecuted, and there our presence produces persecution. This is the case in every country, and will remain so, even in those highly civilized – for instance, France – until the Jewish question finds a solution on a political basis. The unfortunate Jews are now carrying the seeds of Anti-Semitism into England; they have already introduced it into America.

I believe that I understand Anti-Semitism, which is really a highly complex movement. I consider it from a Jewish standpoint, yet without fear or hatred. I believe that I can see what elements there are in it of vulgar sport, of common trade jealousy, of inherited prejudice, of religious intolerance, and also of pretended self-defense. I think the Jewish question is no more a social than a religious one, notwithstanding that it sometimes takes these and other forms. It is a national question, which can only be solved by making it a political world-question to be discussed and settled by the civilized nations of the world in council.

We are a people – one people.

We have sincerely tried everywhere to merge with the national communities in which we live, seeking only to preserve the faith of our fathers. It is not permitted us. In vain are we loyal patriots, sometimes superloyal; in vain do we make the same sacrifices of life and property as our fellow citizens; in vain do we strive to enhance the fame of our native lands in the arts and sciences, or her wealth by trade and commerce. In our native lands where we have lived for centuries we are still decried as aliens, often by men whose ancestors had not yet come at a time when Jewish sighs had long been heard in the country . . .

Oppression and persecution cannot exterminate us. No nation on earth has endured such struggles and sufferings as we have. Jew-baiting has merely winnowed out our weaklings; the strong among us defiantly return to their own whenever persecution breaks out . . . Wherever we remain politically secure for any length of time, we assimilate. I think this is not praiseworthy . . .

Palestine is our unforgettable historic homeland . . . Let me repeat once more my opening words: The Jews who will it shall achieve their State. We shall live at last as free men on our own soil, and in our own homes peacefully die. The world will be liberated by our freedom, enriched by our wealth, magnified by our greatness. And whatever we attempt there for our own benefit will redound mightily and beneficially to the good of all mankind.

Source: https://www.jewishvirtuallibrary.org/jsource/
Zionism/herzl2.html

Document 2

From Vladimir Ze'ev Jabotinsky's 'The Iron Wall', 4 November 1923

Russian Jewish journalist Vladimir Ze'ev Jabotinsky wrote 'The Iron Wall' in 1923 after the British Colonial Secretary Winston Churchill prohibited Zionist settlement on the east bank of the Jordan River.

We cannot offer any adequate compensation to the Palestinian Arabs in return for Palestine. And therefore, there is no likelihood of any voluntary agreement being reached. So that all those who regard such an agreement as a condition sine qua non for Zionism may as well say 'non' and withdraw from Zionism.

Zionist colonisation must either stop or else proceed regardless of the native population. Which means that it can proceed and develop only under the protection of a power that is independent of the native population – behind an iron wall, which the native population cannot breach.

That is our Arab policy; not what we should be, but what it actually is, whether we admit it or not. What need, otherwise, of the Balfour Declaration? Or of the Mandate? Their value to us is that outside Power has undertaken to create in the country such conditions of administration and security that if the native population should desire to hinder our work, they will find it impossible.

And we are all of us, without any exception, demanding day after day that this outside Power, should carry out this task vigorously and with determination.

In this matter there is no difference between our 'militarists' and our 'vegetarians'. Except that the first prefer that the iron wall should consist of Jewish soldiers, and the others are content that they should be British.

We all demand that there should be an iron wall. Yet we keep spoiling our own case, by talking about 'agreement' which means telling the Mandatory Government that the important thing is not the iron wall, but discussions. *Empty rhetoric of this kind is dangerous.* And that is why it is not only a pleasure but a duty to discredit it and to demonstrate that it is both fantastic and dishonest.

Source: https://www.jewishvirtuallibrary.org/jsource/Zionism/ironwall.html

Document 3

From the Hussein–McMahon Correspondence

The Hussein–McMahon Correspondence is a series of letters exchanged between the British High Commissioner in Egypt, Sir Henry McMahon, and the Amir of Mecca, Sharif Hussein, in 1915–16. The British pledge to support Arab independence in the area, which the Arabs maintain included Palestine, is contained in these letters.

Letter from McMahon to Sharif Hussein   24 October 1915

. . . it is with great pleasure that I communicate to you on their (HMG) behalf the following statement, which I am confident you will receive with satisfaction:

The two districts of Mersina and Alexandretta and portions of Syria lying to the west of the districts of Damascus, Homs, Hama and Aleppo cannot be said to be purely Arab, and should be excluded from the limits demanded.

With the above modification, and without prejudice to our existing treaties with Arab chiefs, we accept those limits.

As for the regions lying within those frontiers wherein Great Britain is free to act without detriment to the interests of her ally, France, I am empowered in the name of the Government of Great Britain to give the following assurance and make the following reply to your letter:

(1)   Subject to the above modifications, Great Britain is prepared to recognise and support the independence of the Arabs in all regions within the limits demanded by the Sharif of Mecca.

(2)   Great Britain will guarantee the Holy Places against all external aggression and will recognise their inviolability.

Source: Bernard Reich (ed.), *Arab–Israeli Conflict and Conciliation: A Documentary History* (© Praeger, 1995), 19–25.

Document 4

The Balfour Declaration: 2 November 1917

The Balfour Declaration is a letter from Foreign Secretary Arthur Balfour to British Zionist leader Lord Rothschild, supporting the Zionist project in Palestine.

His Majesty's Government view with favour the establishment in Palestine of a national home for the Jewish people, and will use their best endeavours to facilitate the achievement of this object, it being clearly understood that nothing shall be done which may prejudice the civil and religious rights of existing non-Jewish communities in Palestine, or the rights and political status enjoyed by Jews in any other country.

Source: Bernard Reich (ed.), *Arab–Israeli Conflict and Conciliation:*
A Documentary History (© Praeger, 1995), 29.

Document 5

From the Sykes–Picot Agreement

The Sykes–Picot Agreement was negotiated between Sir Mark Sykes and Georges Picot in January 1916 and defines areas of British and French interests in the territory of the disintegrating Ottoman Empire.

Letter from Sir Edward Gray to Paul Cambon   15 May 1916

1. That France and Great Britain are prepared to recognise and protect an independent Arab State or a Confederation of Arab States in the areas (A) and (B) marked on the annexed map, under the suzerainty of an Arab chief. That in area (A) France, and in area (B) Great Britain, shall have priority of right of enterprise and local loans. That in area (A) France, and in area (B) Great Britain, shall alone supply advisers or foreign functionaries at the request of the Arab State or Confederation of States.
2. That in the blue area France, and in the red area Great Britain, shall be allowed to establish such direct or indirect administration or control as they desire and as they may think fit to arrange with the Arab State or Confederation of States.
3. That in the brown area there shall be established an international administration, the form of which is to be decided upon after consultation with Russia, and subsequently in consultation with the other Allies, and the representatives of the Shareef of Mecca.

Source: Bernard Reich (ed.), *Arab–Israeli Conflict and Conciliation:*
A Documentary History (© Praeger, 1995), 27.

Document 6

From the recommendations of the Peel
Commission July 1937

In 1936 a Royal Commission, headed by Lord Peel, was appointed to investigate the cause of the Arab riots. Its report was published in July 1937 and introduced the notion of partition.

... An irrepressible conflict has arisen between the two national communities within the narrow bounds of one small country. About 1,000,000 Arabs are in strife, open or latent, with some 400,000 Jews. There is no common ground between them. The Arab community is predominantly Asiatic in character, the Jewish community predominantly European. They differ in religion and in language. Their cultural and social life, their ways of thought and conduct, are as incompatible as their national aspirations. These last are the greatest bar to peace. Arabs and Jews might possibly learn to live together in Palestine if they would make a genuine effort to reconcile and combine their national ideals and so build up in time a joint or dual nationality. But this they cannot do. The War and its sequel have inspired all Arabs with the hope of reviving in a free and united Arab world the traditions of the Arab golden age. The Jews similarly are inspired by their historic past. They mean to show what the Jewish nation can achieve when restored to the land of its birth. National assimilation between Arabs and Jews is thus ruled out. In the Arab picture the Jews could only occupy the place they occupied in Arab Egypt or Arab Spain. The Arabs would be as much outside the Jewish picture as the Canaanites in the old land of Israel. The National Home, as we have said before, cannot be half-national. In these circumstances to maintain that Palestinian citizenship has any moral meaning is a mischievous pretence. Neither Arab nor Jew has any sense of service to a single state. . . .

Source: Walter Laqueur (ed.), *The Israel-Arab Reader: A Documentary History of the Middle East Conflict* (Bantam Books, 1968), 56–8.

Document 7

From the MacDonald White Paper: 17 May 1939

The MacDonald White Paper marked the shift of British Palestine policy in a pro-Arab direction. By limiting Jewish immigration and land purchases, the British sought to end the Arab Revolt in light of emerging war in Europe.

His Majesty's Government are convinced that in the interests of the peace and well-being of the whole people of Palestine a clear definition of policy and objectives is essential. . . . It has therefore been necessary for His Majesty's Government to devise an alternative policy, which will, consistently with their obligations to Arabs and Jews, meet the need of the situation in Palestine. Their views and proposals are set forth below under the three heads, (I) The Constitution, (II) Immigration, and (III) Land.

I. – The constitution
. . . His Majesty's Government believe that the framers of the Mandate in which the Balfour Declaration was embodied could not have intended that Palestine should be converted into a Jewish State against the will of the Arab population of the country. . . .

II. – Immigration
. . . If immigration has an adverse effect on the economic position in the country, it should clearly be restricted; and equally, if it has a seriously damaging effect on the political position in the country,

that is a factor that should not be ignored. Although it is not difficult to contend that the large number of Jewish immigrants who have been admitted so far have been absorbed economically, the fear of the Arabs that this influx will continue indefinitely until the Jewish population is in a position to dominate them has produced consequences which are extremely grave for Jews and Arabs alike and for the peace and prosperity of Palestine. . . .

(1) Jewish immigration during the next five years will be at a rate which, if economic absorptive capacity permits, will bring the Jewish population up to approximately one-third of the total population . . .

(2) The existing machinery for ascertaining economic absorptive capacity will be retained, and the High Commissioner will have the ultimate responsibility for deciding the limits of economic capacity. Before each periodic decision is taken, Jewish and Arab representatives will be consulted.

(3) After the period of five years no further immigration will be permitted unless the Arabs of Palestine are prepared to acquiesce in it.

(4) His Majesty's Government are determined to check illegal immigration, and further preventive measures are being adopted. The numbers of any Jewish illegal immigrants who, despite these measures, may succeed in coming into the country and cannot be deported will be deducted from the yearly quotas. . . .

III.   – Land

. . . The Reports of several Commissions have indicated that, owing to the natural growth of the Arab population and the steady sale in recent years of Arab land to Jews, there is now in certain areas no room for further transfers of Arab land, whilst in some other areas such transfers of land must be restricted if Arab cultivators are to maintain their existing standard of life and a considerable landless Arab population is not soon to be created. In these circumstances, the High Commissioner will be given general powers to prohibit and regulate transfers of land. . . .

Source: Walter Laqueur (ed.), *The Israel-Arab Reader: A Documentary History of the Middle East Conflict* (Bantam Books, 1968), 64–75.

Document 8

Plan D: 10 March 1948

Plan D, or Dalet, has become one of the most controversial documents of the 1948 war. Israelis have portrayed it as a set of defensive military measures, while Palestinians see it as proof of a systematic strategy of ethnic cleansing.

I. Introduction

A. The purpose conveyed in this program is domination over the area of the Jewish state and the protection of its borders, as well as of the blocs of Jewish settlement and population outside its borders, against a regular, semi-regular, or small enemy – operating from bases either outside or within the territory of the state.
B. This Plan is based upon three Plans which preceded it, namely:
    a) Plan B, September 1945
    b) Plan of May 1946
    c) The Joshua Plan – 1948
C. Concerning the above-mentioned Plans: the first and second were intended for the first stage of the disturbances, within the country; while the third was intended for the event of invasion by regular forces from neighbouring countries; the purpose of Plan D is to complement the three preceding Plans regarding those matters in which they are deficient and to adapt them to the projected situation likely to come about upon the conclusion of British rule over the country.

II. Basic assumptions

The Plan is based upon the following assumptions:

A. The enemy

1. Projected Composition of Forces
    - A semi-regular force of liberation of the Arab League, acting from bases which it has seized thus far, or which it will seize in the future.
    - The regular forces of the neighbouring countries which will invade across the borders or will act from bases within the country (the Arab Legion).
    - Small local forces operating from bases within the country and across the borders of the Hebrew state. All three of these forces will act simultaneously, following – with tactical coordination – a joint operative program more or less strictly.
2. Projected Operative Goals of the Enemy
    - Isolation, and possibly conquest of the Eastern Galilee, the Western Galilee, and the Negev.
    - Deep penetration into the Sharon and the Hefer Valley in the direction of Kalkilya–Herzliya; Tul Karem–Netanya.
    - Isolation of the three major cities (particularly Tel Aviv).
    - Cutting off the supply of vital and other services, such as water, electricity, and sewage.

B. The British government

The program is based upon the general assumption that, at the time of its operation, government forces will no longer be present in the country. In the event that government forces will still be present in certain bases and areas during the operation of this program, the program will need to be adjusted to this situation in those places. Special appendices will follow concerning this.

C. International forces

This program is based upon the assumption that no international force having effective operative power will be present in the country.

D. Our operative goals

1. To defend against invasion by semi-regular and regular forces by:
    - A fixed system of defence, based upon regional defence, on the one hand; and blocking actions against the primary avenues of access of the enemy, from his territory to the territory of the state – on the other; so as to protect our settlements, essential economic enterprises, property, and the operation of government services within the territory of the state.
    - Counter-attacks, organized in advance, against enemy bases and supply lines in the depth of his territory – both within the borders of the country and in neighbouring countries.
2. To assure freedom of movement, both in the military and economic sense, within the territory of the state and in Jewish centres outside it, by conquering and holding key outposts controlling a number of transport arteries.
3. To prevent the enemy from using advance bases within his territory, which are more convenient to him for launching attacks, by conquering and holding them.
4. Economic pressure upon the enemy with the aim of forcing him to halt activities in certain parts of the country – by imposing a siege on particular cities.
5. Reducing the enemy's ability to engage in small actions by the conquest and domination of selected centres, in the countryside and in the city, within the borders of the state.
6. To seize control of government services and properties lying within the boundaries of the state, and to assure the efficient operation of necessary public services.

III. Definition of missions

In accordance with our operative aims, as described above, the following missions are imposed upon the various forces:

a. Strengthening the fixed defense system of the areas and adapting their activities within a district framework. In addition, blocking off the primary avenues of access of the enemy from his territory to the territory of the state, by suitable activities and arrangements.
b. Stabilizing the defense system.
c. Consolidation in large cities.
d. Control of primary national transportation arteries.
e. Siege against some of the enemy cities.
f. Conquest and dominance of the advance bases in the country.
g. Counter-attack, within and beyond the borders of the country.

IV. The mission in detail

A. *The fixed system of defense*

1. A fixed system of defense – within the rural areas – built upon two fundamental factors: the areas protected for circumferential defense – on the one hand; and blocking the primary avenues of access of the enemy – on the other.
2. Regional defense arrangements in the rural areas, at present primarily intended to repel a small enemy, are to be adapted in terms of planning and fortification to the projected tactical methods of a semi-regular or regular enemy, in accordance with the orders to come from the Operational Branch regarding defense and planning of rural areas.

B. *Placement of defense systems*

So as to assure effective action of the fixed defense system, as well as to assure its rear, the following actions will be performed:

1. Seizing police stations.
2. Control of government services and assuring vital services in each district.
3. Protection of secondary transport arteries.
4. Actions against enemy settlements, which are located within or adjacent to our defense system, with the goal of preventing their use as bases for active armed forces.

C. *Consolidation in large cities*

Consolidation in large cities will be performed in accordance with the following lines:

1. Seizure and domination of centres of government services and property (postal centres, telephone, railroad, police stations, ports etc.)
2. Assurance of all essential public services and enterprises.
3. Seizure and domination of all Arab neighbourhoods lying between our central urban area and the urban centre of the Arabs – particularly those neighbourhoods which dominate the avenues of entrance and exit from the cities. The dominance over these neighbourhoods will be carried out in accordance with the lines that were explained in connection with the destruction of the villages. In the event of resistance, the population will be expelled to the central, Arab urban centre.
4. Surrounding the Arab urban centre, cutting off its means of transport, and cessation of its vital services (water, electricity, gas, etc.) insofar as possible.

D. *Domination over principal national transport arteries*

1. Seizing and controlling those objects that dominate the principal transportation arteries of the country, such as police stations, hydraulic stations, etc. These objects will be converted into fortified outposts which

will serve, in accordance with need, as bases for assuring mobility (this activity will be combined, in many cases, with that of seizing police stations in order to stabilize the fixed defense system).

E. Siege against the enemy cities will be conducted according to the following lines:

1. Blocking of transportation arteries leading thereto, by means of mining, blowing up bridges, and a permanent system of ambushes.
2. If necessary, by seizing the outposts which dominate traffic arteries to the enemy cities and fortifying our units over these outposts.
3. Cutting off vital services, such as: electricity, water, and gas – either by activating economic factors or by means of sabotage.
4. Action from the sea against those cities that are likely to receive supplies from the direction of the sea, with the aim of destroying the craft that bring the supplies and sabotaging the routine of the ports.

F. Conquest and domination of advance bases of the enemy

It is not, generally speaking, the goal of this program to conquer the territory outside the borders of the Hebrew State. However, certain enemy bases which are in immediate proximity to the border and which are likely to serve as jumping points for penetration to key areas inside the state will be temporarily conquered and destroyed, in accordance with the lines sketched above, and will, until the completion of actions, be converted into part of our defense system . . .

G. Counter-Attack, within and outside the borders of the country

Counter-attacks will be used as an additional element in the fixed system of defense, in order to halt and to cause organised attacks to fail by semi-regular or regular enemy forces, from bases within the country or from bases beyond the borders. The counter-attacks will be carried out according to the following lines:

1. Attacks to mislead – that is, while an attack is being conducted by the enemy against a certain area of ours, a counter-attack will be waged in the depths of his own territory, in order to distract the enemy forces in the direction of the counter-attack.
2. Attacks against avenues of transport and supply, in the midst of the enemy – primarily aimed against a regular enemy which invades our borders.
3. Attacks against enemy rear bases, whether inside the country or beyond its borders.

Source: Amir Bar-on, 'The evolution of the Army's role in strategic planning', *Israel Studies*, Vol. 1, No. 2, Fall 1996, 110–14.
Courtesy of Indiana University Press.

Document 9

From the declaration of the establishment of the State of Israel: 14 May 1948

Upon the expiration of the Palestine mandate, the Jewish People's Council declared the establishment of the State of Israel in the territory designated by the UN partition resolution.

. . . On the 29th of November 1947, the United Nations General Assembly passed a resolution calling for the establishment of a Jewish state in Eretz – Israel; the General Assembly required the inhabitants of Eretz-Israel to take such steps as were necessary on their part for the implementation of that resolution. This recognition by the United Nations of the right of the Jewish people to establish their State is irrevocable.

This right is the natural right of the Jewish people to be masters of their own fate, like all other nations, in their own sovereign state.

Accordingly we, the members of the National Council, representing the Jewish people in Palestine and the World Zionist Movement, are assembled today, the day of termination of the British Mandate for Palestine; and by virtue of the natural and historic right of the Jewish people and of the Resolution of the General Assembly of the United Nations, we hereby proclaim the establishment of the Jewish State in Palestine to be called Medinath Yisrael (The State of Israel).

Source: Bernard Reich (ed.), Arab–Israeli Conflict and Conciliation:
A Documentary History (© Praeger, 1995), 76–8.

Document 10

From the Cabinet discussions on the Czech arms deal: 4 October 1955

The Czech arms deal was perceived as one of the key signs that Egypt had shifted from non-alignment to a pro-Soviet position. The Cabinet discussions surrounding the arms deal reflect the globalist Cold War approach of Britain towards regional Middle Eastern tensions.

The Foreign Secretary said it was now known that the Egyptian Government had entered into a contract for the purchase of arms from the Soviet bloc. There were also indications that the Russians were making overtures for the supply of arms to Saudi Arabia, Syria and possibly other Arab countries. The implications of these developments were serious. It seemed likely that with the situation in the Far East stabilised and a situation of stalemate in Europe, the Russians were turning their attention to the Middle East. . . .

The Prime Minister said that these developments might seriously affect our interests in the Middle East as a whole. Indeed, the importance of the developments in Egypt lay in their potential effect on the other Arab States. Our interests were greater than those of the United States because of our dependence on Middle East oil, and our experience in the area was greater than theirs. We should not therefore allow ourselves to be restricted over much by reluctance to act without full American concurrence and support. We should frame our policy in the light of our interests in the area and get the Americans to support it to the extent we could induce them to do so. . . .

Source: PRO CAB/128/29, CM34 (55), 4 October.

Document 11

The Sèvres Protocol: 24 October 1956

Between 22 and 24 October, British, French and Israeli representatives met at Sèvres to lay down the plans for the joint Suez–Sinai campaign.

1. The Israeli forces launch in the evening of 29 October 1956 a large-scale attack on the Egyptian forces with the aim of reaching the Canal zone the following day.
2. On being apprised of these events, the British and French Governments during the day of 30 October 1956 respectively and simultaneously make two appeals to the Egyptian Government and the Israeli Government on the following lines:

    (a) To the Egyptian Government
    - (i)   halt all acts of war
    - (ii)   withdraw all its troops ten miles from the Canal
    - (iii) accept temporary occupation of key positions on the Canal by the Anglo-French forces to guarantee freedom of passage through the Canal by vessels of all nations until a final settlement.

    (b) To the Israeli Government
    - (i)   halt all acts of war
    - (ii)   withdraw its troops ten miles to the east of the Canal.

In addition, the Israeli Government will be notified that the French and British Governments have demanded of the Egyptian Government to accept temporary occupation of key positions along the Canal by Anglo-French forces.

It is agreed that if one of the Governments refused, or did not give its consent, within twelve hours the Anglo-French forces would intervene with the means necessary to ensure that their demands are accepted.

    (c) The representatives of the three Governments agree that the Israeli Government will not be required to meet the conditions in the appeal addressed to it, in the event that the Egyptian Government does not accept those in the appeal addressed to it for their part.

3. In the event that the Egyptian Government should fail to agree within the stipulated time to the conditions of the appeal addressed to it, the Anglo–French forces will launch military operations against the Egyptian forces in the early hours of the morning of 31 October.
4. The Israeli Government will send forces to occupy the western shore of the Gulf of Akaba and the group of islands Tiran and Sanafir to ensure freedom of navigation in the Gulf of Akaba.
5. Israel undertakes not to attack Jordan during the period of operations against Egypt. But in the event that during the same period Jordan should attack Israel, the British Government undertakes not to come to the aid of Jordan.
6. The arrangements of the present protocol must remain strictly secret.
7. They will enter into force after the agreement of the three Governments.

Source: Keith Kyle, *Suez* (St. Martin's Press, New York, 1991), 565.

Document 12

From the national covenant of the Palestine Liberation Organization

On 28 May 1964, Ahmad Shukayri, chairman of the first Palestine Congress, proclaimed the establishment of the Palestine Liberation Organization. The PLO's aims were outlined in a 29-article covenant.

Article 1

Palestine is an Arab homeland bound by strong Arab national ties to the rest of the Arab Countries and which together form the large Arab Homeland.

Article 2

Palestine with its boundaries at the time of the British Mandate is a regional indivisible unit.

Article 3

The Palestinian Arab people has the legitimate right to its homeland and is an inseparable part of the Arab Nation. It shares the sufferings and aspirations of the Arab Nation and its struggle for freedom, sovereignty, progress and unity.

Article 4

The people of Palestine determine its destiny when it completes the liberation of its homeland in accordance with its own wishes and free will and choice.

Article 6

The Palestinians are those Arab citizens who were living normally in Palestine up to 1947, whether they remained or were expelled. Every child who was born to a Palestinian parent after this date whether in Palestine or outside is a Palestinian.

Article 7

Jews of Palestinian origin are considered Palestinians if they are willing to live peacefully and loyally in Palestine.

Article 10

Palestinians have three mottoes: National unity, National mobilization, and Liberation. Once liberation is completed, the people of Palestine shall choose for its public life whatever political, economic or social system they want.

Article 11

The Palestinian people firmly believes in Arab unity, and in order to play its role in realizing this goal, it must, at this stage of its struggle preserve its Palestinian personality and all its constituents. It must strengthen the consciousness of its existence and stand against any attempt or plan that may weaken or disintegrate its personality.

Article 12

Arab unity and the liberation of Palestine are two complementary goals; each prepares for the attainment of the other. Arab unity leads to the liberation of Palestine, and the liberation of Palestine leads to Arab unity. Working for both must go side by side.

Article 13

The destiny of the Arab Nation and even the essence of Arab existence are firmly tied to the destiny of the Palestine question. From this firm bond stems the effort and struggle of the Arab Nation to liberate Palestine. The people of Palestine assume a vanguard role in achieving this sacred national goal.

Article 14

The liberation of Palestine from an Arab viewpoint, is a national duty. Its responsibilities fall upon the entire Arab Nation, governments and peoples, the Palestinian people being in the foreground. For this purpose, the Arab Nation must mobilize its military, spiritual and material potentialities; specifically, it must give to the Palestinian Arab people all possible support and backing and place at its disposal all opportunities and means to enable them to perform their role in liberating their homeland.

Article 16

The liberation of Palestine, from an international viewpoint, is a defensive act necessitated by the demands of self-defence as stated in the charter of the United Nations. That is why the people of Palestine, desiring to befriend all nations which love freedom, justice, and peace, look forward to their support in restoring the legitimate situation to Palestine, establishing peace and security in its territory, and enabling its people to exercise national sovereignty and freedom.

Article 17

The partitioning of Palestine in 1947 and the establishment of Israel are illegal and false regardless of the loss of time, because they were contrary to the wish of the Palestine people and its natural right to its homeland, and in violation of the basic principles embodied in the charter of the United Nations, foremost among which is the right to self-determination.

Article 18

The Balfour Declaration, the Mandate system and all that has been based upon them are considered fraud. The claims of historic and spiritual ties between Jews and Palestine are not in Agreement with the facts of history or with the true basis of sound statehood. Judaism because it is a divine religion is not a nationality with independent existence. Furthermore the Jews are not one people with an independent personality because they are citizens of the countries to which they belong.

Article 19

Zionism is a colonialist movement in its inception, aggressive and expansionist in its goals, racist and segregationist in its configuration and fascist in its means and aims. Israel in its capacity as the spearhead of this destructive movement and the pillar for colonialism is a permanent source of tension and turmoil in the Middle East in particular and to the international community in general. Because of this the people of Palestine is worthy of the support and sustenance of the community of nations.

Source: Bernard Reich (ed.), Arab–Israeli Conflict and Conciliation:
A Documentary History (© Praeger, 1995), 93–6.

Document 13

UNSC Resolution 242: 22 November 1967

Following the Six Day War, the United Nations Security Council adopted a British-sponsored resolution aimed at solving the Arab–Israeli conflict.

The Security Council,

Expressing its continuing concern with the grave situation in the Middle East,

Emphasizing the inadmissibility of the acquisition of territory by war and the need to work for a just and lasting peace in which every State in the area can live in security,

Emphasizing further that all Member States in their acceptance of the Charter of the United Nations have undertaken a commitment to act in accordance with Article 2 of the Charter,

1. Affirms that the fulfilment of Charter principles requires the establishment of a just and lasting peace in the Middle East which should include the application of both the following principles:
2. 1. (i) Withdrawal of Israeli armed forces from territories occupied in the recent conflict; (ii) Termination of all claims or states of belligerency and respect for and acknowledgement of the sovereignty, territorial integrity and political independence of every State in the area and their right to live in peace within secure and recognised boundaries free from threats or acts of force; 2. Affirms further the necessity (a) For guaranteeing freedom of navigation through international waterways in the area; (b) For achieving a just settlement of the refugee problem; (c) For guaranteeing the territorial inviolability and political independence of every State in the area, through measures including the establishment of demilitarized zones; 3. Requests the Secretary-General to designate a Special Representative to proceed to the Middle East to establish and maintain contacts with the States concerned in order to promote agreement and assist efforts to achieve a peaceful and accepted settlement in accordance with the provisions and principles in this resolution; 4. Requests the Secretary-General to report to the Security Council on the progress of the efforts of the Special Representative as soon as possible.

Source: Bernard Reich (ed.), *Arab–Israeli Conflict and Conciliation:*
A Documentary History (© Praeger, 1995), 101–2.

Document 14

From the Khartoum summit: 1 September 1967

Following the Six Day War, the Arab states established the framework for policy vis-à-vis Israel, the conflict and the territories occupied by Israel during the war.

... The Arab heads of state have agreed to unite their political efforts on the international and diplomatic level to eliminate the effects of the aggression and to ensure the withdrawal of the aggressive Israeli forces from the Arab lands which have been occupied since the 5 June aggression. This will be done within the framework of the main principle to which the Arab states adhere, namely: no peace with Israel, no recognition of Israel, no negotiations with it, and adherence to the rights of the Palestinian people in their country.

Source: Bernard Reich (ed.), *Arab–Israeli Conflict and Conciliation: A Documentary History* (© Praeger, 1995), 101.

Document 15

UNSC Resolution 338: 22 October 1973

Following the 1973 October War, the United Nations Security Council adopted Resolution 338 which called for a ceasefire as well as implementation of UNSC Resolution 242.

The Security Council

1. Calls upon all parties to the present fighting to cease all firing and terminate all military activity immediately, no later than 12 hours after the moment of the adoption of this decision, in the positions they now occupy;
2. Calls upon the parties concerned to start immediately after the cease-fire the implementation of Security Council resolution 242 (1967) in all of its parts;
3. Decides that, immediately and concurrently with the cease-fire, negotiations start between the parties concerned under appropriate auspices aimed at establishing a just and durable peace in the Middle East.

Source: Bernard Reich (ed.), *Arab–Israeli Conflict and Conciliation: A Documentary History* (© Praeger, 1995), 116.

Document 16

From Sadat's announcement to the Egyptian National Assembly: 9 November 1977

On 9 November 1977 Egyptian President Anwar Sadat announced to the Egyptian Parliament that he was willing to go to Israel to make peace. This was followed by the Israeli government's invitation and Sadat's unprecedented visit to Jerusalem on November 19th.

. . . I say this frankly, in your presence, to our people, to the Arab nation and to the whole world. We are ready to go to Geneva and to sit down on behalf of peace regardless of all the procedural problems raised by Israel in the hope of spoiling our chances or of exasperating us that we say, as we have done in the past, No, we do not want to go and we shall not go, so that she may appear to the world as the advocate of peace . . .

. . . I am ready to go to Geneva – and I do not conceal this from you who are the representatives of the people and I say it in the hearing of our people and of the Arab nation. You heard me saying that I am prepared to go to the ends of this earth if my doing so will prevent any of my officers or men being killed or wounded. I really am ready to go to the ends of the earth and Israel will be amazed to hear me say that we do not refuse – I am prepared to go to their very home, to the Knesset itself and discuss things with them . . .

Source: Bernard Reich (ed.), *Arab–Israeli Conflict and Conciliation:*
A Documentary History (© Praeger, 1995), 143–4.

Document 17

From the Camp David Accords: 17 September 1978

In September 1978 Egyptian President Anwar Sadat, Israeli Prime Minister Menachem Begin and US President Jimmy Carter held a series of meetings at Camp David which resulted in the so-called Camp David Accords. These accords provided a framework for future negotiations as well as for an Israeli–Egyptian peace treaty.

Framework for peace in the Middle East

. . . To achieve a relationship of peace, in the spirit of Article 2 of the United Nations Charter, future negotiations between Israel and any neighbour prepared to negotiate peace and security with it, are necessary for the purpose of carrying out all the provisions and principles of Resolutions 242 and 338.

Peace requires respect for the sovereignty, territorial integrity and political independence of every state in the area and their right to live in peace within secure and recognized boundaries free from threats or acts of force. Progress toward that goal can accelerate movement toward a new era of reconciliation in the Middle East marked by cooperation in promoting economic development, in maintaining stability, and in assuring security.

Security is enhanced by a relationship of peace and by cooperation between nations which enjoy normal relations. In addition, under the terms of peace treaties, the parties can, on the basis of reciprocity, agree to special security arrangements such as demilitarized zones, limited armament areas, early warning stations, the presence of international forces, liaisons, agreed measures for monitoring, and other arrangements that they agree are useful. . . .

Taking these factors into account, the parties are determined to reach a just, comprehensive, and durable settlement of the Middle East conflict through the conclusion of peace treaties based on Security Council Resolutions 242 and 338 in all their parts. Their purpose is to achieve peace and good neighbourly relations. They recognize that, for peace to endure, it must involve all those who have been most deeply affected by the conflict. They therefore agree for peace not only between Egypt and Israel, but also between Israel and each of its other neighbours which is prepared to negotiate peace with Israel on this basis. . . .

Framework for the conclusion of a peace treaty between Egypt and Israel

In order to achieve peace between them, Israel and Egypt agree to negotiate in good faith with a goal of concluding within three months of the signing of this framework a peace treaty between them:

It is agreed that: The site of negotiations will be under a United Nations flag at a location or locations mutually agreed.

All of the principles of UN resolution 242 will apply in this resolution of the dispute between Israel and Egypt. Unless otherwise mutually agreed, terms of the peace treaty will be implemented between two and three years after the peace treaty is signed. The following matters are agreed between the parties:

(1) the full exercise of Egyptian sovereignty up to the internationally recognized border between Egypt and mandated Palestine;
(2) the withdrawal of Israeli armed forces from the Sinai;
(3) the use of airfields left by the Israelis near Al-Arish, Rafah, Ras en-Naqb, and Sharm el-Sheikh for civilian purposes only, including possible commercial use only by all nations;
(4) the right of free passage by ships of Israel through the Gulf of Suez and the Suez Canal on the basis of the Constantinople Convention of 1888 applying to all nations; the Strait of Tiran and Gulf of Aqaba are international waterways to be open to all nations for unimpeded and nonsuspendable freedom of navigation and overflight;
(5) the construction of a highway between the Sinai and Jordan; and
(6) the stationing of military forces listed below.

. . . After a peace treaty is signed, and after the interim withdrawal is complete, normal relations will be established between Egypt and Israel, including full recognition, including diplomatic, economic and cultural relations; termination of economic boycotts and barriers to the free movement of goods and people; and mutual protection of citizens by due process of law.

Source: Bernard Reich (ed.), *Arab–Israeli Conflict and Conciliation: A Documentary History* (© Praeger, 1995), 146–54.

Document 18

From the Reagan Fresh Start Initiative: 1 September 1982

In the wake of Israel's invasion of Lebanon, the United States put forward a set of proposals to achieve a just and lasting peace known as the Fresh Start Initiative.

... The Lebanon War, tragic as it was, has left us with a new opportunity for Middle East peace. We must seize it now and bring peace to this troubled area so vital to world stability while there is still time. It was with this strong conviction that over a month ago, before the present negotiations in Beirut have been completed, I directed Secretary of State Shultz to again review our policy and to consult a wide range of outstanding Americans on the best ways to strengthen chances for peace in the Middle East. ...

But the opportunities for peace do not begin and end in Lebanon. As we help Lebanon rebuild, we must also move to resolve the root causes of conflict between Arabs and Israelis. The war in Lebanon has demonstrated many things, but two consequences are key to the peace process:

First, the military losses of the PLO have not diminished the yearning of the Palestinian people for a just solution of their claims; and

Second, while Israel's military successes in Lebanon have demonstrated that its armed forces are second to none in the region, they alone cannot bring just and lasting peace to Israel and its neighbours.

... So tonight I am calling for a fresh start. This is the moment for all those directly concerned to get involved – or lend their support – to a workable basis for peace. The Camp David agreement remains the foundation of our policy. Its language provides all parties with the leeway they need for successful negotiations.

I call on Israel to make clear that the security for which she yearns can only be achieved through genuine peace, a peace requiring magnanimity, vision, and courage.

I call on the Palestinian people to recognise that their own political aspirations are inextricably bound to recognition of Israel's right to a secure future.

And I call on the Arab states to accept the reality of Israel and the reality that peace and justice are to be gained only through hard, fair, direct negotiation. ...

Source: Bernard Reich (ed.), *Arab–Israeli Conflict and Conciliation: A Documentary History* (© Praeger, 1995), 175–9.

Document 19

From the Fez Peace Plan: 9 September 1982

In reaction to Reagan's Fresh Start Initiative, the Arab states put forward the Fez Peace Plan at the Arab summit meeting in Fez, Morocco.

... Out of the conference's belief in the ability of the Arab nation to achieve its legitimate objectives and eliminate the aggression, and out of the principles and basis laid down by the Arab summit conferences, and out of the Arab countries' determination to continue to work by all means for the establishment of peace based on justice in the Middle East and using the plan of President Habib Bourguiba, which is based on international legitimacy, as the foundation for solving the Palestinian question and the plan of His Majesty King Fahd ibn Abd al-Aziz which deals with peace in the Middle East, and in light of the discussions and notes made by their majesties, excellencies and highnesses the kings, presidents and emirs, the conference decided to adopt the following principles:

1. The withdrawal of Israel from all Arab territories occupied in 1967 including Arab al-Kuds (Jerusalem)
2. The dismantling of settlements established by Israel on territories after 1967
3. The guarantee of freedom of worship and practice of religious rites for all religions in the holy shrines
4. The reaffirmation of the Palestinian people's right to self-determination and the exercise of its imprescriptible and inalienable national rights under the leadership of the Palestine Liberation Organisation, its sole and legitimate representative, and the indemnification of all those who do not desire to return
5. Placing the West Bank and the Gaza Strip under the control of the UN for a transitory period not exceeding a few months
6. The establishment of an independent Palestinian state with al-Kuds as its capital
7. The Security Council guarantees peace among all states of the region including the independent Palestinian state
8. The Security Council guarantees the respect of these principles.

Source: Bernard Reich (ed.), *Arab–Israeli Conflict and Conciliation:*
A Documentary History (© Praeger, 1995), 179–80.

Document 20

From the Israel–Lebanon agreement: 17 May 1983

Following the 1982 Israeli invasion of Lebanon, the United States tried to broker a peace treaty between the two states. The 17 May agreement fell short of both Israeli and Lebanese requirements and was unilaterally abrogated by Lebanon in 1984.

Article 1.

1. The Parties agree and undertake to respect the sovereignty, political independence and territorial integrity of each other. They consider the existing international boundary between Israel and Lebanon inviolable. 2. The Parties confirm that the state of war between Israel and Lebanon has been terminated and no longer exists. 3. Taking into account the provisions of paragraphs 1 and 2, Israel undertakes to withdraw all its armed forces from Lebanon in accordance with the Annex of the present Agreement.

Article 4.

1. The territory of each Party will not be used as a base for hostile or terrorist activity against the other Party, its territory, or its people. 2. Each
   Party will prevent the existence or organisation of irregular forces, armed
   bands, organisations, bases, offices or infrastructure, the aims and purposes of which include incursions or any act of terrorism into the territory of the other Party, or any other activity aimed at threatening or
   endangering the security of the other Party and safety of its people. To
   this end all agreements and arrangements enabling the presence and func-
   tioning on the territory of either Party of elements hostile to the other
   party are null and void. 3. Without prejudice to the inherent right of
   self-defence in accordance with international law, each Party will refrain:
   a. from organising, instigating, assisting, or participating in threats or
   acts of belligerency, subversion, or incitement or any aggression directed
   against the other Party, its population or property, both within its territory and originating therefrom, or in the territory of the other Party; b.
   from using the territory of a third state; c. from intervening in the internal
   or external affairs of the other Party. 4. Each Party undertakes to ensure
   that preventive action and due proceedings will be taken against persons
   or organisations perpetrating acts in violation of this Article.

Source: Bernard Reich (ed.), Arab–Israeli Conflict and Conciliation:
A Documentary History (© Praeger, 1995), 187–91.

Document 21

The Amman Agreement, or Hussein–Arafat Accord: 11 February 1985

*On 11 February, King Hussein and Yasser Arafat signed an accord in order
to create momentum for resolving the Palestine problem. The PLO's refusal
to accept UN Resolutions 242 and 338 as a basis for negotiation, however,
led to a breakdown in Jordanian–Palestinian relations on 19 February 1986.*

The Government of the Hashemite Kingdom of Jordan and the Palestine
Liberation Organisation have agreed to march together towards the realisation of a just and peaceful settlement of the Middle East problem and to put
an end to the Israeli occupation of the Arab Occupied Territories, including
Jerusalem, in accordance with the following principles:

1. Land in exchange for peace as cited in the UN resolutions, including the
   Security Council resolutions.
2. The Palestinian people's right to self-determination. The Palestinians
   will be able to exercise their inalienable right to self-determination
   when the Jordanians and Palestinians manage to achieve this within
   the framework of an Arab Confederation that it is intended to establish
   between the two states of Jordan and Palestine.

3. Solving the Palestinian refugee problem in accordance with the UN resolutions.
4. Solving all aspects of the Palestine question.
5. Based on this, peace negotiations should be held within the framework of an international conference to be attended by the five UN Security Council permanent member states and all parties to the conflict, including the PLO, which is the Palestinian people's sole legitimate representative, within a joint delegation – a joint Jordanian–Palestinian delegation.

Source: Bernard Reich (ed.), Arab–Israeli Conflict and Conciliation:
A Documentary History (© Praeger, 1995), 194–5.

Document 22

Jordan relinquishes its claim to the West Bank:
31 July 1988

In a televised speech, King Hussein of Jordan declared that he was renouncing Jordan's claim to the West Bank, which had been annexed in 1950 but had come under Israeli occupation in 1967.

. . . The relationship of the West Bank with the Hashemite Kingdom of Jordan in light of the PLO's call for the establishment of an independent Palestinian state, can be confined to two considerations. First, the principled consideration pertaining to the issue of Arab unity as a pan-Arab aim, to which the hearts of the Arab peoples aspire and which they want to achieve. Second, the political consideration pertaining to the extent of the Palestinian struggle's gain from the continuation of the legal relationship of the Kingdom's two banks. Our answer to the question now stems from these two considerations and the background of the clear-cut and firm Jordanian position toward the Palestine question, as we have shown.

Regarding the principle consideration, Arab unity between any two or more countries is an option of any Arab people. This is what we believe. Accordingly, we responded to the wish of the Palestinian people's representatives for unity with Jordan in 1950. From this premise, we respect the wish of the PLO, the sole and legitimate representative of the Palestinian people, to secede from us as an independent Palestinian state.

Source: Bernard Reich (ed.), Arab–Israeli Conflict and Conciliation:
A Documentary History (© Praeger, 1995), 199–203.

Document 23

From the Hamas Charter: 18 August 1988

The Islamic Resistance Movement Hamas was created on 14 December 1987. Its aim is the establishment of an Islamic state in all of Palestine through Jihad.

Article 1

The Islamic Resistance Movement draws its guidelines from Islam; derives from it its thinking, interpretations and views about existence, life and humanity; refers back to it for its conduct; and is inspired by it in whatever step it takes.

Article 6

The Islamic Resistance Movement is a distinct Palestinian Movement which owes its loyalty to Allah, derives from Islam its way of life and strives to raise the banner of Allah over every inch of Palestine. Only under the shadow of Islam could the members of all regions coexist in safety and security for their lives, properties and rights. In the absence of Islam, conflict arises, oppression reigns, corruption is rampant and struggles and wars prevail . . .

Article 10

The Islamic Resistance Movement, while breaking its own path, will do its utmost to constitute at the same time a support to the weak, a defense to all the oppressed. It will spare no effort to implement the truth and abolish evil, in speech and in fact, both here and in any other location where it can reach out and exert influence.

Article 11

The Islamic Resistance Movement believes that the land of Palestine has been an Islamic Waqf throughout the generations and until the Day of Resurrection, no one can renounce it or part of it, or abandon it or part of it. No Arab country nor the aggregate of all Arab countries, and no Arab King or President nor all of them in the aggregate, have that right, nor has that right any organisation or the aggregate of all organisations, be they Palestinian or Arab. . . .

Article 13

Initiatives, the so-called peaceful solutions, and the international conferences to resolve the Palestine problem, are all contrary to the beliefs of the Islamic Resistance Movement. For renouncing any part of Palestine means renouncing part of the religion; the nationalism of the Islamic Resistance Movement is part of its faith, the movement educates its members to adhere to its principles and to raise the banner of Allah over their homeland as they fight their Jihad. . . .

Source: Bernard Reich (ed.), *Arab–Israeli Conflict and Conciliation: A Documentary History* (© Praeger, 1995), 203–12.

Document 24

Palestinian declaration of independence:
15 November 1988

At the height of the intifada, and following Jordan's renunciation of its claim to the West Bank, PLO Chairman Yasser Arafat declared the establishment of an independent State of Palestine at the Palestine National Council in Algiers.

In the name of God, the Compassionate, the Merciful.

Palestine, the land of the three monotheistic faiths, is where the Palestinian Arab people was born, on which it grew, developed, and excelled. The Palestinian people was never separated from or diminished in its integral bonds with Palestine. Thus the Palestinian Arab people ensured for itself an everlasting union between itself, its land, and its history. . . .

When in the course of modern times a new order of values was declared with norms and values fair for all, it was the Palestinian Arab people that had been excluded from the destiny of all other peoples by a hostile array of local and foreign powers. Yet again had unaided justice been revealed as insufficient to drive the world's history along its preferred course. . . .

Despite the historical injustice inflicted on the Palestinian Arab people resulting in their dispersion and depriving them of their right to self-determination, following UN General Assembly Resolution 181 (1947), which partitioned Palestine into two states, one Arab, one Jewish, yet it is this resolution that still provides these conditions of international legitimacy that ensure the right of the Palestinian Arab people to sovereignty and national independence. . . .

Now by virtue of natural, historical, and legal rights and the sacrifices of successive generations who gave of themselves in defense of the freedom and independence of their homeland;

. . . The Palestine National Council, in the name of God, and in the name of the Palestinian Arab people, hereby proclaims the establishment of the State of Palestine on our Palestinian territory with its capital Jerusalem.

The State of Palestine is the state of Palestinians wherever they may be. The state is for them to enjoy in it their collective national and cultural identity, theirs to pursue in it a complete equality of rights. In it will be safeguarded their political and religious convictions and their human dignity by means of a parliamentary democratic system of governance, itself based on freedom of expression and the freedom to form parties. The rights of minorities will be duly respected by the majority, as minorities must abide by decisions of the majority. Governance will be based on principles of social justice, equality and nondiscrimination in public rights on grounds of race, religion, color, or sex under the aegis of a constitution which ensures the role of law and an independent judiciary. Thus all these principles shall

allow no departure from Palestine's age-old spiritual and civilizational herit-
age of tolerance and religious co-existence. . . .

Source: Bernard Reich (ed.), *Arab–Israeli Conflict and Conciliation:*
A Documentary History (© Praeger, 1995), 213–17.

Document 25

Madrid conference letter of invitation: 18 October 1991

The 1990–91 Gulf War opened a window of opportunity for resolving con-
flict in the Middle East. Israel, Jordan, Lebanon, Syria and the Palestinians
were invited to an international peace conference in Madrid, which set up
the framework for further negotiations.

After extensive consultations with Arab states, Israel and the Palestinians,
the United States and the Soviet Union believe that an historic opportunity
exists to advance the prospects for genuine peace throughout the region.
The United States and the Soviet Union are prepared to assist the parties
to achieve a just, lasting and comprehensive peace settlement, through
direct negotiations along two tracks, between Israel and the Arab states,
and between Israel and the Palestinians, based on United Nations Security
Council Resolutions 242 and 338. The objective of this process is real
peace.

Toward that end, the president of the US and the president of the USSR
invite you to a peace conference, which their countries will co-sponsor, followed immediately by direct negotiations. The conference will be convened
in Madrid on October 30, 1991.

. . . Direct bilateral negotiations will begin four days after the opening
of the conference. Those parties who wish to attend multilateral negotiations will convene two weeks after the opening of the conference to organise
those negotiations. The co-sponsors believe that those negotiations should
focus on region-wide issues of water, refugee issues, environment, economic
development, and other subjects of mutual interest.

The co-sponsors will chair the conference, which will be held at ministerial level. Governments to be invited include Israel, Syria, Lebanon and
Jordan. Palestinians will be invited and attend as part of a joint Jordanian–
Palestinian delegation. Egypt will be invited to the conference as a participant. The European Community will be a participant in the conference,
alongside the United States and the Soviet Union and will be represented
by its presidency. The Gulf Cooperation Council will be invited to send its
secretary-general to the conference as an observer, and GCC member states
will be invited to participate in organising the negotiations on multilateral
issues. The United Nations will be invited to send an observer, representing
the secretary-general.

The conference will have no power to impose solutions on the parties or
veto agreements reached by them. It will have no authority to make decisions

for the parties and no ability to vote on issues of results. The conference can reconvene only with the consent of all parties. . . .

Source: Bernard Reich (ed.), *Arab–Israeli Conflict and Conciliation:
A Documentary History* (© Praeger, 1995), 226–8.

Document 26

From the Declaration of Principles: 9 September 1993

Months of secret negotiations in Norway culminated in the signing of the first Israeli–Palestinian agreement known as the Declaration of Principles, or Oslo (I) Accords.

The Government of the State of Israel and PLO team . . . representing the Palestinian people, agree that it is time to put an end to decades of confrontation and conflict, recognize their mutual legitimate and political rights, and strive to live in peaceful coexistence and mutual dignity and security and achieve a just, lasting and comprehensive peace settlement and historic reconciliation through the agreed political process. Accordingly, the two sides agree to the following principles:

Article 1.

> The aim of the Israeli–Palestinian negotiations within the current Middle East peace process is, among other things, to establish a Palestinian Interim Self–Government Authority, the elected Council for the Palestinian people in the West Bank and the Gaza Strip, for a transitional period not exceeding five years, leading to permanent settlement based on Security Council Resolutions 242 and 338.
> It is understood that the interim arrangements are an integral part of the whole peace process and that the negotiations on the permanent status will lead to the implementation of Security Council Resolution 242 and 338.

Article 2.

> The agreed framework for the interim period is set forth in this Declaration of Principles.

Article 3. Elections

1. In order that the Palestinian people in the West Bank and Gaza Strip may govern themselves according to democratic principles, direct, free and general political elections will be held for the Council under agreed supervision and international observation, while the Palestinian police will ensure public order.

2. An agreement will be concluded on the exact mode and conditions of the elections in accordance with the protocol attached to Annex I, with the goal of holding the elections not later than nine months after the entry into force of this Declaration of Principles.
3. These elections will constitute a significant interim preparatory step toward the realisation of the legitimate rights of the Palestinian people and their just requirements.

Article 4. Jurisdiction

Jurisdiction of the Council will cover West Bank and Gaza territory, except for issues that will be negotiated in the permanent status negotiations. The two sides view the West Bank and Gaza Strip as a single territorial unit, whose integrity will be preserved during the interim period.

Article 5. Transitional period and permanent status negotiations

1. The five-year transitional period will begin upon the withdrawal from the Gaza Strip and Jericho area.
2. Permanent status negotiations will commence as soon as possible, but not later than the beginning of the third year of the interim period, between the Government of Israel and the Palestinian people representatives.
3. It is understood that these negotiations shall cover remaining issues, including: Jerusalem, refugees, settlements, security arrangements, borders, relations and cooperation with other neighbours, and other issues of common interest.
4. The two parties agree that the outcome of the permanent status negotiations should not be prejudiced or preempted by agreements reached for the interim period.

Source: Bernard Reich (ed.), *Arab–Israeli Conflict and Conciliation: A Documentary History* (© Praeger, 1995), 230–4.

Document 27

Israeli–Jordanian Peace Agreement: 26 October 1994

On 26 October 1994, Jordanian Prime Minister Abdul–Salam Majali and Israeli Prime Minister Itzhak Rabin met in the Jordan Valley to sign the Israeli–Jordanian Peace Agreement.

Article 1. Establishment of peace.

Peace is hereby established between the State of Israel and the Hashemite Kingdom of Jordan (the Parties) effective from the exchange of the instruments of ratification of this Treaty.

Article 2. General principles.

The Parties will apply between them the provisions of the Charter of the United Nations and the principles of international law governing relations among states in times of peace. In particular: 1. They recognise and will respect each other's sovereignty, territorial integrity and political independence; 2. They recognise and will respect each other's right to live in peace within secure and recognised boundaries; 3. They will develop good neighbourly relations of co-operation between them to ensure lasting security, will refrain from the threat or use of force against each other and will settle all disputes between them by peaceful means; . . .

Article 4. Security.

1.a. Both Parties, acknowledging that mutual understanding and cooperation in security-related matters will form a significant part of their relations and will further enhance the security of the region, take upon themselves to base their security relations on mutual trust, advancement of joint interests and co-operation, and to aim towards a regional framework of partnership in peace. . . . 2. The obligations referred to in this Article are without prejudice to the inherent right of self-defence in accordance with the United Nations Charter. 3. The Parties undertake, in accordance with the provisions of this Article, the following: a. to refrain from the threat or use of force or weapons, conventional, non-conventional or of any other kind, against each other, or of other actions or activities that adversely affect the security of the other Party; b. to refrain from organising, instigating, inciting, assisting or participating in acts or threats of belligerency, hostility, subversion or violence against the other Party; c. to take necessary and effective measures to ensure that acts or threats of belligerency, hostility, subversion or violence against the other Party do not originate from, are not committed within, through or over their territory. . . .

Article 7. Economic relations.

1. Viewing economic development and prosperity as pillars of peace, security and harmonious relations between states, peoples and individual human beings, the Parties, taking note of understandings reached between them, affirm their mutual desire to promote economic co-operation between them, as well as within the framework of wider regional economic cooperation. 2. In order to accomplish this goal, the Parties agree to the following: a. to remove all discriminatory barriers to normal economic relations, to terminate economic boycotts directed at each other, and to co-operate in terminating boycotts directed against either Party by third parties; b. recognising that the principle

of free and unimpeded flow of goods and services should guide their relations, the Parties will enter into negotiations with a view to concluding agreements on economic co-operation, including trade and the establishment of a free trade area, investment, banking, industrial co-operation and labour, for the purpose of promoting beneficial economic relations . . .

Source: Bernard Reich (ed.), *Arab–Israeli Conflict and Conciliation:*
A Documentary History (© Praeger, 1995), 263–73.

Document 28

A performance-based roadmap to a permanent two-state solution to the Israeli–Palestinian conflict

In July 2002 the Quartet put together the so-called Roadmap. However, it was not until the appointment of Mahmoud Abbas as Palestinian prime minister in April 2003 that it was officially initiated. The Roadmap was a performance-based plan in three phases, which ultimately envisaged a safe and secure Israel coexisting with a viable, sovereign and democratic Palestine.

The following is a performance-based and goal-driven roadmap, with clear phases, timelines, target dates, and benchmarks aiming at progress through reciprocal steps by the two parties in the political, security, economic, humanitarian, and institution-building fields, under the auspices of the Quartet [the United States, European Union, United Nations, and Russia]. The destination is a final and comprehensive settlement of the Israel-Palestinian conflict by 2005, as presented in President Bush's speech of 24 June, and welcomed by the EU, Russia and the UN in the 16 July and 17 September Quartet Ministerial statements.

A two-state solution to the Israeli-Palestinian conflict will only be achieved through an end to violence and terrorism, when the Palestinian people have a leadership acting decisively against terror and willing and able to build a practicing democracy based on tolerance and liberty, and through Israel's readiness to do what is necessary for a democratic Palestinian state to be established, and a clear, unambiguous acceptance by both parties of the goal of a negotiated settlement as described below. The Quartet will assist and facilitate implementation of the plan, starting in Phase I, including direct discussions between the parties as required. The plan establishes a realistic timeline for implementation. However, as a performance-based plan, progress will require and depend upon the good faith efforts of the parties, and their compliance with each of the obligations outlined below. Should the parties perform their obligations rapidly, progress within and through the phases may come sooner than indicated in the plan. Non-compliance with obligations will impede progress.

A settlement, negotiated between the parties, will result in the emergence of an independent, democratic, and viable Palestinian state living side by side in peace and security with Israel and its other neighbors. The settlement will resolve the Israel-Palestinian conflict, and end the occupation that began in 1967, based on the foundations of the Madrid Conference, the principle of land for peace, UNSCRs 242, 338 and 1397, agreements previously reached by the parties, and the initiative of Saudi Crown Prince Abdullah – endorsed by the Beirut Arab League Summit – calling for acceptance of Israel as a neighbor living in peace and security, in the context of a comprehensive settlement. This initiative is a vital element of international efforts to promote a comprehensive peace on all tracks, including the Syrian-Israeli and Lebanese-Israeli tracks.

The Quartet will meet regularly at senior levels to evaluate the parties' performance on implementation of the plan. In each phase, the parties are expected to perform their obligations in parallel, unless otherwise indicated.

Phase I: Ending terror and violence, normalizing Palestinian life, and building Palestinian institutions – Present to May 2003

In Phase I, the Palestinians immediately undertake an unconditional cessation of violence according to the steps outlined below; such action should be accompanied by supportive measures undertaken by Israel. Palestinians and Israelis resume security cooperation based on the Tenet work plan to end violence, terrorism, and incitement through restructured and effective Palestinian security services. Palestinians undertake comprehensive political reform in preparation for statehood, including drafting a Palestinian constitution, and free, fair and open elections upon the basis of those measures. Israel takes all necessary steps to help normalize Palestinian life. Israel withdraws from Palestinian areas occupied from September 28, 2000 and the two sides restore the status quo that existed at that time, as security performance and cooperation progress. Israel also freezes all settlement activity, consistent with the Mitchell report.

At the outset of Phase I:

- Palestinian leadership issues unequivocal statement reiterating Israel's right to exist in peace and security and calling for an immediate and unconditional ceasefire to end armed activity and all acts of violence against Israelis anywhere. All official Palestinian institutions end incitement against Israel.
- Israeli leadership issues unequivocal statement affirming its commitment to the two-state vision of an independent, viable, sovereign Palestinian state living in peace and security alongside Israel, as expressed by President Bush, and calling for an immediate end to violence against Palestinians everywhere. All official Israeli institutions end incitement against Palestinians.

Security

- Palestinians declare an unequivocal end to violence and terrorism and undertake visible efforts on the ground to arrest, disrupt, and restrain individuals and groups conducting and planning violent attacks on Israelis anywhere.
- Rebuilt and refocused Palestinian Authority security apparatus begins sustained, targeted, and effective operations aimed at confronting all those engaged in terror and dismantlement of terrorist capabilities and infrastructure. This includes commencing confiscation of illegal weapons and consolidation of security authority, free of association with terror and corruption.
- GOI takes no actions undermining trust, including deportations, attacks on civilians; confiscation and/or demolition of Palestinian homes and property, as a punitive measure or to facilitate Israeli construction; destruction of Palestinian institutions and infrastructure; and other measures specified in the Tenet work plan.
- Relying on existing mechanisms and on-the-ground resources, Quartet representatives begin informal monitoring and consult with the parties on establishment of a formal monitoring mechanism and its implementation.
- Implementation, as previously agreed, of U.S. rebuilding, training and resumed security cooperation plan in collaboration with outside oversight board (U.S.–Egypt–Jordan). Quartet support for efforts to achieve a lasting, comprehensive cease-fire.
- All Palestinian security organizations are consolidated into three services reporting to an empowered Interior Minister.
- Restructured/retrained Palestinian security forces and IDF counterparts progressively resume security cooperation and other undertakings in implementation of the Tenet work plan, including regular senior-level meetings, with the participation of U.S. security officials.
- Arab states cut off public and private funding and all other forms of support for groups supporting and engaging in violence and terror.
- All donors providing budgetary support for the Palestinians channel these funds through the Palestinian Ministry of Finance's Single Treasury Account.
- As comprehensive security performance moves forward, IDF withdraws progressively from areas occupied since September 28, 2000 and the two sides restore the status quo that existed prior to September 28, 2000. Palestinian security forces redeploy to areas vacated by IDF.

Palestinian institution-building

- Immediate action on credible process to produce draft constitution for Palestinian statehood. As rapidly as possible, constitutional committee circulates draft Palestinian constitution, based on strong parliamentary democracy and cabinet with empowered prime minister, for public comment/debate. Constitutional committee proposes draft document for submission after elections for approval by appropriate Palestinian institutions.

- Appointment of interim prime minister or cabinet with empowered executive authority/decision-making body.
- GOI fully facilitates travel of Palestinian officials for PLC and Cabinet sessions, internationally supervised security retraining, electoral and other reform activity, and other supportive measures related to the reform efforts.
- Continued appointment of Palestinian ministers empowered to undertake fundamental reform. Completion of further steps to achieve genuine separation of powers, including any necessary Palestinian legal reforms for this purpose.
- Establishment of independent Palestinian election commission. PLC reviews and revises election law.
- Palestinian performance on judicial, administrative, and economic benchmarks, as established by the International Task Force on Palestinian Reform.
- As early as possible, and based upon the above measures and in the context of open debate and transparent candidate selection/electoral campaign based on a free, multi-party process, Palestinians hold free, open, and fair elections.
- GOI facilitates Task Force election assistance, registration of voters, movement of candidates and voting officials. Support for NGOs involved in the election process.
- GOI reopens Palestinian Chamber of Commerce and other closed Palestinian institutions in East Jerusalem based on a commitment that these institutions operate strictly in accordance with prior agreements between the parties.

Humanitarian response

- Israel takes measures to improve the humanitarian situation. Israel and Palestinians implement in full all recommendations of the Bertini report to improve humanitarian conditions, lifting curfews and easing restrictions on movement of persons and goods, and allowing full, safe, and unfettered access of international and humanitarian personnel.
- AHLC reviews the humanitarian situation and prospects for economic development in the West Bank and Gaza and launches a major donor assistance effort, including to the reform effort.
- GOI and PA continue revenue clearance process and transfer of funds, including arrears, in accordance with agreed, transparent monitoring mechanism.

Civil society

- Continued donor support, including increased funding through PVOs/NGOs, for people to people programs, private sector development and civil society initiatives.

Settlements

- GOI immediately dismantles settlement outposts erected since March 2001.
- Consistent with the Mitchell Report, GOI freezes all settlement activity (including natural growth of settlements).

Phase II: Transition – June 2003–December 2003

In the second phase, efforts are focused on the option of creating an independent Palestinian state with provisional borders and attributes of sovereignty, based on the new constitution, as a way station to a permanent status settlement. As has been noted, this goal can be achieved when the Palestinian people have a leadership acting decisively against terror, willing and able to build a practicing democracy based on tolerance and liberty. With such a leadership, reformed civil institutions and security structures, the Palestinians will have the active support of the Quartet and the broader international community in establishing an independent, viable, state.

Progress into Phase II will be based upon the consensus judgment of the Quartet of whether conditions are appropriate to proceed, taking into account performance of both parties. Furthering and sustaining efforts to normalize Palestinian lives and build Palestinian institutions, Phase II starts after Palestinian elections and ends with possible creation of an independent Palestinian state with provisional borders in 2003. Its primary goals are continued comprehensive security performance and effective security cooperation, continued normalization of Palestinian life and institution-building, further building on and sustaining of the goals outlined in Phase I, ratification of a democratic Palestinian constitution, formal establishment of office of prime minister, consolidation of political reform, and the creation of a Palestinian state with provisional borders.

- **International Conference:** Convened by the Quartet, in consultation with the parties, immediately after the successful conclusion of Palestinian elections, to support Palestinian economic recovery and launch a process, leading to establishment of an independent Palestinian state with provisional borders.

  - Such a meeting would be inclusive, based on the goal of a comprehensive Middle East peace (including between Israel and Syria, and Israel and Lebanon), and based on the principles described in the preamble to this document.
  - Arab states restore pre-intifada links to Israel (trade offices, etc.).
  - Revival of multilateral engagement on issues including regional water resources, environment, economic development, refugees, and arms control issues.

- New constitution for democratic, independent Palestinian state is finalized and approved by appropriate Palestinian institutions. Further elections, if required, should follow approval of the new constitution.
- Empowered reform cabinet with office of prime minister formally established, consistent with draft constitution.
- Continued comprehensive security performance, including effective security cooperation on the bases laid out in Phase I.
- Creation of an independent Palestinian state with provisional borders through a process of Israeli-Palestinian engagement, launched by the international conference. As part of this process, implementation of prior agreements, to enhance maximum territorial contiguity, including further action on settlements in conjunction with establishment of a Palestinian state with provisional borders.
- Enhanced international role in monitoring transition, with the active, sustained, and operational support of the Quartet.
- Quartet members promote international recognition of Palestinian state, including possible UN membership.

Phase III: Permanent status agreement and end of the Israeli-Palestinian conflict: 2004–2005

Progress into Phase III, based on consensus judgment of Quartet, and taking into account actions of both parties and Quartet monitoring. Phase III objectives are consolidation of reform and stabilization of Palestinian institutions, sustained, effective Palestinian security performance, and Israeli-Palestinian negotiations aimed at a permanent status agreement in 2005.

- **Second International Conference:** Convened by Quartet, in consultation with the parties, at beginning of 2004 to endorse agreement reached on an independent Palestinian state with provisional borders and formally to launch a process with the active, sustained, and operational support of the Quartet, leading to a final, permanent status resolution in 2005, including on borders, Jerusalem, refugees, settlements; and, to support progress toward a comprehensive Middle East settlement between Israel and Lebanon and Israel and Syria, to be achieved as soon as possible.
- Continued comprehensive, effective progress on the reform agenda laid out by the Task Force in preparation for final status agreement.
- Continued sustained and effective security performance, and sustained, effective security cooperation on the bases laid out in Phase I.
- International efforts to facilitate reform and stabilize Palestinian institutions and the Palestinian economy, in preparation for final status agreement.
- Parties reach final and comprehensive permanent status agreement that ends the Israel-Palestinian conflict in 2005, through a settlement

negotiated between the parties based on UNSCR 242, 338, and 1397, that ends the occupation that began in 1967, and includes an agreed, just, fair, and realistic solution to the refugee issue, and a negotiated resolution on the status of Jerusalem that takes into account the political and religious concerns of both sides, and protects the religious interests of Jews, Christians, and Muslims worldwide, and fulfills the vision of two states, Israel and sovereign, independent, democratic and viable Palestine, living side-by-side in peace and security.

- Arab state acceptance of full normal relations with Israel and security for all the states of the region in the context of a comprehensive Arab-Israeli peace.

Source: Press Statement, Office of the Spokesman, Washington, DC, released on 30 April 2003.

Document 29

Excerpts from the 2014 Gaza ceasefire agreement

This ceasefire agreement between Israel and Hamas was reached through Egyptian mediation and brought to an end the 2014 Gaza War. Although it remains unpublished, some details were released to the press, providing the following outline.

Immediate steps

- Hamas and the other terrorist groups in Gaza halt all rocket and mortar fire into Israel.
- Israel stops all military action, including air strikes, ground operations and targeted killings.
- The Palestinian Authority will lead coordination of the reconstruction effort in Gaza with international donors, including the European Union, Qatar, Turkey and Norway. Saudi Arabia is also likely to be a major donor, with the expectation in Jerusalem being that unlike Qatar, it will take pains to ensure that its funds will not be directed to Hamas, but rather to build up the PA.
- Israel is expected to narrow the security buffer – a no-go area for Palestinians that runs along the inside of the Gaza border – reducing it from 300 meters to 100 meters if the truce holds. The move will allow Palestinians more access to farmland close to the border.
- Israel will extend the fishing limit off Gaza's coast from 3 miles to 6 miles, with the possibility of widening it gradually if the truce holds. Ultimately, the Palestinians want to return to a full 12-mile international allowance.

- Israel agrees to open the Erez and Kerem Shalom crossings to the supervised transfer of goods, including humanitarian aid and reconstruction equipment, into the Gaza Strip.

Channel 2 reported that a three-person committee made up of Maj.-Gen. Yoav Mordechai, the coordinator of government activities in the territories, UN Mideast envoy Robert Serry and PA Prime Minister Rami Hamdallah will supervise the process and determine what goods are allowed in.

Israel is demanding the tight monitoring of imports of construction materials like cement and cast iron to make sure they are used to rebuild homes, not destroyed terror tunnels, as well as ensuring that weapons, ammunition and any "dual-use" goods are prevented from entering Gaza.

Longer-term issues to be discussed

- Israel will demand that the reconstruction and rehabilitation of Gaza be linked to the enclave's demilitarization, as called for under previous Israeli-Palestinian agreements.

Jerusalem's formula will be that the extent of building above ground in Gaza must be linked to the degree to which "underground" Gaza is dismantled.

- Hamas wants Israel to release hundreds of Palestinian prisoners rounded up in Judea and Samaria following the abduction and murder of Naftali Fraenkel, Gil-Ad Shaer and Eyal Yifrah in June. Among those arrested were some 60 prisoners freed in the Gilad Schalit deal, and 37 Palestinian parliamentarians, including 35 affiliated with Hamas.
- Israel will demand the return of the remains of slain IDF soldiers Oron Shaul and Hadar Goldin.
- Hamas wants to rebuild an airport and seaport in Gaza, as well as the transfer of funds to allow it to pay 40,000 police, government workers and other administrative staff who have largely been without salaries since late last year. The funds were frozen by the Palestinian Authority.

Source: http://www.jpost.com/Arab-Israeli-Conflict/
Outline-of-Protective-Edge-cease-fire-agreement-with-Hamas-372560

Glossary

Aliyah (Hebrew: ascent) Wave of Jewish immigration to Palestine and, later, to Israel.

an-Nakba (Arabic: the disaster) Term for the Palestinian experience in the 1948 war, alluding to the Arab defeat and the Palestinian refugee situation.

Arab Higher Committee The main institution of the Palestinian–Arab political leadership in 1936 under the chairmanship of Hajj Amin al-Husseini. Outlawed on 1 October 1937 for its role in the 1936 Arab Revolt.

Arab League Established in 1945 by Egypt, Iraq, Lebanon, Saudi Arabia, Syria, Transjordan and Yemen to promote Arab cooperation and coordination as well as providing a united political front.

Arab Legion Army formed in Transjordan in 1920–21 by the British. Precursor of the Jordanian Army.

Arab Liberation Army Arab force during the 1947–48 Arab–Israeli war.

Arab Peace Plan Proposed by Saudi Crown Prince Abdullah; adopted by Arab League on 28 March 2002; calls for full normalization in the context of a final settlement; plan did not stand a chance as undermined by a series of suicide bombings.

Ashkenazi/Ashkenazim Jews of East European origin.

Axis of Evil Term coined by George W. Bush referring to Iran, Iraq and North Korea and their allies such as Syria; states seen as sponsoring terrorism or possessing weapons of mass destruction and the intent to use them.

Bar Lev Line Unofficial name for the system of Israeli fortresses along the Suez Canal during the time of the War of Attrition, 1968–69.

Black September Confrontation between the Jordanian Army and Palestinian guerrillas in Jordan in September 1970, as a result of which the PLO was expelled from Jordan and relocated its headquarters to Beirut, Lebanon.

CAPS Comprehensive Agreement on Permanent Status.

Cedar Revolution Popular, pro-democracy revolution in Lebanon against the Syrian presence and involvement in the assassination of Prime Minister Rafiq al-Hariri.

Circassians Originally from the area of the Caucasus, many emigrated to the Ottoman Empire when the Russians took control. The Muslim

Circassians settled in Syria, Jordan and Palestine where they assimilated with the local population.

Dalet   Hebrew letter of the alphabet, corresponding to D.

DFLP   Democratic Front for the Liberation of Palestine.

Diaspora   Term for 'dispersion' of the Jews.

DOP   Declaration of Principles; also known as the Oslo Accord.

Druze   Originally an offshoot of Ismaili Shi'ism, but considered by most to have seceded from Islam. Their spiritual guide was the Fatimid Caliph Hakim in the eleventh century. The Druze stress moral and social principles rather than ritual and ceremony. Most settled in Lebanon, Syria and Palestine.

Elon Peace Plan   Proposed by Binyamin Elon in response to Sharon's disengagement plan: calls for annexation of the West Bank and Gaza Strip.

Eretz Yisrael (Hebrew: Land of Israel)   Hebrew name of Palestine in its original mandate boundaries (including Jordan).

FAPS   Framework Agreement on Permanent Status.

Fatah   Palestinian guerrilla organization founded in 1957 in Kuwait by, amongst others, Yasser Arafat. Became the core of the PLO.

Fedayeen (Arabic: commandos)   Generally means Palestinian guerrillas.

Geneva Accord   Peace plan put forward by Yossi Beilin and Yasser Abed Rabbo: it is a detailed permanent status agreement drawing the borders close to the 4 June 1967 boundary.

Green Line   Armistice frontiers in 1949; pre-1967 Six Day War Israeli state boundary.

Gush Emunim (Hebrew: Bloc of Believers)   Religious Zionist movement established in the wake of the Six Day War, whose aims include, among others, to integrate the territories gained in that war into the Israeli state on the grounds that they are part of the Land of Israel.

Haganah (Hebrew: defence)   Jewish underground organization established in 1920 following the Arab riots and British failure to defend the Jews. It became the core of the Israel Defence Force upon the declaration of the State of Israel in 1948.

Hamas (Arabic acronym for Islamist Resistance Movement)   Founded in 1987 in the Gaza Strip; opposes peace with Israel; wants an Islamic state in Palestine.

Hashemites   Clan of the Qureish tribe from whom the Prophet Mohammed is descended. Has come to refer to the Sharifs of Mecca, who supplied the kings for the Hejaz, Iraq and Jordan.

Hebron Agreement   Concluded in January 1997 between Israel and the PA; calls for Israeli redeployment from Hebron within 10 days and the assumption of responsibility by the Palestinian police.

Herut   Israeli party established in 1948 by veterans of the Irgun; headed by Menachem Begin; advocated an activist approach to the Arab states as well as assertion of Jewish rights on both sides of the Jordan River.

Histadrut   General Labour Federation in Israel. Established in 1920 for Jewish workers; opened its doors to Arab workers in 1969.

Hizbollah (Arabic: Party of God) Lebanese Shi'a resistance movement established in the wake of the 1982 Israeli invasion of Lebanon.

IDF Israel Defence Force.

intifada (Arabic: shaking off) Name given to the Palestinian uprising against Israeli occupation which began on 9 December 1987 and lasted until the signing of the 1993 Oslo Accords between the PLO and Israel.

Irgun Zvai Leumi (Hebrew: National Military Organization) Jewish extremist underground organization founded in 1937. After the 1939 White Paper the Irgun directed its operations against the British. In 1946 the Irgun blew up the British Army Command and the Palestine Government Secretariat in the King David Hotel.

Jewish Agency Formally established in 1929 to facilitate Jewish immigration to Palestine, to advance the Hebrew language and culture, to purchase land in Palestine, to develop Jewish agriculture and settlements and to fulfil Jewish religious needs in Palestine. Also functioned as a quasi-government internationally until those functions were taken over by the Israeli government in 1948.

Kach Militant nationalist and religious Zionist Israeli party.

Kataib (Arabic: phalanx) Paramilitary youth movement in Lebanon established in 1936 by Pierre Gemayel, George Naccache, Charles Helou and Shafiq Wasif to work for Lebanese independence. Evolved into a Maronite Christian organization with a party and militia devoted to preserving the Christian character of Lebanon.

Kibbutz Collective agricultural settlement in Israel based upon equal sharing in both production and consumption; product of the difficult living conditions in Palestine at the beginning of the century as well as the socialism adhered to by the Zionist leaders at that time.

Land of Israel Movement Established in the aftermath of the 1967 Six Day War in opposition to Israeli withdrawal from the Occupied Territories.

Lehi A Jewish underground organization.

Lebanon First Netanyahu's policy of sidelining the Palestinians and Syrians in favour of the Lebanese in order to advise a peace agreement without territorial concessions.

National Religious Party Established in 1955 when the two religious Zionist parties Mizrahi and Hapoel HaMizrahi merged; aimed at restoring religious values and the Torah as Israel's constitution; believes in Jewish historical rights to the whole of Palestine; is in favour of settlement of the West Bank.

NATO North Atlantic Treaty Organization.

OPEC Organization of Petroleum Exporting Countries.

PCP Palestine Communist Party.

PFLP Popular Front for the Liberation of Palestine.

PLA Palestine Liberation Army.

PLC Palestinian Legislative Council.

PLO Palestine Liberation Organization.

PNA   Palestine National Authority.

PNC   Palestine National Council.

PNM   Palestinian National Movement.

PSA   Permanent Status Agreement.

Roadmap   Put forward by United States, EU, UN and Russia in mid-2002; performance-based three-phased plan for Israeli–Palestinian peace; was officially initiated with appointment of Mahmoud Abbas as Palestinian Prime Minister so that neither the United States nor Israel had to deal with Arafat; never fully implemented.

Sephardim   Eastern or Oriental Jews.

SLA   South Lebanese Army.

Sumud (Arabic: steadfastness)   Term used to describe the Palestinian pursuit of unity and endurance of hardship during the intifada.

Tehiya (Hebrew: renaissance)   Militant nationalist Israeli party; broke away from the Likud Party in 1978 in opposition to the Camp David peace agreement.

Territorial maximalism   Agenda pursued by religious Zionists and right-wing Israelis to integrate the territories occupied after 1967 into Israel on either religious or security grounds. Sees Israel's boundary as the Jordan River.

Transjordan   The area east of the Jordan River; included in the British mandate; in 1921 the British established Transjordan; in 1948 the name was changed to the Hashemite Kingdom of Jordan.

UNC   Unified National Command.

UNEF   United Nations Emergency Force.

UNSC   United Nations Security Council.

UNSCOP   United Nations Special Committee on Palestine.

Wafd   Egyptian nationalist party; evolved from the Egyptian delegation sent to negotiate Egyptian independence from the British in 1919; was in power in 1924, 1928, 1930, 1936–37, 1942–44, 1950 and 1952.

Wailing Wall/Western Wall   Built by King Herod in 20 BC as the western wall of the Temple in Jerusalem; only remnant of the temple after its destruction by the Romans in AD 70; most hallowed site in Judaism.

Waqf   Muslim religious foundation or endowment.

War on Terror   Initiated by US President George W. Bush in response to the 11 September 2001 attacks; war on terror, terrorism and terrorists aimed at eliminating the Al-Qaeda network and supporters; includes the overthrow of the Taliban in 2001 and Saddam Hussein in 2003.

West Bank Barrier   Wall or fence of separation between Israel and the West Bank; runs roughly along the given line; construction began late 2002 under the Sharon government.

Yishuv (Hebrew: settlement)   The Jewish settlement in Palestine before the establishment of the State of Israel.

Yom Kippur (Hebrew: Day of Atonement)   After the Sabbath, the most important of the Jewish holy days; marked by 24 hours of fasting and prayer.

Zero-sum   Belief that the gain of one party to a conflict automatically translates into the loss of the other party, thus making compromise difficult.

Further reading

There are numerous books covering the whole period of the Arab–Israeli conflict. Of these five in particular stand out in terms of scope and scholarship: Mark Tessler, *A History of the Israeli–Palestinian Conflict* (Bloomington, IN, 1994), Yezid Sayigh, *Armed Struggle and the Search for State: The Palestinian National Movement, 1949–1993* (Oxford, 1997), Avi Shlaim, *The Iron Wall: Israel and the Arab World* (London, 2000), Benny Morris, *Righteous Victims: A History of the Zionist-Arab Conflict 1881–2001* (New York, 2001), and James Gelvin, *The Israeli-Palestinian Conflict: One Hundred Years of War* (Cambridge, 2014). Books on the early phase of the Arab–Zionist conflict over Palestine from 1882 until 1948 deal broadly with three subjects: Zionism, Palestinian nationalism and British policy. Good general histories of the intellectual roots and developments of Zionism include Shlomo Avineri, *The Making of Modern Zionism: The Intellectual Origins of the Jewish State* (New York, 1981), Walter Lacqueur, *A History of Zionism: From the French Revolution to the Establishment of the State of Israel* (New York, 1972), David Vital's trilogy, *The Origins of Zionism* (Oxford, 1975), *Zionism: The Formative Years* (Oxford, 1982), and *Zionism: The Crucial Phase* (Oxford, 1987) as well as David Engel, *Zionism* (New York, 2009). Interesting additions to the general literature include Jehuda Reinharz and Anita Shapira (eds.), *Essential Papers on Zionism* (London, 1996), which comprises a wide range of essays on specific turning points in Zionist history from different historiographical perspectives, Anita Shapira's in-depth analysis of the defensive ethos in Zionism in her book *Land and Power: The Zionist Resort to Force* (New York, 1992) and Mitchell Cohen, *Zion and State: Nation, Class and the Shaping of Modern Israel* (Oxford, 1987) which looks at the struggle between the Zionist Left and Right.

While books on Zionism are abundant, good books on Palestinian nationalism during the mandate period are hard to find. The development towards a distinctly Palestinian nationalism is discussed by Yehoshua Porath in his books *The Emergence of the Palestinian Arab Nationalist Movement, 1918–1929* (London, 1974), *The Palestinian Arab National Movement 1929–1939: From Riots to Rebellion* (London, 1977), and *In Search of Arab Unity, 1930–1945* (London, 1986) as well as in Muhammad Y. Muslih, *The Origins of Palestinian Nationalism* (New York, 1988), while the effects of key personalities such as Hajj Amin al-Husayni and events such as the Arab Revolt upon Palestinian nationalism are extremely well analyzed by Philip Mattar, *The Mufti of Jerusalem: Al-Hajj Amin al-Husayni and the Palestinian National Movement* (New York, 1988) and Ted Swedenburg, *Memories of Revolt: The 1936–1939 Rebellion and the Palestinian National Past* (Fayetteville, 2003). Two worthwhile books looking at the shortcomings of Palestinian leaders and society are Ann Mosely Lesch, *Arab Politics in Palestine, 1917–1939: The Frustration of a National Movement* (Ithaca, NY, 1979) and Issa Khalaf, *Politics in Palestine: Arab Factionalism and Social Disintegration, 1939–1948* (Albany, NY, 1991). Finally, useful sections on early Palestinian identity and leaders can also be found in Pamela Ann Smith, *Palestine and the Palestinians, 1876–1983* (London, 1984) as well as Rashid Khalidi, *Palestinian Identity: The Construction of Modern National Consciousness* (New York, 1997) and Baruch Kimmerling and Joel S. Migdal, *The Palestinian People; A History* (Cambridge, MA, 2003).

British policy in Palestine is discussed by Nicholas Bethell, *The Palestine Triangle: The Struggle between the British, the Jews and the Arabs, 1935–1948* (London, 1979), Bernard Wasserstein, *The British in Palestine: The Mandatory Government and the Arab-Jewish Conflict, 1917–1929* (Oxford, 1990), and Naomi Shepherd, *Ploughing Sand: British Rule in Palestine, 1917–1948* (New Brunswick, 2000). A comprehensive analysis of British policy during the Second World War can be found in Ronald Zweig, *Britain and Palestine during the Second World War* (Suffolk, 1986) while Michael Cohen focuses on the final phase of the mandate in *Palestine – Retreat from the Mandate: The Making of British Policy, 1936–1945* (London, 1978). Two of the more interesting aspects of the British mandate are the Jewish Revolt and illegal Jewish immigration. A good book on the former is David A. Charters, *The British Army and Jewish Insurgency in Palestine, 1945–1947* (New York, 1989) while books on the Jewish paramilitary organizations include J. Bowyer Bell, *Terror Out of Zion: Irgun Zvai Leumi, LEHI and the Palestinian Underground, 1929–1949* (Dublin, 1977). For an insider's view, Menachem Begin, *Revolt: Story of the Irgun* (New York, 1977) is recommended. On the subject of illegal immigration, useful books include Jon and David Kimche's very readable account *The Secret Roads: The 'Illegal' Migration of a People, 1938–1948* (New York, 1954) as well as Ze'ev Venia Hadari, *Second Exodus: The Full Story of Jewish Illegal Immigration to Palestine, 1945–1948* (London, 1991). By far the most academic study of this subject which sets immigration in a broader context is Dina Porat, *The Blue and Yellow Stars of David: The Zionist Leadership in Palestine and the Holocaust, 1939–1945* (Cambridge, 1990).

The period of the end of the mandate has been attractive to both diplomatic and regionalist historians, most of whom have focused on Palestine as a reflection of the decline of Britain and the rise of the United States. Good works on this subject are Zvi Ganin, *Truman, American Jewry and Israel, 1945–1948* (New York, 1979), Evan M. Wilson, *Decision on Palestine: How the US Came to Recognize Israel* (Stanford, CA, 1979), Michael

Cohen, *Palestine and the Great Powers, 1945–1948* (Princeton, NJ, 1982), W. Roger Louis, *The British Empire and the Middle East, 1945–1951: Arab Nationalism, the United States and Postwar Imperialism* (Oxford, 1984), and W. Roger Louis and Robert W. Stookey, *The End of the Palestine Mandate* (Austin, TX, 1985).

The 1948 war and the establishment of the State of Israel is discussed by Uri Milstein, *History of Israel's War of Independence* (Lanham, 1996), Joseph Heller, *The Birth of Israel, 1945–49: Ben Gurion and His Critics* (Gainesville, 2000), David Tal, *War in Palestine 1948: Strategy and Diplomacy* (London 2004), and Efrat Ben-Ze'ev, *Remembering Palestine in 1948: Beyond National Narratives* (Cambridge, 2011). Its impact upon the Palestinians is detailed in Walid Khalidi, *All that Remains: the Palestinian Villages Occupied and Depopulated by Israel in 1948* (Washington DC, 1992) and Salim Tamari, *Jerusalem 1948: The Arab Neighbourhoods and Their Fate in the War* (Bethlehem, 1999). The 1948 war was one of the first areas targeted by revisionist historians. Important Israeli contributions include Benny Morris, *The Birth of the Palestinian Refugee Problem, 1947–1949* (Cambridge, 1987), Simha Flapan, *The Birth of Israel: Myths and Realities* (New York, 1987), Avi Shlaim, *Collusion across the Jordan: King Abdullah, the Zionist Movement, and the Partition of Palestine* (Oxford, 1988), Ilan Pappé, *The Making of the Arab-Israeli Conflict, 1947–1951* (London, 1994), Ilan Pappé, *Ethnic Cleansing of Palestine* (Oxford, 2006), and Benny Morris, *1948: A History of the First Arab-Israeli War* (New Haven, 2008). Important Palestinian contributions include Nur Masalha, *Expulsion of the Palestinians: The Concept of 'Transfer' in Zionist Political Thought 1882–1948* (London, 1992), Salim Tamari and Elia Zureik, *Reinterpreting the Historical Record: The Uses of Palestinian Refugee Archives for Social Science Research and Policy Analysis* (Jerusalem, 2001), and Nur Masalha, *The Palestinian Nakba: Decolonizing History, Narrating the Subaltern, Reclaiming Memory* (London, 2012).

Books on the Suez crisis range from those looking at the Israeli perspective such as Mordechai Bar-On, *The Gates of Gaza: Israel's Road to Suez and Back, 1955–1957* (New York, 1994), Benny Morris, *Israel's Border Wars, 1949–1956* (Oxford, 1993), Moshe Dayan's first-hand account *Diary of the Sinai Campaign* (London, 1996) to the Egyptian perspective presented by Mohammed Heikal's *Cutting the Lion's Tail: Suez through Egyptian Eyes* (London, 1986). Other good analyses are Keith Kyle, *Suez* (New York, 1991), S.I. Troen and M. Shemesh (eds.), *The Suez-Sinai Crisis 1956: Retrospective and Reappraisal* (London, 1990), Michael Oren, *Origins of the Second Arab-Israeli War: Egypt, Israel and the Great Powers 1952–56* (London, 1992), and Simon C. Smith, *Reassessing Suez 1956: New Perspectives on the Crisis and Its Aftermath* (Aldershot, 2008). The most useful collection of documents on this period is Anthony Gorst and Lewis Johnman, *The Suez Crisis* (London, 1997).

The Suez crisis is conventionally seen as the entry point for the Cold War and superpower involvement in the Arab–Israeli conflict. The role of the superpowers is discussed by Fawaz Gerges, *The Superpowers and the*

Middle East: Regional and International Politics, 1955–1967 (Boulder, CO, 1994), Galia Golan, *Moscow and the Middle East: New Thinking on Regional Conflict* (New York, 1992), Mohammed Heikal, *The Sphinx and the Commissar: The Rise and Fall of Soviet Influence in the Middle East* (New York, 1978), and Yezid Sayigh and Avi Shlaim (eds.), *The Cold War and the Middle East* (Oxford, 1997).

Good books on the 1967 June War include the in-depth, thoroughly researched, day-by-day account by Michael Oren, *Six Days of War: June 1967 and The Making of the Modern Middle East* (New York, 2002) and Ami Gluska, *The Israeli Military and the Origins of the 1967 War: Government, Armed Forces and Defence Policy 1963–67* (London, 2006). The Arab perspective is advanced by Ibrahim Abu Lughod, *The Arab–Israeli Confrontation of June 1967: An Arab Perspective* (Evanston, IL, 1987), Elias Sam'o, *The June 1967 Arab–Israeli War: Miscalculation or Conspiracy?* (Wilmette, IL, 1971), and Moshe Shemesh, *Arab Politics, Palestinian Nationalism, and the Six Day War: The Crystallization of Arab Strategy and Nasser's Descent to War 1957–1967* (Brighton, 2008). Good retrospective re-evaluations are Richard Parker (ed.), *The Six Day War: A Retrospective* (Gainesville, VA, 1996) and J. Roth, *The Impact of the Six Day War: A Twenty Year Assessment* (Basingstoke, 1988).

Books that deal with the 1973 war include Michael Brecher, *Decisions in Crisis: Israel 1967 and 1973* (Berkeley, CA, 1980) and Ray Maghroori, *The Yom Kippur War* (Washington, DC, 1981). Important Egyptian contributions to the literature have come from journalist Mohammed Heikal, *The Road to Ramadan* (London, 1975) and Field Marshall Mohamed El-Gamasy, *The October War* (Cairo, 1993). They stand alongside Israeli accounts such as Chaim Herzog, *The War of Atonement: The Inside Story of the Yom Kippur War* (London, 2003). A reconsideration of the 1973 War was undertaken by P.R. Kumaraswamy (ed.), *Revisiting the Yom Kippur War* (Portland, OR, 2000), and Richard B. Parker (ed.), *The October War: A Retrospective* (Gainesville, 2001).

Compared to the 1973 war, Israel's 1982 invasion of Lebanon generated a much larger body of literature. Good analyses of the war can be found in George Ball, *Error and Betrayal in Lebanon: An Analysis of Israel's Invasion of Lebanon and the Implications for US–Israeli Relations* (Washington, DC, 1984), Yair Evron, *War and Intervention in Lebanon* (London, 1987), Itamar Rabinovich, *The War for Lebanon, 1970–1985* (New York, 1985), Richard Gabriel, *Operation Peace for Galilee: The Israel–PLO War in Lebanon* (New York, 1984), Zeev Schiff and Ehud Ya'ari, *Israel's Lebanon War* (London, 1984), and Kirsten E. Schulze, *Israel's Covert Diplomacy in Lebanon* (Basingstoke, 1998).

Because the literature on the individual wars often only addresses the Palestinians in passing, it is important to broaden this particular aspect through further reading. In addition to Yezid Sayigh's previously mentioned excellent book, useful books on the PLO include John W. Amos, *Palestinian Resistance: Organisation of a National Movement* (New York, 1980), Helena

Cobban, *The Palestine Liberation Organisation: People, Power, and Policies* (Cambridge, 1984), Alain Gresh, *The PLO: The Struggle Within: Towards an Independent Palestinian State* (London: 1985), Shaul Mishal, *The PLO Under Arafat: Between Gun and Olive Branch* (New Haven: 1986), Barry Rubin, *Revolution Until Victory?: The Politics and History of the PLO* (Cambridge, 1994), and Alan Hart, *Arafat: A Political Biography* (London, 1994).

The *intifada* has engendered its own body of literature, which has been more journalistic and anecdotal than scholarly in nature. The most readable and analytic accounts of the uprising are Don Peretz, *intifada: The Palestinian Uprising* (Boulder, CO, 1990), Zeev Schiff and Ehud Ya'ari, *intifada: The Palestinian Uprising – Israel's Third Front* (London, 1989), and Zachary Lockman and Joel Beinin, *The Palestinian Uprising Against Israeli Occupation* (London, 1989).

The most authoritative books on Hizbollah are Hala Jaber's, *Hezbollah: Born with a Vengeance* (New York, 1997), Amal Saad-Ghorayeb's *Hizbullah: Politics and Religion* (London, 2001), Ahmed Nizar Hamzeh's, *In the Path of Hizbullah* (New York, 2004), Naim Qassem's, *Hizbullah: The Story from Within* (London, 2005), Augustus Richard Norton, *Hezbollah: A Short History* (Princeton, 2007), and Matthew Levitt, *Hezbollah: the Global Footprint of Lebanon's Party of God* (London, 2013). For further reading on Hamas, see Shaul Mishal and Avraham Sela, *The Palestinian Hamas: Vision, Violence and Coexistence* (New York, 2000), Khaled Khroub, *Hamas: Political Thought and Practise* (Washington, 2000), Andrea Nüsse, *Muslim Palestine: The Ideology of Hamas* (London, 2002), Matthew Levitt, *Hamas: Politics, Charity and Terrorism in the Service of Jihad* (New Haven, 2006), and Jeroen Gunning, *Hamas in Politics: Democracy, Religion, Violence* (London, 2007). The latter is particularly interesting as it challenges the image of Hamas as inflexible and dogmatic.

The first step on the road to peace between Israel and the Arabs came with the 1978 Camp David Accords. Good analyses of the issues and negotiations can be found in Yaacov Bar Siman Tov, *Israel and the Peace Process, 1977–1982: In Search of Legitimacy for Peace* (Albany, NY, 1994), Shibley Telhami, *Power and Leadership in International Bargaining: The Path to the Camp David Accords* (New York, 1990), and William Quandt, *Camp David: Peace Making and Politics* (Washington, DC, 1986) as well as in the first-hand accounts of Moshe Dayan, *Breakthrough: A Personal Account of the Egypt–Israel Peace Negotiations* (New York, 1981), Ezer Weizman, *The Battle for Peace* (New York, 1981), and Ibrahim Kamel, *The Camp David Accords: A Testimony* (London, 1986).

Books on the Madrid and Oslo peace processes have been written by many participants such as Hanan Ashrawi, *This Side of Peace: A Personal Account* (New York, 1995), Shimon Peres, *Battling for Peace: A Memoir* (London, 1995), Mohamed Heikal, *Secret Channels: The Inside Story of Arab–Israeli Peace Negotiations* (London, 1996), Uri Savir, *The Process: 1,100 Days That Changed the Middle East* (New York, 1998), and Itamar Rabinovich, *The Brink of Peace: the Israeli-Syrian negotiations* (Princeton,

1998). Academic analyses are provided by Ziva Flamhaft, *Israel on the Road to Peace: Accepting the Unacceptable* (Boulder, CO, 1996), Rashid al-Madfai, *Jordan, the United States and the Middle East Peace Process, 1974–1991* (Cambridge, 1993), Moshe Maoz, *Syria and Israel: From War to Peacemaking* (Oxford, 1995), Joel Peters, *Pathways to Peace: The Multilateral Arab–Israeli Peace Talks* (London, 1996), Edward Said, *Peace and its Discontents: Gaza-Jericho, 1993–1995* (London, 1995), Yehuda Lukacs, *Israel, Jordan and the Peace Process* (New York, 1997), George Giacaman and Dag Jorund Lønning (eds.), *After Oslo: New Realities, Old Problems* (London, 1998), and Adnan Abu Odeh, *Jordanians, Palestinians and the Hashemite Kingdom in the Middle East Peace Process* (Washington, 1999). The collapse of the Oslo process and the eruption of the second *intifada* resulted in further books revisiting the peace process. Interesting analyses are provided by Edward Said, *The End of the Peace Process: Oslo and After* (London, 2000), Tim Youngs, *The Middle East Crisis: Camp David, the 'Al-Aqsa intifada' and the Prospects for the Peace Process* (London, 2001), J.W. Wright Jr, *Structural Flaws in the Middle East Peace Process: Historical Contexts* (New York, 2002), Wendy Pearlman, *Occupied Voices: Stories of Everyday Life from the Second intifada* (New York, 2003), Oded Balaban, *Interpreting Conflict: Israeli–Palestinian Negotiations at Camp David II and Beyond* (New York, 2005), Avraham Sela, *Non-State Peace Spoilers and the Middle East Peace Efforts* (2005), Tanya Reinhart, *Road Map to Nowhere: Israel/Palestine since 2003* (London, 2006), Yoram Meital, *Peace in Tatters: Israel, Palestine and the Middle East* (Boulder, 2006), Douglas Sturkey, *The Limits of American Power: Prosecuting a Middle East Peace* (2007), Daniel Kurtzer, *Negotiating Arab-Israeli Peace: American Leadership in the Middle East* (2008), Ghassan Khatib, *Palestinian Politics and the Middle East Peace Process: Consensus and Competition in the Palestinian Negotiating Team* (2010), and Sari Nuseibeh, *What Is a Palestinian State Worth?* (2011). Fascinating personal insights are provided by Bill Clinton, *My Life* (New York, 2004), Dennis Ross, *Missing Peace: The Inside Story of the Fight for Middle East Peace* (New York, 2005), and Gilead Sher, *Israeli – Palestinian Negotiations 1999–2004: Within Reach* (New York, 2006) while a good broader analysis covering a longer period can be found in Galia Golan's book *Israeli Peacemaking since 1967: Factors behind the Breakthroughs and Failures* (London, 2014).

The 2006 Lebanon War generated a comparatively limited number of books: Gilbert Achcar, *The 33-Day War: Israel's War on Hizbollah in Lebanon and Its Consequences* (2007), Anthony Cordesman, *Lessons of the 2006 Israeli-Hezbollah War* (2007), and Cathy Sultan, *Tragedy in South Lebanon: The Israel-Hezbollah War of 2006* (2009). Equally limited have been the books of the Gaza wars: Ilan Pappé, *Gaza in Crisis: Reflections on Israel's War against the Palestinians* (2010) and Gideon Levy, *The Punishment of Gaza* (2010).

References

The place of publication is London unless otherwise stated.

Abbas, Mahmoud, *Through Secret Channels*, Garnet Publishing, Reading, 1995.

Abu Amr, Ziad, *Islamic Fundamentalism in the West Bank and Gaza*, Indiana University Press, Bloomington, 1994.

Abu Lughod, Ibrahim, *The Arab-Israeli Confrontation of June 1967: An Arab Perspective*, Northwest University Press, Evanston, 1987.

Abu Odeh, Adnan, *Jordanians, Palestinians and the Hashemite Kingdom in the Middle East Peace Process*, United States Institute of Peace Press, Washington, 1999.

Adan, Avraham, *The Yom Kippur War: An Israeli General's Account*, Drum Books, New York, 1986.

Ajami, Fuad, *The Arab Predicament: Arab Political Thought and Practice since 1967*, Cambridge University Press, Cambridge, 1981.

Alteras, Isaac, *Eisenhower and Israel: US-Israeli Relations, 1953–1960*, University Press of Florida, Gainesville, 1993.

Amos, John W., *Palestinian Resistance: Organisation of a National Movement*, Pergamon, New York, 1980.

Antonius, George, *The Arab Awakening: The Story of the Arab National Movement*, Capricorn Books, New York, 1965.

Ashrawi, Hanan, *This Side of Peace: A Personal Account*, Simon & Schuster, New York, 1995.

Avineri, Shlomo, *The Making of Modern Zionism: The Intellectual Origins of the Jewish State*, Basic Books, New York, 1981.

Bailey, Sidney D., *Four Arab-Israeli Wars and the Peace Process*, Macmillan, 1990.

Ball, George, *Error and Betrayal in Lebanon: An Analysis of Israel's Invasion of Lebanon and the Implications for US-Israeli Relations*, Foundation for Middle East Peace, Washington, DC, 1984.

Bar On, Mordechai, *The Gates of Gaza: Israel's Road to Suez and Back, 1955–1957*, St. Martin's Griffin, New York, 1994.

Bar Siman Tov, Yaacov, *The War of Attrition*, Columbia University Press, New York, 1980.

Bar Siman Tov, Yaacov, *Israel and the Peace Process, 1977–1982: In Search of Legitimacy for Peace*, State University of New York Press, Albany, 1994.

Bar Zohar, Michael, *Ben Gurion: A Biography*, Weidenfeld & Nicolson, New York, 1978.

Becker, Jillian, *The PLO: Rise and Fall of the Palestine Liberation Organisation*, St. Martin's Press, New York, 1984.

Begin, Menachem, *Revolt: Story of the Irgun*, Nash Publishing Company, New York, 1977.

Bell, J. Boyer, *Terror Out of Zion: Irgun Zvai Leumi, LEHI and the Palestinian Underground, 1929–1949*, Academy Press, Dublin, 1977.

Benziman, Uzi, *Sharon: An Israeli Caesar*, Robson Books, 1987.

Bethell, Nicholas, *The Palestine Triangle: The Struggle Between the British, the Jews, and the Arabs, 1935–1948*, Deutsch, 1979.

Black, Ian and Morris, Benny, *Israel's Secret Wars: The Untold History of Israeli Intelligence*, Hamish Hamilton, 1991.

Blumenthal, Max, 'Politicide in Gaza: How Israel's Far Right Won the War', *Journal of Palestine Studies*, Vol. 44, No. 1, Autumn 2014.

Brand, Laurie A., *Palestinians in the Arab World: Institution Building and the Search for State*, Columbia University Press, New York, 1988.

Brecher, Michael, *The Foreign Policy System of Israel: Setting, Images, Process*, Yale University Press, New Haven, 1972.

Brecher, Michael, *Decisions in Crisis: Israel 1967 and 1973*, University of California Press, Berkeley, 1980.

Bregman, Ahron and el-Tahri, Jihan, *The Fifty Years War: Israel and the Arabs*, PenguinBooks/BBC Books, 1998.

Brown, L. Carl, 'Origins of the Crisis', in Richard Parker (ed.), *The Six-Day War: A Retrospective*, University Press of Florida, Gainesville, 1996.

Brynen, Rex, *Sanctuary and Survival: The PLO in Lebanon*, Westview Press, Boulder, 1990.

Caplan, Neil, *Futile Diplomacy, Volume I: Early Arab-Zionist Negotiation Attempts, 1913–1931*, Frank Cass, 1983.

Caplan, Neil, *Futile Diplomacy, Volume II: Arab-Zionist Negotiations and the End of the Mandate*, Frank Cass, 1986.

Charters, David A., *The British Army and Jewish Insurgency in Palestine, 1945–1947*, New York, 1989.

Chorev, Harel, 'The Road to Operation Protective Edge: Gaps in Strategic Perception', *Israel Journal of Foreign Affairs*, Vol. VIII, No. 3, 2014.

Clinton, Bill, *My Life*, Alfred A. Knopf, New York, 2004.

Cobban, Helena, *The Palestine Liberation Organization: People, Power, and Policies*, Cambridge University Press, 1984.

Cohen, Michael J., *Palestine: Retreat from the Mandate: The Making of British Policy, 1936–1945*, Paul Elek, 1978.

Cohen, Michael J., *Palestine and the Great Powers 1945–1948*, Princeton University Press, Princeton, 1982.

Cohen, Michael J., *The Origins and Evolution of the Arab-Israeli Conflict*, University of California Press, 1987.

Cohen, Mitchell, *Zion and State: Nation, Class and the Shaping of Modern Israel*, Blackwell, Oxford, 1987.

Cohen, Raymond, *Culture and Conflict in Egyptian-Israeli Relations: A Dialogue of the Deaf*, Indiana University Press, Bloomington, 1990.

Corbin, Jane, *The Norway Channel: The Secret Talks That Led to the Middle East Peace Accord*, Atlantic Monthly Press, New York, 1994.

Dayan, Moshe, *Diary of the Sinai Campaign 1956*, Sphere Books, 1967.

Dayan, Moshe, *Breakthrough: A Personal Account of the Egypt-Israel Peace Negotiations*, Knopf, New York, 1981.

Drezon-Tepler, Marcia, *Interest Groups and Political Change in Israel*, State University of New York Press, Albany, 1990.

Dumper, Michael, *The Politics of Jerusalem since 1967*, Columbia University Press, New York, 1997.

Eban, Abba, *Personal Witness: Israel through My Eyes*, Jonathan Cape, 1992.

Eden, Anthony, *The Suez Crisis of 1956*, Beacon Press, Boston, 1968.

Eisenberg, Laura Z., *My Enemy's Enemy: Lebanon in Early Zionist Imagination 1900–1948*, Wayne State University Press, Detroit, 1994.

Eisenhower, Dwight D., *The White House Years: Waging Peace, 1956–61*, Doubleday, Garden City, NY, 1965.

Evron, Yair, *The Middle East: Nations, Superpowers and Wars*, Praeger, New York, 1973.

Evron, Yair, *War and Intervention in Lebanon*, Croom Helm, 1987.

Flamhaft, Ziva, 'Israel and the Arab-Israeli Peace Process in the 1990s', in A. Lazin and Gregory S. Mahler (eds.), *Israel in the Nineties: Development and Conflict*, University of Florida Press, Gainesville, 1996.

Flamhaft, Ziva, *Israel on the Road to Peace: Accepting the Unacceptable*, Westview Press, Boulder, 1996.

Flapan, Simha, *The Birth of Israel: Myths and Realities*, Pantheon Books, New York, 1987.

Ford, Gerald, *A Time to Heal*, Allen, 1979.

Fraser, T.G., *The Arab-Israeli Conflict*, St. Martin's Press, New York, 1995.

Freedman, Robert O., *The Intifada: Its Impact on Israel, the Arab World, and the Superpowers*, Florida International University, Miami, 1991.

Gabriel, Richard, *Operation Peace for Galilee: The Israel-PLO War in Lebanon*, Hill and Wang, New York, 1984.

El-Gamasy, Mohamed, *The October War*, American University of Cairo Press, Cairo, 1993.

Gambill, Gary C., 'Hezbollah and the Political Ecology of Postwar Lebanon', *Mideast Monitor*, Vol. 1, No. 3, 2006.

Ganin, Zvi, *Truman, American Jewry and Israel 1945–1948*, Holmes & Meier, New York, 1979.

Garfinkle, Adam, *Politics and Society in Modern Israel: Myths and Realities*, M.E. Sharpe, 1997.

Gerges, Fawaz A., *The Superpowers and the Middle East: Regional and International Politics, 1955–1967*, Westview Press, Boulder, 1994.

Giacaman, George and Lønning, Dag Jorund (eds.), *After Oslo: New Realities, Old Problems*, Pluto Press, 1998.

Golan, Galia, *Moscow and the Middle East: New Thinking on Regional Conflict*, Council on Foreign Relations Press, New York, 1992.

Golani, Motti, 'The Historical Place of the Czech-Egyptian Arms Deal, Fall 1955', *Middle Eastern Studies*, Vol. 31, No. 4, October 1995.

Goldschmidt, Arthur Jr., *A Concise History of the Middle East* (5th edition), Westview Press, Boulder, 1996.

Gorst, Anthony and Johnman, Lewis, *The Suez Crisis*, Routledge, 1997.

Greffenius, Steven, *The Logic of Conflict: Making War and Peace in the Middle East*, Sharpe, Armonk, 1993.

Gresh, Alain, *The PLO: The Struggle Within: Towards an Independent Palestinian State*, Zed Books, 1988.

Gunning, Jeroen, *Hamas in Politics: Democracy, Religion, Violence*, Hurst, 2007.

Hadari, Ze'ev Venia, *Second Exodus: The Full Story of Jewish Illegal Immigration to Palestine, 1945–1948*, Vallentine Mitchell, 1991.

Hamzeh, Ahmed Nizar, *In the Path of Hizbullah*, Syracuse University Press, New York, 2004.

Harris, William, *Faces of Lebanon: Sects, Wars and Global Extensions*, Marcus Wiener, Princeton, 1997.

Hart, Alan, *Arafat: A Political Biography*, Sidgwick & Jackson, 1994.

Heikal, Mohamed H., *The Cairo Documents: The Inside Story of Nasser and his Relationships with World Leaders*, Doubleday, New York, 1973.

Heikal, Mohamed H., *The Road to Ramadan*, Balantine, New York, 1977.

Heikal, Mohamed H., *The Sphinx and the Commissar: The Rise and Fall of Soviet Influence in the Middle East*, Harper & Row, New York, 1978.

Heikal, Mohamed H., *Autumn of Fury: The Assassination of Sadat*, Random House, New York, 1983.

Heikal, Mohamed H., *Cutting the Lion's Tail: Suez through Egyptian Eyes*, Andre Deutsch, 1986.

Heikal, Mohamed H., *Secret Channels: The Inside Story of Arab-Israeli Peace Negotiations*, Harper Collins, 1996.

Heller, Joseph, *The Birth of Israel 1945–49: Ben Gurion and His Critics*, University Press of Florida, Gainesville, 2000.

Heller, Mark, *A Palestinian State: The Implications for Israel*, Harvard University Press, Cambridge, Mass, 1983.

Hersh, Seymour M., 'Annals of National Security: Watching Lebanon: Washington's Interests in Israel's War', *New Yorker*, 21 August 2006.

Herzog, Chaim, *The War of Atonement: The Inside Story of the Yom Kippur War*, Greenhill, 2003.

Hopwood, Derek, *Egypt: Politics and Society, 1945–90* (3rd edition), Routledge, 1991.

Hudson, Michael C., *Arab Politics: The Search for Legitimacy*, Yale University Press, New Haven, 1977.

Hunter, Robert F., *The Palestinian Uprising: A War by Other Means* (2nd edition), University of California Press, Berkeley, 1993.

Jaber, Hala, *Hezbollah: Born with a Vengeance*, Columbia University Press, New York, 1997.

Jansen, Michael, *The Battle of Beirut: Why Israel Invaded Lebanon*, Zed Press, 1982.

Kamel, Ibrahim, *The Camp David Accords: A Testimony*, KPI, 1986.

Karsh, Efraim. 'Rewriting Israel's History', *Middle East Quarterly*, June 1996.

Karsh, Efraim, *Fabricating Israeli History: The 'New Historians'*, Frank Cass, 1997.

Khalaf, Issa, *Politics in Palestine: Arab Factionalism and Social Disintegration 1939–1948*, State University of New York, Albany, 1991.

Khalidi, Rashid, *Palestinian Identity: The Construction of Modern National Consciousness*, Columbia University Press, New York, 1997.

Khalidi, Rashid, 'The Palestinians and 1948: The Underlying Causes of Failure', in Eugene L. Rogan and Avi Shlaim (eds), *The War for Palestine*, Cambridge University Press, Cambridge, 2001.

Khalidi, Walid, 'Plan Dalet: Masterplan for the Conquest of Palestine', *Journal of Palestinian Studies*, Vol. 18, No. 1, 1988.

Khroub, Khaled, *Hamas: Political Thought and Practise*, Institute of Palestine Studies, Washington, 2000.

Kimche, David, *The Last Option*, Weidenfeld & Nicolson, 1991.

Kimche, Jon and Kimche, David, *The Secret Roads: The 'Illegal' Migration of a People 1938–1948*, Secker & Warburg, New York, 1954.

Kimmerling, Baruch and Migdal, Joel S., *The Palestinian People: A History*, Harvard University Press, 2003.

King, John, *Handshake in Washington: The Beginning of Middle East Peace?*, Ithaca Press, Garnet Publishing, 1994.

Kissinger, Henry, *Years of Upheaval*, Little, Brown, Boston, 1982.

Klieman, Aaron, *Statecraft in the Dark: Israel's Practice of Quiet Diplomacy*, Westview Press, Boulder, 1988.

Kumaraswamy, P.R. (ed.), *Revisiting the Yom Kippur War*, Frank Kass, Portland, 2000.

Kyle, Keith, *Suez*, St. Martin's Press, New York, 1991.

Lall, Arthur S., *The UN and the Middle East Crisis, 1967*. Columbia University Press, New York, 1968.

Laqueur, Walter (ed.), *The Israel-Arab Reader: A Documentary History of the Middle East Conflict*, Bantam Books, 1968.

Laqueur, Walter, *A History of Zionism: From the French Revolution to the Establishment of the State of Israel*, MFJ Books, New York, 1972.

Laqueur, Walter, *Confrontation: The Middle East and World Politics*, New York Times Books, New York, 1974.

Lesch, Ann Mosely, *Arab Politics in Palestine, 1917–1939: The Frustration of a Nationalist Movement*, Cornell University Press, Ithaca, 1979.

Lesch, Ann Mosely, *The Palestinian Uprising – Causes and Consequences*, United Field Staff International Reports, Asia, No. 1, 1988–89.

Levey, Zach, 'Anglo-Israeli Strategic Relations, 1952–56', *Middle Eastern Studies*, Vol. 31, No. 4, October 1995.

Levy, Gideon, *The Punishment of Gaza*, Verso, London and New York, 2010.

Lipson, Charles, 'American Support for Israel: History, Sources, Limits', *Israel Affairs*, Vol. 2, Nos. 3 and 4, Spring/Summer 1996.

Lockman, Zachary and Beinin, Joel, *Intifada: The Palestinian Uprising against Israeli Occupation*, I.B. Tauris, 1989.

Louis, W. Roger, *The British Empire and the Middle East 1945–1951: Arab Nationalism, the United States and Postwar Imperialism*, Clarendon, Oxford, 1984.

Louis, W. Roger and Stokey, Robert W., *The End of the Palestine Mandate*, Tauris, 1985.

Lukacs, Yehuda, *Israel, Jordan and the Peace Process*, Syracuse University Press, New York, 1997.

MacBride, Sean, *Israel in Lebanon: The Report of the International Commission to Enquire into Reported Violations of International Law by Israel During Its Invasion of Lebanon*, Ithaca Press, 1983.

Al-Madfai, Rashid, *Jordan, the United States and the Middle East Peace Process, 1974–1991*, Cambridge University Press, 1993.

Maghroori, Ray, *The Yom Kippur War*, University Press of America, Washington, 1981.

Maoz, Moshe, *Syria and Israel: From War to Peacemaking*, Clarendon Press, Oxford, 1995.

Masalha, Nur, *Expulsion of the Palestinians: The Concept of 'Transfer' in Zionist Political Thought 1882–1948*, Institute for Palestine Studies, London, 1992.

Mattar, Philip, *The Mufti of Jerusalem: Al-Hajj Amin al-Husayni and the Palestinian National Movement*, Columbia University Press, New York, 1988.

McDowell, David, *Palestine and Israel: The Uprising and Beyond*, I.B. Tauris, 1989.

Medzini, Meron, *Israel's Foreign Relations, 1979–80*, Ministry of Foreign Affairs, Jerusalem, 1984.

Meir, Golda, *My Life: The Autobiography of Golda Meir*, Futura Publications Ltd, Aylesbury, 1975.

Meital, Yoram, *Peace in Tatters: Israel, Palestine and the Middle East*, Lynne Rienner, Boulder, 2006.

Milstein, Uri, *History of Israel's War of Independence*, University Press of America, Lanham, 1996.

Mishal, Shaul, *The PLO Under Arafat: Between Gun and Olive Branch*, Yale University Press, New Haven, 1986.

Mishal, Shaul and Sela, Avraham, *Hamas: A Behavioral Profile*, The Tami Steinmetz Center for Peace Research, Tel Aviv, 1997.

Mishal, Shaul, and Sela, Avraham, *The Palestinian Hamas: Vision, Violence and Coexistence*, Columbia University Press, New York, 2000.

Morris, Benny, *The Birth of the Palestinian Refugee Problem, 1947–1949*, Cambridge University Press, Cambridge, 1987.

Morris, Benny, *1948 and After: Israel and the Palestinians*, Oxford University Press, Oxford, 1990.

Morris, Benny, *Israel's Border Wars, 1949–1956*, Clarendon Press, Oxford, 1993.

Al-Moualem, Walid, 'Fresh Light on the Syrian-Israeli Negotiations: An interview with Ambassador Walid al-Moualem', *Journal of Palestine Studies*, Vol. 26, No. 2, 1997.

Muslih, Muhammad Y., *The Origins of Palestinian Nationalism*, Columbia University Press, New York, 1988.

Netanyahu, Benjamin, *A Place Among Nations: Israel and the World*, Bantam Books, New York, 1993.

Newman, David (ed.), *The Impact of Gush Emunim: Politics and Settlement in the West Bank*, St. Martin's Press, New York, 1985.

Norton, Augustus Richard, *Hezbollah: A Short History*, Princeton University Press, Princeton, 2007.

Nüsse, Andrea, *Muslim Palestine: The Ideology of Hamas*, Routledge Curzon, 2002.

O'Neil, Bard E., *Armed Struggle in Palestine: A Politico-Military Analysis*, Westview Press, Boulder, 1978.

Oren, Michael, *The Origins of the Second Arab-Israeli War: Egypt, Israel and the Great Powers, 1952–56*, Frank Cass, 1992.

Oren, Michael, *Six Days of War: June 1967 and the Making of the Modern Middle East*, Oxford University Press, New York, 2002.

Ovendale, Ritchie, *The Origins of the Arab-Israeli Wars* (2nd edition), Longman, 1992.

Pappé, Ilan, *The Making of the Arab-Israeli Conflict, 1947–1951*, I.B. Tauris, 1994.

Pappé, Ilan (ed.), *The Israel/Palestine Question*, Routledge, 2006.

Parker, Richard (ed.), *The Six-Day War: A Retrospective*, University Press of Florida, Gainesville, 1996.

Parker, Richard (ed.), *The October War: A Retrospective*, University of Florida Press, Gainesville, 2001.

Pearlman, Wendy, *Occupied Voices: Stories of Everyday Life from the Second Intifada*, Nation Books, New York 2003.

Peleg, Ilan, *Begin's Foreign Policy, 1977–83: Israel's Move to the Right*, Greenwood Press, New York, 1987.

Peres, Shimon, *Battling for Peace: A Memoir*, Random House, New York, 1995.

Peretz, Don, *Intifada: The Palestinian Uprising*, Westview Press, Boulder, 1990.

Peretz, Don, *The Arab-Israel Dispute*, Facts on File, New York, 1996.

Peri, Yoram, *Between Battles and Ballots: Israeli Military in Politics*, Cambridge University Press, Cambridge, 1983.

Peri, Yoram, 'Coexistence or Hegemony? Shifts in the Israeli Security Concept', in Dan Caspi, Abraham Diskin, and Emanuel Gutman (eds.), *The Roots of Begin's Success: The 1981 Israeli Elections*, Croom Helm, 1984.

Peters, Joel, *Pathways to Peace: The Multilateral Arab-Israeli Peace Talks* RIIA, 1996.

Picard, Elizabeth, *Lebanon: A Shattered Country*, Holmes & Meier, 1996.

Porat, Dina, *The Blue and Yellow Stars of David: The Zionist Leadership in Palestine and the Holocaust, 1939–1945*, Harvard University Press, Cambridge, Mass., 1990.

Porath, Yehoshua, *The Emergence of the Palestinian Arab Nationalist Movement, 1918–1929*, Cass, 1974.

Porath, Yehoshua, *The Palestinian Arab National Movement 1929–1939: From Riots to Rebellion*, Cass, 1977.

Porath, Yehoshua, *In Search of Arab Unity 1930–1945*, Cass, 1986.

Qasem, Naim, *Hizbullah: The Story from Within*, Saqi, 2005.

Quandt, William, *Camp David: Peace Making and Politics*, Brookings Institution, Washington, 1986.

Rabie, Mohamed, *US-PLO Dialogue: Secret Diplomacy and Conflict Resolution*, University Press of Florida, Gainesville, 1995.

Rabinovich, Itamar, *The War for Lebanon, 1970–1985* (revised edition), Cornell University Press, New York, 1985.

Rabinovich, Itamar, *The Road Not Taken: Early Arab-Israeli Negotiations*, Oxford University Press, New York, 1991.

Rabinovich, Itamar, *The Brink of Peace: The Israeli-Syrian Negotiations*, Princeton University Press, Princeton, 1998.

Rabinovich, Itamar and Reinharz, Yehuda, *Israel in the Middle East*, Oxford University Press, Oxford, 1984.

Reinharz, Yehuda and Shapira, Anita (eds.), *Essential Papers on Zionism*, Cassel, 1996.

Rivlin, Paul, 'Economics and the Gaza War', *Middle East Economy*, Vol. 4, No.8, 31 August 2014.

Roth, J., *The Impact of the Six Day War: A Twenty Year Assessment*, Macmillan, Basingstoke, 1988.

Rubin, Barry, *Revolution Until Victory?: The Politics and History of the PLO*, Harvard University Press, Cambridge, 1994.

Rynhold, Jonathan and Waxman, Dov, 'Ideological Change and Israel's Disengagement from Gaza', *Political Science Quarterly*, Vol. 123, No. 1, Spring 2008.

Saad-Ghorayeb, Amal, *Hizbullah: Politics and Religion*, Pluto, 2001.

Safran, Nadav, *From War to War: The Arab-Israeli Confrontation, 1948–1967*, Pegasus, Indianapolis, 1969.

Safran, Nadav, *Israel: The Embattled Ally*, Harvard University Press, Cambridge, 1978.

Said, Edward W., *The Question of Palestine*, Vintage, 1992.

Said, Edward W., *The Politics of Dispossession: The Struggle for Palestinian Self-Determination 1969–1994*, Chatto & Windus, 1994.

Said, Edward, *Peace and Its Discontents: Gaza-Jericho 1993–1995*, Vintage, 1995.

Said, Edward, *The End of the Peace Process: Oslo and After*, Granta, 2000.

Sam'o, Elias, *The June 1967 Arab-Israeli War: Miscalculation or Conspiracy?*, Wilmette, 1971.

Savir, Uri, *The Process: 1,000 Days That Changed the Middle East*, Random House 1998.

Sayigh, Yezid, *Arab Military Industry: Capability, Performance, and Impact*. Brassey's, 1992.

Sayigh, Yezid, *Armed Struggle and the Search for State: The Palestinian National Movement, 1949–1993*, Clarendon, Oxford, 1997.

Sayigh, Yezid and Shlaim, Avi (eds.), *The Cold War and the Middle East*, Clarendon Press, Oxford, 1997.

Schiff, Zeev, *A History of the Israeli Army*, Sidgwick & Jackson, 1987.

Schiff, Zeev, 'Israel After the War', *Foreign Affairs*, Vol. 70, Spring 1991.

Schiff, Zeev and Ya'ari, Ehud, *Israel's Lebanon War*, George Allen & Unwin, 1984.

Schiff, Zeev and Ya'ari, Ehud, *Intifada: The Palestinian Uprising – Israel's Third Front*, Simon and Schuster, 1989.

Schulze, Kirsten E., *Israel's Covert Diplomacy in Lebanon*, Macmillan, 1998.

Schulze, Kirsten E., 'Camp David and the Al-Aqsa Intifada: An Assessment of the State of the Israeli-Palestinian Peace Process, July–December 2000', *Studies in Conflict and Terrorism*, Vol. 24, No. 3, 2001.

Schulze, Kirsten E., 'Israeli-Lebanese Relations: A Future Imperfect?', in Kail C. Ellis (ed.), *Lebanon's Second Republic*, University Press of Florida, Gainesville, 2002.

Shalev, Aryeh, *Israel and Syria: Peace and Security on the Golan*, Westview Press, Boulder, 1994.

Shamir, Eitan and Hecht, Eado, 'A War Examined – Gaza 2014: Israel's Attrition vs. Hamas' Exhaustion', *Parameters*, Vol. 44, No. 4, Winter 2014–2015.

Shapira, Anita, *Land and Power: The Zionist Resort to Force*, Oxford University Press, New York, 1992.

Sharett, Moshe, *Yoman Ishi* (Personal Diary), 8 volumes, Sifriyat Maariv, Tel Aviv, 1978.

Shemesh, Moshe, *The Palestinian Entity 1959–1974: Arab Politics and the PLO*, Frank Cass, 1988.

Shlaim, Avi, *Collusion Across the Jordan: King Abdullah, the Zionist Movement, and the Partition of Palestine*, Clarendon Press, Oxford, 1988.

Shlaim, Avi, 'Israeli interference in Internal Arab Affairs: The Case of Lebanon', in Giacomo Luciani and Ghassan Salame (eds.), *The Politics of Arab Integration*, Croom Helm, 1988.

Shlaim, Avi, 'The Debate About 1948', *International Journal for Middle East Studies*, Vol. 27, 1995.

Shlaim, Avi, *The Iron Wall: Israel and the Arab World*, Allen Lane, 2000.

Smith, Charles D., *Palestine and the Arab-Israeli Conflict* (3rd edition), St. Martin's Press, New York, 1996.

Smith, Pamela Ann, *Palestine and the Palestinians, 1876–1983*, Croom Helm, 1984.

Sofer, Sasson, *Begin: An Anatomy of Leadership*, Oxford University Press, Oxford, 1988.

Sprinzak, Ehud, *The Ascendance of Israel's Radical Right*, Oxford University Press, Oxford, 1991.

Stahl, Adam, 'Israeli Policy, Strategy and the 2012 Eight-Day War', *Infinity Journal*, Vol. 5, No. 1, 2015.

Stein, Kenneth W., *The Land Question in Palestine, 1917–1939*, University of North Carolina Press, Chapel Hill, 1984.

Strand, Trude, 'Tightenting the Noose', *Journal of Palestine Studies*, Vol. 43, No. 2, Winter 2014.

Tamari, Salim, 'The Palestinian Movement in Transition: Historical Reversals and the Uprising', in Rex Brynen (ed.), *Echoes of the Intifada: Regional Repercussions of the Palestinian-Israeli Conflict*, Westview Press, Boulder, 1991.

Tamari, Salim, *Jerusalem 1948: The Arab Neighbourhoods and Their Fate in the War*, Institute of Jerusalem Studies, Bethlehem, 1999.

Tamari, Salim and Zureik, Elia, *Reinterpreting the Historical Record: The Uses of Palestinian Refugee Archives for Social Science Research and Policy Analysis*, Institute of Jerusalem Studies, Jerusalem, 2001.

Telhami, Shibley, *Power and Leadership in International Bargaining: The Path to the Camp David Accords*, Columbia University Press, New York, 1990.

Tessler, Mark, *History of the Israeli-Palestinian Conflict*, Indiana University Press, Bloomington, 1994.

Teveth, Shabtai, *Ben Gurion and the Palestinian Arabs: From Peace to War*, Oxford University Press, Oxford, 1985.

Troen, Selwyn Ilan, and Shemesh, Moshe (eds.), *The Suez-Sinai Crisis, 1956: Retrospective and Reappraisal*, Frank Cass, 1990.

Victor, Barbara, *Hanan Ashrawi: A Passion for Peace*, Fourth Estate, 1995.

Vital, David, *The Origins of Zionism*, Clarendon, Oxford, 1975.

Vital, David, *Zionism: The Formative Years*, Clarendon, Oxford, 1982.

Vital, David, *Zionism: The Crucial Phase*, Clarendon, Oxford, 1987.

Wasserstein, Bernard, *The British in Palestine: The Mandatory Government and the Arab-Jewish Conflict, 1917–1929*, Blackwell, 1990.

Weizman, Ezer, *The Battle for Peace*, Bantam Books, 1981.

Wells Jr, Samuel F., 'The Clinton Administration and Regional Security: The First Two Years', *Israel Affairs*, Vol. 2, Nos. 3 and 4, Spring/Summer 1996.

Wilson, Evan, *Decision on Palestine: How the US Came to Recognize Israel*, Hoover Institution Press, Stanford, 1979.

Wright Jr, J.W., *Structural Flaws in the Middle East Peace Process: Historical Contexts*, Palgrave, 2002.

Yaniv, Avner, *Dilemmas of Security: Politics, Strategy and the Israeli Experience in Lebanon*, Oxford University Press, Oxford, 1987.

Yaniv, Avner (ed.), *National Security and Democracy in Israel*, Lynne Rienner, Boulder, 1993.

Yapp, Malcom, *The Near East since the First World War*, Longman, 1991.

Youngs, Tim, *The Middle East Crisis: Camp David, the 'Al-Aqsa Intifada' and the Prospects for the Peace Process*, House of Commons Press, 2001.

Zartman, I. William, *Ripe for Resolution: Conflict and Intervention in Africa*, Oxford University Press, Oxford, 1989.

Zartman, I. William (ed.), *Elusive Peace: Negotiating an End to Civil Wars*, The Brookings Institution, Washington DC, 1995.

Zweig, Ronald W., *Britain and Palestine During the Second World War*, Boydell Press, Suffolk, 1986.

Index